Empire's Proxy

America and the Long 19th Century

GENERAL EDITORS
David Kazanjian, Elizabeth McHenry, and Priscilla Wald

Empire's Proxy

American Literature and U. S. Imperialism in the Philippines

Meg Wesling

NEW YORK UNIVERSITY PRESS

New York and London

NEW YORK UNIVERSITY PRESS
New York and London
www.nyupress.org

LIBRARY OF CONGRESS CATALOGING-IN-PUBLICATION DATA
Wesling, Meg.
Empire's proxy : American literature and U. S. imperialism in the Philippines / Meg
Wesling.
 p. cm. — (America and the long 19th century)
Includes bibliographical references and index.
ISBN 978-0-8147-9476-0 (alk. paper)
ISBN 978-0-8147-9477-7 (pbk. : alk. paper)
ISBN 978-0-8147-9478-4 (e-Book)
1. American literature—19th century—History and criticism.   2. Imperialism
in literature.   3. Philippine literature (English)   4. Americans—Philip-
pines.   5. American literature—Filipino American authors—History and
criticism.   6. National characteristics, American, in literature.   7. United States—
Relations—Philippines.   8. Philippines—Relations—United States.   I. Title.
PS217.I47W48   2011
810.9'358599032—dc22   2010021006

References to Internet Web sites (URLs) were accurate at the time of
writing. Neither the author nor New York University Press is responsible
for URLs that may have expired or changed since the manuscript was
prepared.

New York University Press books are printed on acid-free paper,
and their binding materials are chosen for strength and durability.
We strive to use environmentally responsible suppliers and materials to the
greatest extent possible in publishing our books.

Manufactured in the United States of America
c 10 9 8 7 6 5 4 3 2 1
p 10 9 8 7 6 5 4 3 2 1

THE
AMERICAN
LITERATURES
INITIATIVE

A book in the American Literatures Initiative (ALI), a collaborative
publishing project of NYU Press, Fordham University Press, Rutgers
University Press, Temple University Press, and the University of Virginia
Press. The Initiative is supported by The Andrew W. Mellon Foundation.
For more information, please visit www.americanliteratures.org.

For Rachel and Ida

Contents

Acknowledgments

For the completion of this book, as well as for the myriad pleasures experienced along the way, I owe thanks to so many friends, colleagues, and kindred spirits. Though this project is not the direct outgrowth of my dissertation work, its contours were clearly shaped by the skillful help of my committee members at Cornell University. Sunn Shelley Wong offered advice and direction with insight, patience, and thoughfulness. Biodun Jeyifo asked rigorous questions with good humor and a keen sense of curiosity, and set a lovely example for rigorous scholarly exchange. Hortense Spillers offered expertise and enthusiasm at every turn. Mary Pat Brady gave invaluable advice when it was most necessary. For these things, I thank them wholeheartedly. While at Cornell, I also benefitted from the friendship and mentorship of many other colleagues. Benedict Anderson, Eric Cheyfitz, Brett de Bary, Salah Hassan, Biddy Martin, Barry Maxwell, and Natalie Melas provided intellectual stimulation and political camaraderie throughout my time there. Amy Villarejo and Andrea Hammer helped to brighten the long winters with good food and great humor. Most importantly, my time in Ithaca would not have been nearly so grand without the companionship, both intellectual and emotional, of so many: Akin Adesokan; David Agruss; Sze-Wei Ang; Amanda Carreiro; Zahid Chaudhary; Iftikhar, Elizabeth, and Rehan Dadi; Yvette de Boer; Jennifer Good; Javier Lezaun; Sheetal Majithia; Carol Maxwell Miller; Kristina Paszek; Anastasia Riehl; Saadia Toor; and Chi-ming Yang.

I had the good fortune to return to Cornell as a fellow at the Society for the Humanities in 2007–8. Not only was it delightful to be back in Ithaca, but the collaboration of the fellows at the A. D. White House cannot be underestimated. I am so grateful to have had the experience, and I owe special thanks to Brett de Bary for her graceful leadership, and to all of the fellows, particularly Max Cavitch, Tsitsi Jaji, Anne-Marie François, Charlie Kronengold, Chris Nealon, Simone Pinet, Rachel Prentice, Phoebe

Sengers, and C. J. Wan-ling Wee. Among the more fortuitous blessings of that year was the chance to get to know Denise Riley, for whose friendship and example I am particularly grateful. Lastly, we would never have enjoyed that year so well without the warmth and resourcefulness of Lisa Patti, Mary Ahl, and Amy Staples.

Before moving to Ithaca, I was lucky to start my graduate work in Pittsburgh, and while my time there was too short, those years were absolutely delightful in every way. Holly McCullough and Trina Brown, Matt Weiss and Marie Norman, Henry and Karen Thorne, and Danielle and Chuck Staresinic continue to make homecomings to the Golden Triangle among the trips I most enjoy; Hope Celani, Manon desGroseilliers, Shari Barnett, and Ashley Smith each remind me why I'm proud to be part of the Yinzer diaspora. My mentors and colleagues in literary and cultural theory at Carnegie Mellon, particularly Doug Davis, John Eperjesi, Samantha Fenno, Sharon Gamari-Tabrizi, Elizabeth Heffelfinger, Courtney Maloney, Kathleen Newman, David Shumway, Kristina Straub, Angela Todd, and Mimi Van Ausdall, provided inspiration, intellectual motivation, and exceptional camaraderie.

Since my arrival in San Diego, I've been blessed to have wonderful mentors, colleagues, students, and friends who've helped to make California feel like home. Lisa Lowe has extended her kindness as a mentor and friend, and her sense of intellectual curiosity and professional generosity has been an inspiration. Michael Davidson, John D. Blanco, Shelley Streeby, and Nicole Tonkovitch all provided crucial feedback and solidarity along the way. Natalia Molina, Ian Fusselman, and Michael Molina opened their home and hearts to me, for which I continue to be grateful. Hildie Kraus read every page of this manuscript with a librarian's eye for detail and a friend's generosity of spirit. Roberto Tejada brought his exceptional intellect and infectious laughter to every encounter. Colleen and Phil Grossfield provided a sense of family in Southern California, and I'm grateful for their friendship. I also thank Rae Armantrout, Sarah Shun-lien Bynum, Sara Cassetti, Jan Estrellado, Camille Forbes, Ken Foster, Cathy Gere, Rosemary George, Larissa Heinrich, Roshanak Kheshti, Lisa Lampert-Weissig, Martha Lampland, Margaret Loose, Luis Martín-Cabrera, Alanna Aiko Moore, Nayan Shah, Kathryn Shevelow, Anna Joy Springer, Don Wayne, and Nina Zhiri, who have each, in different ways, made UCSD and San Diego a productive and pleasant place to live and work.

Away from San Diego, but close in spirit and solidarity, a number of friends and colleagues have inspired and sustained me in different ways.

Robyn Wiegman inspired much of what made this book possible; first as teacher, then as mentor and friend, she offered her insight, feedback, and critical acumen with quick humor and no small amount of sass. Eric Lott provided enthusiastic support and merriment. Rey Chow, Donald Pease, and Vicente Rafael all provided feedback at crucial points along the way. Progress on this book was aided by having the opportunity to present portions to audiences at UCSD and elsewhere; such experiences were crucial in shaping the contours of the arguments offered here. In particular, I am grateful to members of Lesbian and Gay Studies at Yale University; Feminist, Gender, and Sexuality Studies at Cornell University; and the Institute for Advanced Study at Indiana University, for initiating these opportunities. Important support, both intellectual and financial, was provided by numerous people and agencies. Thank you to Ivona Hedin at the Institute for Advanced Study at Indiana University for her hospitality there. The Office of Academic Diversity and Equal Opportunity provided a Faculty Career Development Grant in the fall of 2006, which gave me leave time for research at the Library of Congress and the National Archives and Records Administration. Also in 2006, the Hellman Foundation provided financial support for the travel to those archives. The Academic Senate at UCSD provided numerous grants that funded the archival research for this book, as well as conference travel so that I could share the material with scholars elsewhere.

Eric Zinner and Ciara McLaughlin, of New York University Press, displayed a commendable commitment to editorial excellence in moving this book from proposal to print. Series editors Priscilla Wald, David Kazanjian, and Elizabeth McHenry offered enthusiasm for the project. I thank all of them for their hard work and expertise. Special thanks are due to Abraham Ignacio and the HATI-an Archives for use of the images contained in this book.

Most important, I would like to thank the friends and family who have provided the support, generosity, companionship, and constancy for which I feel so lucky. Shena Potter Jaffee and Chrissy Nichols continue to be dear to me after all of these years. The friendship, generosity, and hilarity of David Agruss and Chi-ming Yang have sustained me throughout the ups and downs of academic life. Bridget Clarke never ceases to amaze me with her capacity for empathy and her appreciation of the absurd. Flamine Rouger and Isabelle Jourdan have taught me more about the human capacity for kindness, humor, and hospitality than anyone I know. Thank you to each of you for knowing what this book means.

Linda and Dom Seta, Team Brown, Casey Gilmore, Scott and Sarah Fullen, and my lively extended family have filled my life with love and laughter. Janet, Wayne, and the amiable Nichols clan have extended that circle and added to the fun. Sue and Tom Fullen and Mark Wesling have been unfailing in their support and enthusiasm. Stephanie and Gil Kaufman made their home my own, time and again; Emmett and Grace have opened my heart in so many ways. I thank you for sharing so much of your lives with me. Ida Louise came as the sweetest possible reward after the solitary work of writing, and fills each day with laughter and wonder. Lastly, Rachel Nichols came along and changed so much, in a wonderful way. Thank you for your efforts as research assistant, bibliographer, editor, and interlocutor. Thank you for making everything seem possible, and for providing so many reasons to look forward to each new day.

Introduction

Educated Subjects: Literary Production,
Colonial Expansion, and the Pedagogical
Public Sphere

In an impassioned speech delivered to Congress on January 9, 1900, Albert J. Beveridge, a Republican senator from Indiana, argued for the manifold advantages of U.S. dominion over the Philippine Islands. Addressing his remarks specifically to the anti-imperialist critics among his fellow senators, Beveridge outlined an expansionist doctrine based on the moral, material, and religious import of the territory:

> The Philippines are ours forever. . . . And just beyond the Philippines are China's illimitable markets. We will not retreat from either. We will not repudiate our duty in the archipelago. We will not abandon our opportunity in the Orient. We will not renounce our part in the mission of our race, trustee under God, of the civilization of the world. And we will move forward to our work, not howling at regrets like slaves whipped to their burdens, but with gratitude for a task worthy of our strength and thanksgiving to Almighty God that He has marked us as His chosen people, henceforth to lead in the regeneration of the world.[1]

Mixing financial gain with religious righteousness, Beveridge's appeal was meant to inspire both fear and desire among his colleagues. The speech begins by calling to mind the prosperity to be gained in extraterritorial expansion, both in the labor and resources of the Philippines and in the islands' strategic placement in Pacific trade routes. Lest such financial concerns be taken for imperialistic greed, however, Beveridge links this material wealth to an imagined divine "duty" for Americans as a "chosen people." Admonishing his critics as cowards who would "retreat" from expansion and "renounce" that duty, he glorifies the project in racialized terms, marking the "forward movement" of empire as the privilege of Anglo-American freedom by characterizing anti-imperialists as "slaves" who replace gratitude with regret. Dismissing his critics as unworthy of this "mission of [the] race," Beveridge dismisses, too, the violence of this imperialistic advancement as a historically inevitable conflict and triumph, part of the "regeneration of the world" through the necessary supremacy of Anglo-Saxon "civilization."

Beveridge's comments on the Senate floor were notable but not unusual in their succinct interweaving of the religious, racial, and historical within a logic of imperial expansion. Rather, Beveridge offered an exemplary model of imperialist excitement at the turn of the century, one that melded racialized fears about the erosion of white dominance in the face of Asian immigration and African American enfranchisement with opportunistic dreams of new markets and U.S. global naval power, all articulated through the religious and moral discourse of the divine supremacy of "Anglo-Saxon civilization." In this respect, he simply offered a more vitriolic version of the paternalistic terms President William McKinley himself had used in 1898 when he announced that God had appeared to him in a dream and counseled him to "educate the Filipinos, and uplift and civilize and Christianize them."[2] Importantly, in this formulation McKinley chose to disregard several crucial points about Philippine history and its entanglements with Spanish colonialism, including the fact that many of the islands' inhabitants were Christian and had experienced long, though uneven, access to formalized education on the islands, both in local schools run by Spanish friars, and, after the Education Reform Law of 1863, in a system of compulsory primary education in Spanish. Nevertheless, McKinley's appeal to the discourse of uplift through religious missionary work and education echoed the logic Beveridge propounded so forcefully in Congress, a logic that proved to be a crucial part of rallying support for the imperialist cause.[3]

Against these views, those opposed to the imperialist project lamented the continuing U.S. involvement in the Philippines. Some saw in it the degradation of the very "American" ideals of democracy and independence that expansionists championed, while others expressed alarm at the possibility that Filipino incorporation into the national body would threaten the supremacy of Anglo-Saxon culture. Such are the concerns voiced at the outset of an 1898 article by Andrew Carnegie urging against the "inconvenience" of empire, where he posed the questions: "Is the Republic, the apostle of Triumphant Democracy, of the rule of the people, to abandon her political creed and endeavor to establish in other lands the rule of the foreigner over the people, Triumphant Despotism? Is the Republic to remain one homogeneous whole, one united people, or to become a scattered and disjointed aggregate of widely separated and alien races?"[4] In voicing his fear of "triumphant despotism," Carnegie echoed a number of critics who feared that the U.S. involvement in territories outside of the continent would irretrievably degrade the Constitution and weaken the republic, rendering it indistinguishable from the European monarchical system. William Dean Howells, the foremost literary critic of the period, concurred by confessing his shame at the deception implicit in the government and media coverage of the Spanish-American War as a liberation struggle, offering, "Our war for humanity has unmasked itself as a war for coaling stations."[5] Where material interest was masquerading as liberation struggle, such critics saw the duplicitous nature of the imperial program not as a logical outcome of the nationalist project but as a violation of its founding principles.

This book takes up the competing logics of imperialism, as espoused by expansionists like McKinley and Beveridge and anti-imperialists like Carnegie and Howells, in order to gauge the effects of such logics in the consolidation of another turn-of-the-century enterprise—the consolidation of the academic discipline of English. For, while Beveridge's racialized rhetoric, resounding in the halls of Congress, may seem far from the literary inquiries in progress in the towers of academe, they were united by a particular, and particularly timely, logic of cultural transmission, a pragmatic notion of culture as an ameliorative and powerful force in the formation of citizens and the submission of colonial subjects. As importantly, they drew upon a conceptualization of education as the moral imperative of American citizens, and the most effective means of managing or "rehabilitating" racialized subjects—immigrants, African Americans, Native Americans, and Filipinos alike—within the framework of middle-class Protestant Americanism. Within the new phase of extracontinental U.S. expansion, it was the power of education that was called upon to manage the contradiction between colonial despotism and national independence by framing the violent intervention of the United States in the Philippines through the paradigm of tutelage, in which Filipinos were regarded as the beneficiaries of the civilizing effects of American political and cultural tradition. Indeed, so powerful was the "romance of the common school" that the actual schoolhouse itself became the signifier of Americanism. "Model school buildings thoroughly equipped with books, pictures, maps, globes, etc., . . .will have an influence not securable by force of arms," one American officer asserted; "the school buildings should be models, both interior and exterior—the stamp of Americanism on each town."[6]

With the defeat of the Spanish flotilla in Manila Bay by U.S. Admiral George Dewey in August 1898, the U.S. military occupation of Philippines began. Under the terms of the Treaty of Paris, ratified in February 1899, Spain ceded Puerto Rico, Cuba, and Guam, and for an additional $20 million, sold the Philippines to the United States; with the annexation of Hawai'i that same year, this marked the first steps in the United States' extracontinental expansion, a new phase beyond the geographical limits of the doctrine of Manifest Destiny that called into question the status of the United States as a global imperial power on the one hand, and an exceptionalist nation committed to the principles of freedom and democracy on the other. Before the Treaty of Paris had even been ratified by the U.S. Senate, McKinley issued his plan for continued rule in the Philippines via his Proclamation of Benevolent Assimilation, in which he declared U.S. sovereignty over the islands and assured Filipinos that the Americans came "not as invaders or conquerors, but as friends, to protect the natives in their homes, in their employments, and in their personal and religious rights." Almost immediately, American teachers were thrust into the foreground as agents of the project, mobilizing a discourse of education for self-government meant to justify a prolonged colonial occupation and to mask the violent resistance to U.S. intervention. Influenced by progressive theories of educational reform as well as the history of Protestant missionary zeal in Asia, U.S. government officials emphasized the role of education in the moral and practical maintenance of the colony.

Such policies had immediate practical as well as ideological implications. The report issued in 1900 by the First Philippine Commission, a five-member group sent by McKinley to evaluate the conditions in the Philippines, asserted, "Undoubtedly a well-directed system of education will prove one of the most forceful agencies for elevating Filipinos, materially, socially, and morally, and preparing them for a large participation in the affairs of government."[7] The provision for universal public education was established by the Philippine Commission in January 1901, and there was much fanfare around the democratic impulse reflected in such schools; American journalists at home, in particular, were quick to remind readers that three centuries of Spanish colonial rule in the islands had failed to establish universal, free public education, and that the masses of Filipino subjects were but "poor, illiterate savages." One journalist opined that: "At no very distant date, I hope, when the suspicious nature of these people is satisfied, the work being done in the schools here will have its effect. It will then be one of the most potent forces in bringing about a reconciliation, and go far toward convincing the natives that American sovereignty means enlightenment, progress, civilization, and the fullest measure of independence consistent with their safety and well-being."[8] Juxtaposed with the images of decadent Spanish rulers and reticent Filipino subjects, American teachers were portrayed as an efficient army of democratizing and civilizing agents, armed with the scientific and moral superiority to uplift their new charges. This indicates a more powerful intent beyond the efficacy of U.S. schoolhouses themselves, however. Exceeding the actual material impact of this new system of education was the ideological force of the educational apparatus as a disciplinary regime; teacher, schoolhouse, and textbook were each paraded as signifiers of the exceptionalism of the American occupation.

From the beginning, the opening of the public school system thus established education as the governing metaphor for the colonial state-building project. The school was invested with an ideological weight far more profound than its practical aspects suggested. In the much-lauded transition through which, "almost overnight, soldiers became teachers," the architects of the U.S. occupation envisioned the colonial project as a pedagogical mission, in which Filipinos were not a subject population but pupils who would benefit from the care of American teachers as representatives of the moral, cultural, and political superiority of the United States.[9] By rehearsing, time and again, the continued U.S. authority over the islands as an educational imperative, supporters of the occupation could offer self-congratulatory summaries of the imperial project as "an altruistic experiment" whose beneficiaries were Filipinos themselves, not the American business interests who saw the islands as the necessary gateway to new markets in China.[10] Thus the opening of a public school system and the imposition of English were deemed "eloquent proof of the good wishes of America toward the Philippines," and, in the words of one editorialist, taken as evidence that "the march of civilization is making steady progress."[11]

Resituating the Field of American Letters

This book tells the story of the simultaneous emergence of the U.S. overseas empire and the emergence of the field of American literature. Its argument links these two events in order to consider how the literary object functioned, in the context of overseas empire, as a kind of proxy: a substitute or stand-in for the colonizing subject, who remained a numerical minority in the Philippines, and for a whole ensemble of cultural values, assumptions, and ideals that, in the late nineteenth century, came to be consolidated in the literary object. As I discuss in greater detail in chapter 2, a crucial part of this process was the constellation of reading, writing, and publishing practices through which, by the late nineteenth century, the book became invested with the specific cultural values of white, middle-class Americans while effectively erasing its own partisan affiliations. Thus was the American literary object poised to serve as the exemplar of Americanism, even as the version of "American" it represented was, of course, quite historically specific and marked by domestic hierarchies of race, gender, and class.

In examining the coincident histories of imperial expansion in the Philippines and literary humanism in the United States, *Empire's Proxy* thus investigates the contingent relationship between the fields of American literature in the United States and the study of American literature in the context of colonial rule in the Philippines. Literature, I argue, served two functions as an apparatus of imperial rule. First, American literature was held up as evidence of the cultural and moral superiority of America's Anglo-Saxon civilization, thus providing the ideological justification through which the United States' imperial interventions were recast as "civilizing" missions. Just as important, however, the literary text itself was understood to function as an ameliorative force, offering the promise of moral uplift and mental discipline that became crucial to the project of colonial rule in the U.S.-occupied Philippines. These developments indicate that the initial formations of the field of American literature as it became institutionalized in schools across the United States in the last years of the nineteenth century were shaped in part in response to the ideological, political, and material practices of the United States' extraterritorial expansion after the Spanish-American War.

The esteemed literary and cultural critic E. San Juan Jr. has lamented that that "no American intellectual of any stature has expended the energy to investigate exactly how 'humane letters' were used for over half a century to 'Americanize' and pacify the only U. S. colony in Asia."[12] In fact, *Empire's Proxy* aims to consider just that history. It does so, however, in a complementary fashion; that is, its purpose is both to trace the efficacy of American letters to the colonial project in the Philippines, and to consider how the demand for a body of American literary texts to serve such a purpose was generative both of the field of American literary study and a canon of American letters. That is, the materialist, historical approach of my study also traces how the project of "pacification" both helped define the purpose of American literary study as an ennobling, transformative effort with both intellectual rigor and moral value, and contributed to the consolidation of an archive of "classic" American literary texts that were understood to embody those values. Decisions regarding what constituted the "American canon," at least at this initial period around 1900, were not affected only by admissions standards for Harvard and Yale, though those were essential sources of authority.[13] By tracing the mutual implications between field-formation of American literature at home and its instruction in the newly acquired territories, I suggest that it became crystallized as well through the daily, seemingly mundane choices made by administrators, teachers, and colonial functionaries, along with textbook publishers, soldiers, and collaborating Filipino elites. This ensemble of actors on the stage of colonial development came to produce a collective discourse about the meaning of American letters and what sort of training, guidance, and legitimacy they could provide. That this "canon" was produced by colonial administrators, textbook manufacturers, and other functionaries in the educational apparatus of the colonies, before the project of American literature had fully acquired such value in the United States, is demonstrated by the way in which American literature was called upon to embody qualities that, in schools across the United States, were still attributed to classical languages. David Barrows, the American appointed to serve as superintendent of schools in the Philippines, made this hierarchy clear when he specified that: "While in the United States we depend, in our training of the youth, upon Latin and Greek for giving breadth of mind and depth of intellectual and moral insight, here in the Philippines we must depend upon English literature for these same purposes. It is believed that English is adequate to impart these essentials of education, both in disciplinary and spiritual aspects."[14]

Empire's Proxy thus serves as a complement to work like San Juan Jr.'s, which richly explores the effect of the U.S. colonial education system on later Philippine–U.S. literary and political relations, but has less to say

about the specific contours of that system as it took shape after 1898. I in-
tend that the archive presented here will contribute to the understanding of
the complicity between empire and American letters that his readings suggest. Likewise, this study brings to the field of American literature a set of
questions like those posed by Gauri Viswanathan, who has so compellingly
demonstrated how the field of English literature was established in India in
advance of its installation in the schools of Britain. To no small degree, the
function of the literary in India was replicated in the use of American literature in the Philippines, and many of the humanist functions associated with
the literary in that moment of colonial rule: "the shaping of character," for
example, and "the disciplines of ethical thinking," were drawn upon as an
example for U.S. administrators in the Philippines.[15] That said, there were
significant differences between the two systems. While I explore this relation in more detail in chapter 1, let me chart this distinction with two brief
examples here. For one thing, the U.S. educational model in the Philippines
also had a quite different precedent in schools like the Hampton Institute,
the Tuskegee Normal and Industrial Institute, and the Carlisle Indian Industrial Training School, which aimed to "rehabilitate" African American
and Native American students not through literature but through labor.
Another important distinction is that the priority given to American literature in the Philippines was symptomatic of the desire among U.S. officials
to distance themselves from the example of British colonial rule, which they
deemed openly exploitative. American literature was understood to be emblematic of the core values of the republic, as distinct from the excesses of
European imperialism. The American literary object thus stood at an ideological crossroads, both drawing upon the achievements of Anglo-Saxon
tradition as justification for Anglo-American rule, and marking the exceptionalism through which U.S. sovereignty in the islands would be recast as
an extension of U.S. republicanism.

Focusing on the imperial composition of American letters serves also
to diversify and reframe the traditional historical scholarship on the field
history of English and American literature. Extant histories of these fields,
such as Gerald Graff's institutional history of literary study, Arthur Applebee's account of the evolution of English instruction, Michael Warner's
history of American letters, and Kermit Vanderbilt's study of the profession of American literature, have provided painstaking and persuasive
narratives of the origins of the discipline of English in the contemporary
academy, and of American literary study at all levels of the curriculum in
the United States.[16] For the most part, however, this work has taken as its

focus the curricular developments and literary tastes of New England; as such, this archive has had little to say about the extranational motivations for, or implications of, such developments. *Empire's Proxy* tells a different story, one that locates the institutional origins of American literary study not only in the common schools of Massachusetts and the late nineteenth-century curricular reforms at Harvard and Yale, but also in the maintenance of the new American empire, in schoolrooms in Manila and on teacher-transports across the Pacific. In so doing, it draws upon the critical work by scholars of American studies whose interventions have provided a critical paradigm for the conceptual undoing of American exceptionalism, while insisting upon the historical and institutional specificity of American literary study as distinct from the more recent interdisciplinary field of American studies.[17] Such extranational connections are crucial to understanding the politics of literary study and are particularly timely in our contemporary climate in which the necessity, utility, and possibilities of the humanities are increasingly called into question.

Imperial Culture and the Making of Educated Subjects

As part of the ideological justification for the expansionist project, the literary object was invested with a pedagogical, transformative power to create a population of educated subjects in myriad ways. In one sense, "educated subjects" refers to the notion that the United States' "benevolent" colonial rule would serve to make Filipinos into modern, "civilized" subjects through their institutional and cultural education. In this process, literary instruction played a central role in the educational system in the occupied Philippines. I examine this history in order to consider why the literary was imagined to serve as a privileged site for the molding of colonial subjects, particularly at a time when the consolidation of the field of English was itself very new in public schools across the United States. Despite the beginnings of field-consolidation in New England in the 1890s, by 1901 literature continued to be unevenly taught across regions and school districts in the United States, with only 32 percent of secondary students in New York enrolled in literature courses, for example, as opposed to 73 percent in Massachusetts. Latin continued to be a more important subject than English in American high schools for several years.[18] In the Philippines, however, the introduction of the study of English and American literature accompanied the imposition of the English language as the lingua franca of democracy. Within a few years of the reopening of public schools in the Philippines, courses in American and English literature were required of all advanced students. Primary and intermediate instruction similarly focused on the dissemination of the English language as a colonial idiom through the use of American spellers and primers whose format relied upon heavy excerpting from American authors.[19] The goals of such study were stated explicitly in the literary anthologies printed for use in the Philippines, which asserted that "the greatest benefit to be derived from the study of poetry is the Inculcation of High Ideals—Love of Country, Self-Sacrifice, Devotion to Truth and Duty, and the Appreciation of the Beautiful."[20] Such work, it was presumed, could more efficiently be performed by the instruction of literary texts than by any other means.

Historians, legal scholars, feminist critics, and others have written extensively about the U. S. colonial state in the Philippines and its legacies in U. S.–Philippine relations beyond Philippine independence.[21] Their work has enlarged our understanding of the historical and material conditions that motivated the U. S. colonial state-building project. There is also admirable work that illuminates how the race and gender politics inscribed in late nineteenth-century notions of "savage" and "civilized" created the cultural conditions in which such an occupation could not only be attempted, but made to conform to the nationalist paradigm of American exceptionalism.[22] This study draws upon such work, but complements it with a more focused understanding of how that dichotomy between savage and civilized was leveraged through the institutional form of the colonial school; it was through the paradigm of a humanist education that such schools aimed first to teach Filipinos that they were not civilized and then, under the guidance of American sovereignty, to "civilize" them as modern colonial subjects.

In this process, the imposition of English, both language and literature, was essential. The centrality of English was rationalized through reference to the linguistic multitude of the Philippines. Advisors to the educational system insisted that because the local languages were too dissimilar and were shared too infrequently among the population, a unified system of education in the native vernacular would be impossible. "The native dialects," one officer concluded, "must therefore be abandoned as a basis of instruction."[23] As we shall see in chapter 1, this linguistic "chaos" was also used as a mark against Philippine sovereignty, since a nation of many languages, it was insisted, must be a divided nation. But such assertions of the practicality and expediency of English belie the intense ideological force that the imposition of English would entail. Along with assertions of the practical value of English came a companion logic of English as the bearer of cultural value and moral authority, and it is in this sense that the literary became central to the ideological project of the U.S. occupation. With the acquisition of its territories in the Pacific and the Atlantic, the United States embarked upon a new phase of colonial expansion, one that would be characterized not by American settlement, as with westward expansion on the continent, but by market investment and military dominance. In the absence of a majority white American population, the literary came to serve as a powerful proxy for the American colonial authority, working as a mobile model of the Americanism to which Filipinos were expected to adapt. Unlike the minority African American and Native American populations in the United States, whose training was supervised by a vigilant, dominant white society and its legal and extralegal practices of exclusion and intimidation, in the Philippines there could be no integration into the American public, no absorption of its cultural norms through the living example of white, middle-class culture. Unable to be incorporated into white, middle-class American culture, Filipinos could not be influenced by their proximity to its power, or by the perceived persuasiveness of its example. Instead, American literature came to serve as both example and exemplar of the Americanism that McKinley and his pro-imperialist supporters believed to be necessary for Philippine sovereignty. In this sense, it presented an ideal Americanism, the perfection of national culture to which no singular colonial representative could aspire.

While the first concern of this book is to consider the importance of the American literary tradition to the project of colonial dominance in the Philippines, the second is to trace how the imperial origins of American literary study resonate with the field we know today. Here, I use the phrase "educated subjects" to consider the emergence of English and American literary study as a respectable academic subject whose origins are intertwined with the process of nation-building at home and colonial management abroad. Scholars of American studies have recently redirected our attention to the critical place of U.S. empire in the emergence of that field, thus laying the groundwork for the questions I ask here about the particular relations between U.S. colonialism, humanism, and literary study. Despite this important paradigm shift in American studies, however, histories of the field-formation of American literature in the United States, its institutionalization in secondary and university curricula, and the selection and standardization of central "canonical" texts have largely remained limited to the framework of the nation.

As historians of the field have documented, the first courses in English and American literature emerged in college curricula in the late nineteenth century, with the turn of the century witnessing a proliferation of doctoral dissertations, college textbooks, and literary anthologies dedicated to defining the field of American literature. Such courses combined the "scientific" research methods of philology with older traditions of rhetoric, oratory, and belles lettres into a newly consolidated discipline of English, endowed with the twin values of mental rigor and moral uplift. Most accounts locate the origins of American literary study in the common schools of Massachusetts and the college entrance requirements of Harvard and Yale, in order to situate the development of the field within a regional contest between the literary centers of New York and Boston and a national context of increased standardization, both academic and professional. While these developments are a crucial part of the history of the field, by linking Massachusetts and Manila I seek to complement this narrative by telling a different story, one that complicates the linear narrative of origin by asking how the practical and ideological work of colonial dominance figured into the emergence of the discipline of English in the United States, and how the cultural and moral values associated with literary study gained their significant nationalist currency in relation to the imperial project. Understanding such connections is crucial, both for a more accurate assessment of the political, social, and intellectual stakes that animated the field's consolidation and to better understand how those interests have driven the field in the long century of its growth. One of the principal aims of this book, then, will be to flesh out the generative nature of this synchronicity between field-formation "at home" and literary instruction abroad, in order to ask what difference it might make to our understanding of the field's current form and functions when we locate the fact of empire at its center.

The third focus of this book is concerned with another sense of subject, looking beyond the academic subject of American literature to the paradigm of tutelage as a model for producing Filipinos as modern subjects who would comply with their subjection to the authority of the United States colonial apparatus. Here I explore what Louis Althusser has isolated as the "ambiguity" implicit in the multiple modern senses of the subject. It refers first to a "free" subject who is "author of and responsible for its actions"; at the same time, it also indicates "a subjected being, who submits to a higher authority, and is therefore stripped of all freedom except that of freely accepting his submission."[24] The apparent contradiction between these meanings is actually a necessary and constitutive paradox; for Althusser, the first meaning is in fact only the "reflection of the effect" of the second, as the "free" subject is not free at all, but interpellated as such "in order that he shall (freely) accept his subjection, i.e. in order that he shall make the gestures and actions of his subjection 'all by himself.' There are no subjects except by and for their subjection. That is why they 'work all by themselves.'"[25]

This understanding is particularly relevant in the history of the American colonial Philippines, where alongside the actual imposition of English education as an institutional force, the paradigm of tutelage functioned as a more generalized model, envisioning Filipinos as willing students under the guidance and direction of benevolent Americans. Vociferous debates about Filipinos' readiness for self-government demonstrate the utility of the paradigm of colonial tutelage as a temporary measure through which the U.S. government could set the terms under which independence would finally be granted. William H. Taft held that the U.S. colonial government would instruct Filipinos in self-government, thereby assuring an eventual state of independence that, because it rested with American administrators and legislators to ascertain when Filipinos had successfully learned this most important lesson, could be continually and indefinitely postponed according to the convenience of the U.S. government. Though Taft, then governor-general of the Philippines, insisted publicly that the American civil government in the Philippines would be simply a short apprenticeship in independent government until a Filipino government could be established, he undermined these assurances in no uncertain terms, remarking in private that Filipinos would need "fifty or one hundred years" of close supervision to "develop anything resembling Anglo-Saxon political principles and skills."[26] Such discussions animate the very paradox Althusser describes, in which it would only be Filipinos' ready assimilation to the codes of middle-class Protestant Americanism—that is, their willing submission to the authority of American rule—that would indicate their achievement of a sufficient level of civilization to be entrusted with independence. Quite literally, their independence, it was promised, would be granted when they could be trusted to submit "freely," "all by themselves." Such notions reiterate a founding mythology about the distinctions between Anglo-Saxon and Filipino capabilities, justifying the disenfranchisement of and rule over Filipino subjects through a logic of comparative developmental delay.

What should be clear by such testimony is that Filipinos' actual "capacity" for self-government was able to be questioned only because the logic of racial progress was such that, within the United States, people of Asian descent were already understood to be further behind on the evolutionary scale toward civilization. The legal exclusion of Chinese workers and residents in the United States had been established in 1882, but harassment of and prejudice against Asian residents dated from much earlier.[27] Indispensable to the steady growth of an expanding and industrializing U.S. nation, Asian workers were reviled as racial and cultural Others, as sources of contagion, vice, and crime, and the legal enforcement of discriminatory policies against Asian workers served the very instrumental purpose of keeping them "other" to the national body even as they contributed immeasurably to the expansion of its geographical terrain, resources, and wealth. Within such logic, the idea that Filipinos were a "backward" people, "savage," "tribal," and "uncivilized," resonated with powerful racial and cultural stereotypes that had already formed the conditions for the legal and institutional discrimination against Asians.

At the same time, just as the labor of Asian workers was indispensable to the massive industrialization that had produced the nation's tremendous wealth, the question of U.S. sovereignty in the Philippines in 1898 had little to do with Filipinos' perceived inability to go it alone. Militarily, the islands were regarded as an opportunity for greater U.S. influence in the Pacific. Fears about European commercial and military influence in China made the prospect of U.S. naval bases in the Philippines an attractive possibility.[28] More significantly, business interests in the Philippines were influential in making the case for continued, unfettered access to the resources of the island. The period of economic depression between 1893 and 1897 elevated anxieties about Americans' ability to consume the products of an increasingly efficient productive capacity, and markets in China and Japan were seen as a solution for the problem of overproduction. As the historian Brooks Adams advised, "The expansion of any country must depend on the market for its surplus product; and China is the only region which now promises almost boundless possibilities of absorption, especially in the way of iron for its railroads."[29] Cotton, iron, and other goods were increasingly exported to China in the last decade of the century; the United States' total exports to China grew from $4 million in 1890, to almost $12 million in 1897.[30] Even Albert J. Beveridge, hyperbolic defender of U.S. empire, admitted that the imperial cause was one of both "opportunity and duty" and urged U.S. lawmakers to repeal all duties on

Philippine goods and open the Philippines to "all American markets."[31] Consequently, racialized understandings of Filipinos as unfit for independence were inextricably linked to the exploitation of both the human labor and the material resources that the islands would provide.

Within this context, the educational paradigm was a crucial lens through which the exploitative colonial relationship could be recast as a benevolent civilizing mission. When President McKinley denied the material benefits of laying claim to the islands by claiming that "we could not leave them to themselves—they were unfit for self-government," he was implicitly reshaping Euro-American cultural fears about Asian vice by depicting Filipinos as errant children who needed the paternalistic guidance of the white American authority.[32] Within the new embrace of the Anglo-Americanism as an "imperial race," the educational project expanded upon a more general model in which Filipinos were imagined as students and white Americans as teachers in the lessons of racial uplift, self-government, and Anglo-Protestant civilization. Through such programs, the school system was instrumental both as the "most effective solution" toward the "social transformation of the people" and as the signifier or benevolent dominance in the reinforcement of a racialized hierarchy, imagined as benevolent dominance, on the part of the U.S. civil government in the archipelago.[33] Clearly, then, the utopian promise of public education was a defining one for U.S. colonial administrators. As Dean Worcester wrote in 1914, in his two-volume study of the Philippines, "No work accomplished since the American occupation is of more fundamental and far-reaching importance than that of the Bureau of Education."[34]

Literary Histories of Philippine–U.S. Relations

At the same time that the United States was working to establish its public school system as an apparatus of colonial rule in the Philippines, it was opening schools in Puerto Rico, Cuba, and Hawai'i as well. As parts of the newly acquired island territories, each island was assigned a commission of American politicians and educators who reported back to President McKinley and who outlined the shared principles that guided the educational apparatus in the island territories: expansion of primary education, extensive lessons on hygiene, moral behavior, and civic duty, and the introduction of English as the language of business and commerce.[35] In Puerto Rico and Hawai'i, as in the Philippines, administrators of the civil governments and the school system regarded the natives as members of "less fortunate races" and imagined that the role of the school was to provide a proper moral compass to its students, as well as to cultivate an appreciation for the achievements of Anglo-American civilization. In each case, too, school administrators insisted that the native populations were not simply willing, but "exceedingly anxious to learn to read, write, and speak the English language."[36] To this end, American teachers were recruited to teach in the islands, enlisted in "great armies of instruction" to do work that was "in every respect pioneer work" and thus to serve as agents of Manifest Destiny beyond the continental borders of the United States.[37]

Despite the apparent similarities, however, the status of each island in its differential relation to the United States meant that while their initial organizing structures were similar, the education systems and curricular impositions that evolved were quite different. One difference was the attitude toward instruction in English. While each of the school systems focused on English education, in Puerto Rico this instruction was bilingual for the first years of the colonial government, and the debates about, and contestations of, the primacy of English education continued well beyond the first superintendents' efforts to foreground English as the primary language of instruction. Henry K. Carroll, special commissioner for the United States to Puerto Rico, argued that "the attachment to [Spanish] has long and strong roots. It will not do and it is not necessary to take any harsh measures against it. . . . Both Spanish and English may be used side by side for years to come."[38] This policy was written into the curriculum by the head of Puerto Rico's Bureau of Education in 1900, when he prepared the first set of teachers' manuals outlining instruction in both Spanish and English; he offered that "the justification of the study of two languages lies in the fact that one is the mother tongue of the great majority of the pupils of the Island. . . . The other language is destined to be the business and political language of this Island, and should be taught in order that the rising generation may have the same advantages in a business, professional or political career as their compatriots of the mainland."[39]

To be sure, it was at every point made clear that the pedagogical priority was granted to English. Maj. Gen. Guy Henry, the military governor of Puerto Rico, authorized that all secondary and postsecondary graduates be examined in English, and that teachers who spoke English receive preferential treatment for promotion; teachers of English were paid higher wages than other instructors, and all Puerto Rican teachers were required to learn English during separate training periods and summer teachers' retreats.[40] Moreover, the curricular substitution of U.S. history and geography for what had formerly been Spanish and insular history and geography courses made explicit the end goal of this instruction.[41] However, the focus on bilingual education departed significantly from the program under way in the Philippines. As I explain in greater detail in chapter 1, in the Philippines the U.S. education system insisted on the absolute sovereignty of English; arguments asserting the racial and linguistic diversity of the islands were among those most often repeated as proof of the necessity of U.S. rule as a means toward eventual self-government. At no point was instruction authorized in Spanish, not to mention Tagalog or any other of the native languages. Rather, colonial administrators insisted that English would be the necessary "medium of transmission" of both "modern modes of thought" and "modern civilization."[42] It was in the Philippines that English came to bear a strong moral weight, and was imagined to be a civilizing agent in its own right. English, as I explain in chapter 1, was proposed as the "alchemy" by which recalcitrant and "backward" Filipino subjects would be transformed into willing modern political subjects.

Perhaps a more significant difference is visible at the level of curriculum design. In Puerto Rico, Cuba, and Hawai'i, the educational programs that developed slanted heavily toward manual and industrial education. José-Manuel Navarro reports that in Puerto Rico, the administrators borrowed from the curricular models established at Hampton and Tuskegee; as early as 1900, Richard Henry Pratt, the head of the Carlisle School, sent a set of educational models to Gen. John Eaton, the first U.S. commissioner of education there.[43] In addition, Booker T. Washington opened the doors of Tuskegee to cohorts of Cuban students in 1899, and Puerto Rican students in 1900, all as part of a plan for inculcating a love of industry, thrift, and modesty, with the goal of "instituting American culture and American educational ideals in Porto Rico."[44]

In Hawai'i, too, the emphasis of the U.S.-run educational system was decidedly on vocational education.[45] American missionaries had begun to establish schools in Hawai'i as early as the 1820s, bringing with them new religious doctrine, educational ideals, and devastating disease. Upon the annexation of the islands in 1898, the enactment of a compulsory education law aimed to bring under more direct American influence the diversity of populations who had been recruited or compelled to the islands as cheap labor for the highly profitable system of agricultural export. Doubtless the great force of these business interests in the political affairs of the islands had much to do with the vocational orientation of the educational system; this was spelled out quite clearly by Katherine M. Cook, chief of the Office of Education's Division of Special Problems, in saying that the schools' objective to provide "the ability to make good in some type of productive labor" was "responsive to the particular situation in Hawai'i whose industrial system demands unskilled and low-cost workers, almost wholly of the agricultural variety." "Academic programs," Cook asserted, "have not proved successful in meeting the problem in Hawaii."[46] Despite the grand rhetoric about education for moral uplift and participation in the upward mobility of American democracy, Cook reiterated her point in asserting that "the need then as now is for unskilled labor. . . . A school program limited to the usual academic subjects would ignore almost entirely the very heart of the life work of the Islands."[47] This was, in no uncertain terms, a curriculum designed for servitude and labor, and in that regard it differed little from those at the Hampton Institute and the Tuskegee Institute, which had established programs of reading, writing, and vocational training as the way to efficiently assimilate Native American and African American students.

Peter Schmidt has demonstrated that the educational institutions of the territories acquired in 1898 borrowed from the model of racial uplift in schools across the post-Reconstruction South, and in turn reinforced such practices as legitimate social policy. In describing what he calls "Jim Crow colonialism," Schmidt argues compellingly that it was through the adaptation of those models in the colonial context that Jim Crow segregation became codified as national policy that then expanded beyond the South to inform the national discourse of Progressive educational reform. Thus was the expansion of Progressive education to the colonies inextricably linked to the revivification of Reconstruction's policies of racial uplift, reanimating that "paradoxical mix of citizen-building and subjection at the heart of Progressivist discourse at home and abroad."[48] It is all the more striking, then, that the curriculum in the Philippines developed in quite a different direction. Fred Atkinson, the first superintendent of education, wrote to Booker T. Washington to solicit his advice about the project of Filipino education; before the commencement of his work in the islands, Atkinson visited Hampton, Tuskegee, and Carlisle to assess them as models of the potential for the education of "inferior races." Likewise, his successor, David Barrows, toured several Native American reservation schools with the idea that these would prove to be useful models for the organization of schools in rural and mountainous areas of the islands.

Instead, he ended his tour convinced that the Native American reservation schools had been unsuccessful in winning the hearts and minds of the students. As I explore in more detail in chapters 1 and 2, Barrows set out quite deliberately to create a curriculum that would focus heavily on English-language acquisition and, for the more advanced students, American literature study as the mechanisms through which Filipinos would be persuaded about the benefits of continued U.S. rule and convinced of the superiority of American civilization.

Why, then, might administrators in the Philippines have decided upon a humanistic curriculum, particularly during a period when industrial education was deemed more advantageous for racialized populations in the United States and its other newly acquired territories? The crucial distinction was the question of eligibility for citizenship, which, combined with the factors of racial difference and geographical distance, presented the literary object as a practical and efficient tool of colonial rule. In theory, Hawai'ians became eligible for U.S. citizenship upon annexation in 1898; Puerto Ricans were made U.S. citizens only in 1917. However, from the first, school administrators advocated for Puerto Rican statehood quite explicitly and vociferously. In contrast, the administrators of the school system in the Philippines insisted that Filipinos were racially unassimilable and that the purpose of the colonial system in the Philippines was to secure the favorable conditions for U.S. "development" there, to establish a strategic military presence, and to prepare the islands for self-government. Nominal independence, at least, was the spoken intention for the Philippines, even if its timeline and structure were never formalized. Moreover, they argued that the departure of U.S. troops would leave the islands vulnerable to a despotic colonial rule by some other European power, and the departure of the civil government would constitute the "abandonment" of the natives, who were referred to as children in need of American parental protection.

Such paternalistic notions had everything to do with the racialized status of Filipinos and the context of late nineteenth-century fears of the "yellow peril" and restrictions on Asian immigration. Filipinos were considered "nationals" and could migrate to the United States freely after 1898 and were exempted from Asian exclusion laws. As such, they were aggressively targeted by labor recruiters in Hawai'i and in the United States, with a dramatic period of migration in the first decades of the century, such that by 1930 there were 30,470 Filipinos in California alone.[49] At the same time, Filipinos in the United States were subject to harassment, labor intimidation, and unfair restrictions in housing, marriage, and other basic living conditions. It is in the context of these restrictions and the anxieties about racial mixing that underpinned them that the mobilization of the literary was deemed efficacious in providing a persuasive ideological basis for the asserted superiority of Anglo Americanism.

Rather than an anticipated statehood, the strategy in the Philippines was one of "Filipinization": the "gradual substitution of Filipino personnel for American administrators and clerks in the colonial government." Whereas tax and tariff laws in Puerto Rico contributed to an administrative and educational system in which political power was highly centralized, consolidated largely in the hands of American officials and a few Puerto Rican elites, when U.S. officials in the Philippines were unable to generate the income they desired through similar tariff laws, they were forced to develop a less-centralized model of colonial administration, giving nominal control to provincial governments led by Filipino elites. The result, according to Julian Go, was that the process of "Filipinization" depended upon a much more fluid, amorphous strategy of winning the collaboration of Filipino elites; this necessitated a decentralized and delicate organization of domination.[50] The moral mandate of a literary humanist education was thus a strategic part of the colonial apparatus that promised gradual independence and Filipino autonomy while assuring the ideological assimilation of Filipinos to the cultural values of Americanism. In literary education, Filipinos were supposed to absorb the cultural, political, and moral values of an emergent middle-class white Americanism, as well as learn submission to, if not gratitude for, the authority of the United States' government. Through the strategy of Filipinization, the civil government attempted to assure Filipinos' complicity with the American values taught through the educational system so urgently established under U.S. rule. As Renato Constantino has argued, "education became miseducation because it began to de-Filipinize the youth, taught them to regard American culture as superior to any other, and American society as the model par excellence for Philippine society."[51]

Imperialism and the Pedagogical Public Sphere

The conditions in which colonial tutelage in the Philippines could come to be so instrumental at the end of the nineteenth century were marked by a particular investment in the transformative, even rehabilitative power of education. The idea that education was fundamentally linked to citizenship dates back to the founding of the republic, and the cultural weight assigned to the status of educated versus noneducated individuals overlaps with the class, race, and gender distinctions that have been at the center of negotiations about whose cultural traditions count, and which social groups would see their practices abstracted as the national culture. Education, in other words, was an issue both of cultural definition and of social control long before it became, in the late nineteenth century, the privileged tool of liberal white "progressive" reformers seeking to intervene in the political and cultural traditions of working-class, immigrant, and nonwhite peoples. Among the Founding Fathers, Thomas Jefferson noted the nationalist significance of education both in the formation of a ruling class and in the establishment of democracy; attempting to implement a new system of education in Virginia, he proposed the Bill for the More General Diffusion of Knowledge in 1779, arguing that a free society depended upon public schools as the basis of a well-educated and thus autonomous citizenry.[52] In a move indicative of significant opposition to the idea of public funding of mass education, Virginia failed to pass Jefferson's bill, and it was only after the Civil War, nearly a century later, that it instituted the large-scale public education that Jefferson proposed. Benjamin Franklin, too, designed a system of pragmatic education in his 1750 proposal for an English School in Philadelphia, where reading in English would be primary, so as to "early acquaint [students] with the Meaning and Force of Words" and "the Understandings or Morals of the Youth, May at the same Time be improv'd."[53] Franklin emphasized a curriculum in English, rather than in classical languages, as a pragmatic measure, asserting that "tho' unacquainted with any ancient or foreign Tongue, [students] will be Masters of their own, which is of more immediate and general Use."[54] The utility of mastery in reading and writing in English followed in later years by instruction in mathematics, geography, and drawing, would lay the foundation for an educated and therefore autonomous population who, despite little knowledge of classical languages, would have great success in the more practical skills necessary for civic participation.

While Jefferson and Franklin envisioned different paths toward the shaping of a citizenry of a limited participatory democracy, both saw education as essential to the selective cultivation of that citizenry, and looked to education as an institution that would promote the interests of the Anglo-American propertied class and safeguard those interests by defining them not as particular interests at all, but rather as legitimately national ones. Against these elitist, philosophical affirmations of the importance of education to the democratic mission of the United States stands the history in which literacy was a criminal offense among captive African Americans, thus doubly enforcing the equation between citizenship and education by making illiteracy a condition used to justify and perpetuate the system of slavery. The enduring and strategic hypocrisy of this standard is highlighted in a formative moment of Frederick Douglass's autobiographical *Narrative*, in which he performs his own mastery of writing by transcribing the words of Hugh Auld, "If you teach that nigger (speaking of myself) how to read, there would be no keeping him. It would forever unfit him to be a slave."[55] Mimicking the words of his captor, Douglass points to the entrenched logic of education and domination within a very different relationship, in which the withholding of certain forms of knowledge constituted a part of a broader program of repression.

Such examples are merely grounding points meant to indicate the extent to which the function of education in the United States has been to absorb some subjects into the national body while excluding others; in particular, the cultivation or denial of literacy has been a primary apparatus for including or excluding select communities as citizens and as national subjects. But the origins of literary study and the nationalist implications of the field of English as it developed at the end of the nineteenth century involved much more than the expansion of literacy training; its emergence also depended upon the standardization of English as the primary language of that democracy, unofficial and yet violently enforced. Lastly, it required the widespread acceptance of the literary as a new organ of national culture, part of a corpus of shared cultural texts assumed to impart a common body of knowledge and, implicitly, provide a shared system of values among the nation's disparate populations.

This fundamentally new place of education at the center of the social production of the citizen in the late nineteenth century marks the formation of what I will call the *pedagogical public sphere*.[56] By this I mean to indicate several intertwined developments. The first was the unprecedented importance education held in the social imaginary at the end of the nineteenth century, as the institution that might address social discord and guarantee the smooth functioning of a representative democracy. Until the early nineteenth century, formal education was the privilege of the very few, and public schools, when they existed, were charged mainly to teach basic reading, writing, and arithmetic at the primary level.[57] The great expansion of educational facilities in the nineteenth century, particularly after the disestablishment of the church in 1833, marked the growing importance of the school as the site for the formation of a working democracy. The most notable champion of this shift was Horace Mann, who, acting in the newly created post of secretary to the Massachusetts State Board of Education, regarded the public-school movement as "the great equalizer" that would eradicate poverty, sickness, and crime.[58] With a critical eye toward the American class system, Mann reported that "[universal education] gives each man the independence and the means by which he can resist the selfishness of other men. It does better than to disarm the poor of their hostility towards the rich; it prevents being poor."[59] Mann thus conceived of the common school as a force of individualism and independence that would contribute to the vitality of American culture by teaching a common set of beliefs and knowledges. As importantly, the school would be a primary civic institution entrusted with the formation of new citizens and, simultaneously, new publics.

At issue for Mann and other supporters of the public education movement was both the extension of education to better fit the masses for citizenship and the standardization of training adapted to the newly expanding middle class. Of the reforms that Mann championed, most notable was the standardization he sought through the professionalizing of the school. The training of teachers in normal schools, the organization of the curriculum into progressive grades, and compulsory attendance were all part of Mann's vision.[60] In its new function as the sole place for the child's early education, the school functioned, as Richard Brodhead has noted, as the "tutelary adjunct" of the middle-class home, reinforcing the school as an essential "training ground" for citizens of the republic, while expanding the standardization essential to the consolidation of a national culture compatible with, or indeed elaborated from, the norms of Anglo-American domesticity.[61] Such a development points to the disciplinary power of the school, mobilized not in the name of religion but according to the disciplinary structures, habits, and values of an emergent middle-class culture. As the education historian Lawrence Cremin notes:

> The school performed many functions: it provided youngsters with an opportunity to become literate in a standard American English via the Webster speller and the McGuffey readers; it offered youngsters a common belief system combining undenominational Protestantism and nonpartisan patriotism; it afforded youngsters an elementary familiarity with simple

arithmetic, bits and pieces of literature, history, geography, and some rules
of life at the level of the maxim and proverb; it introduced youngsters to an
organized subsociety other than the household and church that observed
such norms as punctuality, achievement, competitiveness, fair play, merit,
and respect for adult authority.[62]

Cremin's description of the intellectual, moral, and physical discipline entrusted to the common school clearly marks its role as the training ground
for the growing managerial class, and the formation of a dominant national
culture aligned with the sensibilities of the expanding middle class. The
school functioned as a primary institutional force in buttressing the "intellectual and moral leadership" that, as Antonio Gramsci has illustrated, is
essential in assuring the supremacy of a particular social group. Gramsci
argues that a social group may "dominate" antagonistic forces through violent means, but it must always also create institutions through which it
"leads" as well, by educating the desires, sensibilities, and ideological values
of its subjects.[63] Thus, by the middle of the nineteenth century, the school
had solidified its role both as an arbiter of national culture and as the site
for producing its citizens; in other words, it functioned as a site for the social formation of citizens as subjects, both by the inculcation of a common,
standardized body of information as the condition of the subject's legibility
as a citizen, and by enforcing the state's authority over its subjects as one
of tutelage. By the end of the nineteenth century, there was a common-
sense belief in the essential role of the school and in the utility of the basic
skills that could be learned there, a belief reflected in the fact that by 1900,
primary enrollment reached 94 percent.[64] Not only was literacy fundamental to citizenship, but the exercise of civil responsibilities, according to
nineteenth-century reformers, depended upon skillful instruction of those
responsibilities to the public—in other words, a pedagogical intervention
into the public sphere in which educators would guide individuals into the
duties of citizenship.

Accompanying the growing importance of the school was a shift in the
content of such training, particularly as the school adapted to the role of
managing the social and economic transformations of the second half of
the century. Thus the second aspect of the citizen's education that I mean
to highlight in referencing the pedagogical public sphere is the new role of
the literary that worked to extend the values of the white middle class as
it differentiated those values from the cultural traditions of other populations that were selectively included or excluded from recognition within

the national body. Among the many social and material dislocations of the last quarter of the century—industrialization, labor unrest, new patterns of immigration from Europe and Asia, as well as urbanization, emancipation, and woman suffrage—the function of literature as part of a humanist education became increasingly important as a tool for defending the primacy of Anglo-American cultural traditions, and for initiating the nation's racialized Others into those traditions. Christopher Newfield has written eloquently about this functioning by noting that "all humanisms have been, in some way, *disciplinary* humanism, constructing manageable subjects. All humanisms have been, in some way, *supremacist* humanisms, entangled in the user's attempts to justify the superiority of a national status, an opposition to strangers, a way of life."[65] As Newfield has demonstrated, historically the liberal arts were regarded as the "expression of human freedom," *liberal* referring to the arts that could occupy the leisure time of a class not obliged to work—that is, slave-owning and elite classes.[66]

Building upon the legacy of Romantic humanists of the early nineteenth century, humanism posited the liberal arts as the artist's freedom from commerce and industrialism, a meaning that, by the end of the century, contributed to the strong associative link between literature and cultural and moral value. But such values continued to advance the interests of another leisured class, striving to normalize the dominance of American middle-class identity in "its difference from—and superiority to—other classes."[67] In the expansion of the school as an apparatus of civil authority and cultural training and the extension of literary education as a part of the public school's mission, the literary served both of these functions, extending the authority of the white, American middle class, its supremacy over other classes, and its authority to discipline and subject. Within the late nineteenth-century pedagogical formation of the state, the category of literature was invested with the power of cultural training, an assimilative force meant to keep at bay the frightening disjunctures signaled by the increasingly visible evidence of racial and cultural difference. Inasmuch as access to education was crucially linked to access to the privileges of citizenship and participation in the representative democracy, the function of the humanities in the newly invented public school serves as an adept and alarming barometer of the formation of a late nineteenth-century national culture.

In addition to the new importance of education in the social imaginary and the role of the literary in extending the values of the white middle class as those of the nation more broadly, the third sense of the pedagogical public sphere that I mean to highlight here is the metaphoric and literal functioning of education as a strategy of containment. Despite the temptation to understand the history of education as one of progressively expanding opportunity for a widening number of people, it is important to acknowledge the ample evidence that this expansion was, at best, uneven and contradictory.[68] The truth about the movement toward universal public education in the nineteenth century was that it was not universal at all, but limited by race and segregated by class and gender. Inasmuch as the culture of education that developed in the second half of the nineteenth century was part of a larger project of defining the nation in the midst of enormous changes among its citizenry and its landscape, one need not look far to see plainly that the main function of education for many populations was the imposition of the habits and norms of middle-class Anglo-American life, at the expense of their own cultural traditions, livelihoods, and sometimes even their lives.[69]

Particularly after the Civil War, education became a primary mechanism for social containment and cultural assimilation, imagined as the institution poised for the "rehabilitation" of newly freed African Americans and the "pacification" of Native Americans. In these instances, the function of education as a medium of social control was rendered more apparent. Institutions such as the Hampton Normal and Agricultural Institute in Virginia, which was established in 1868 for the manual training of African Americans, were organized according to the logic of domestic tutelage, in which it was believed that African Americans would benefit morally from the labor exacted from them at the school, as well as from their emulation of the codes of middle-class, white domesticity. While operating as a normal school that trained teachers for black schools in the South, Hampton also stuck to a rigid curriculum of industrial and agricultural training. Despite the criticism of other community members, including one who insisted that it was the "height of foolishness" to think that former slaves needed training to work, Hampton's founder and headmaster, Gen. Samuel Chapman Armstrong, insisted upon the efficacy of industrial training over an academic curriculum, saying that "it will pay in a *moral* way. It will make them men and women as nothing else will. It is the only way to make them Christians."[70] Such sinister visions formed the flip side to Mann's ideals of education as the handmaiden of independence; these schools were crucial to the maintenance of unequal social and material relations between white Americans and African Americans, fashioning programs in the "domestic arts" and agricultural labor while scripting this "progressive" education as the fulfillment of political independence for African Americans.

Among the many tragedies that accompanied Hampton's strict adherence to a vocational curriculum was the fact that many of these skills, particularly the aspects of industrial training, were already anachronistic in the quickly industrializing economy. As Laura Wexler has demonstrated, "the individualized, small-scale, low-capital, unmechanized operations that Hampton taught . . . [were] in actuality outmoded most as soon as [they were] learned. It was training for a second-class career at best and more likely for domestic service or low-level, nonunion labor."[71] The point, however, was that the training itself, not the job it would later enable its owner to take up, revealed the moral imperative behind the curriculum and the school. Similarly, as the history of forced education for Native Americans bears witness, for example, the "democracy" promised by the common school was one of violent deracination and forced submission to white hegemony, at an extraordinary cost in human life.[72] As at Hampton, industrial training was deemed necessary for Native Americans, whose pacification was attempted through the (often compulsory) attendance of Native children at residential schools where they were expected to adopt the dress, language, eating habits, and daily regimen of their white counterparts.[73] In some cases, Native children were forced into hard labor at school, so as to provide for the material gain of the institution that held them captive. Other times, they were farmed out as domestics to white families. The proliferation of such examples demonstrates the power of education in a white cultural imaginary for envisioning the annihilation of cultural difference and the "assimilation" of nonwhite subjects in their roles in a highly racially segregated social formation. This pedagogical intervention underscores how, despite the curricular differences, by the end of the nineteenth century it was the book and not the sword that was understood to solve the "Native problem," thus setting a strong precedent for the U.S. occupation of the Philippines, where a tutelary paradigm of "benevolent assimilation" insisted on the necessity of moral, intellectual, and political training for Filipinos as the condition of their eventual independence.

By referring to the pedagogical public sphere, I mean to highlight these multiple facets that characterized the expansion of education as an institutional force linked to the privileges of citizenship, cultural and political legibility, and bodily freedom. Contingent upon this conceptualization of the educated citizen is the governing metaphor of education as tutelage, a force in the "rehabilitation" of the nation's other publics. As should be clear, I do not refer to a utopian vision of public discourse where individuals debate the common good. I do not mean, to use Jürgen Habermas's words, "a realm of our social life in which something approaching public opinion can be formed [and where] access is guaranteed to all citizens."[74] Quite the contrary: I use the phrase precisely to isolate the contradictions most thoughtfully articulated by Nancy Fraser: the concept of the public sphere, as outlined by Habermas, is both essential as a analytic for "theorizing the limits of democracy," and limited as an explanatory concept in that it refers only to an idealized version of democratic access while erasing the histories of multiple counterpublics.[75]

Thus, my concerns echo George Eley's critique of the concept of the public sphere as an idea through which the bourgeoisie marked their interests and their public institutions as universal. That is to say, the public sphere operates as a function of hegemony to mark as public, as "popular," the interests of a specific class.[76] Operating on both discursive and institutional levels, the "pedagogical public sphere" characterized a moment when the state's hegemonic function was mobilized through the school (on the institutional level) as well as through a pedagogical discourse in which the interests of the middle class were extended, often violently, as a form of progressive tutelage. Including the history of U.S. expansion into the Pacific diversifies this frame, responding to the call of scholars like Anna Brickhouse, who urges that we "reenvision the nineteenth-century public sphere itself as a plurality of competing and often mutually antagonistic public spheres."[77] This book hopes to broaden the scope of these competing public spheres to include one important part of this newly reframed story. This is one of transpacific contact and textual imposition—what I define in chapter 1 as the literary imperative—through which the meanings of American culture were redefined in the late nineteenth and early twentieth centuries. In accounting for the extranational circulation of American literature and its use as an instrument of colonial dominance, I will demonstrate, our geographical and ideological understandings of late nineteenth-century and early twentieth-century American literatures become increasingly vexed.

By the 1890s, as I have argued, the question was not whether the state should take up the task of educating its citizenry but how it would do so. In this function it was crucial that the state seem to represent and speak to and for all of its citizens equally, even while it worked to maintain specific and uneven social relations. As Gramsci again reminds us:

In reality, the State must be conceived of as an "educator," in as much as it tends precisely to create a new type or level of civilisation. Because one is acting essentially on economic forces, reorganising and developing the apparatus of economic production, creating a new structure, the conclusion must not be drawn that superstructural factors should be left to themselves, to develop spontaneously, to a haphazard and sporadic germination. The State, in this field, too, is an instrument of "rationalisation," of acceleration, and of Taylorisation. It operates according to a plan, urges, incites, solicits, and "punishes."[78]

Here we see most clearly Gramsci's delineation of the importance of the ideological—the superstructural—in the maintenance of power. Far from superfluous, it is the realm in which the state "educates," which is to say, creates its subjects in the double sense: authorizing them as subjects while subjecting them to its authority. Put another way, Gramsci reminds us that the ideological cannot be relegated to the realm of "mere ideas" or understood as the superstructural *effect* of economic relations; rather, ideology is the field upon which the struggle for dominance is fought and won. While the expansionist interests of the state competed for domination through military struggle abroad, it competed on a different terrain altogether for what Gramsci calls "intellectual and moral leadership" both at home and in the newly acquired territories. The former struggle was located firmly on a group of islands that McKinley himself reported not to have been able to locate on a map, but the second took place not only in the archipelago but also across the United States, where the legitimation of the imperial project brought to the fore the instability of the proclaimed superiority of the U.S. republic and posed questions about the content of American national culture.

It is in this shift that the field of American letters took shape, emerging at the core of the new curriculum. I hope to demonstrate how the literary served as a crucial site for determining what counted as a legitimate national public by determining which texts would constitute the nation's cultural traditions, becoming, ideally and ideologically if not practically, the basis for a shared national culture. In linking the formation of American literary culture, and the national identity it worked to consolidate, to the imperial project in the Philippines, this book illuminates the transpacific connections between the diverse publics in the United States and its colonial sites in the Philippines. The school, as an institution in the emergence of the bourgeois public sphere, has been a primary site for that

competition. Likewise, the notion of the pedagogical as a vector for social relations—that is, the notion that individuals were to be instructed
in their proper place as national subjects—participates in the contesta-
tory discourse between versions of the public sphere. It is this sense of
the pedagogical public sphere—the rhetorical force of the pedagogical as
a conceptual framework for producing the citizen's lived relation to national culture—that provided the framework for the modern history of
American letters.

My book connects these curricular developments in the United States
with the imperial educational framework in the occupied Philippines in
order to explore the transnational publics that emerged after 1898. One
limitation of such a study is that there is a great deal of emphasis on the
administrative and ideological designs of the colonial project in the Philippines and less emphasis on the process of reception and resistance to
those designs. Indeed, it could be argued that the book's focus on the perspectives and decisions of the colonizing power—the colonial functionaries, the political operatives, and the American teachers themselves—risks
reenacting the violence of the colonial paradigm by effacing the paths of
resistance that Filipinos invented and navigated in response to this imposition. I have tried to address the question of the varied responses to
the imposition of English and of American literature in the Philippines by
pointing to patterns of literary and literary-critical production among Filipino and Filipino American writers, particularly in chapters 4 and 5. But
I have accorded much greater detail and emphasis to the language, mechanisms, and assumptions of the colonizers here for two distinct reasons.
Tracing reception for determinations of resistance, while necessary, is also
a theoretically compromised task. For the most part, collected responses
of students of the American educational system have been eerily upbeat
about the legacy of the "Thomasites," as American teachers in the Philippines were called, and the curriculum of texts and ideals they designed
for the colonial educational project.[79] Such texts complicate any binary
the critic might hope to map between an unequivocal U.S. dominance on
the one hand and Filipino resistance on the other. That said, the question of resistance has been documented to useful ends elsewhere. In the
context of the Philippines, Vicente Rafael's study of the nationalist plays
that emerged in response to the U.S. census project in the Philippines,
and John D. Blanco's exploration of the political and cultural forms that
emerged to contest Spanish colonial rule at the end of the nineteenth century, are especially important contributions. In particular, Rafael's focus

on the seditionist plays, written in the Tagalog vernacular and popular among working-class and nationalist elites, illuminates a specific mode in which Filipinos contested the epistemological and administrative paradigms of American colonial rule; Blanco's analysis of the counterhistories of colonial rule illuminates how the crisis in colonial hegemony gave rise to political expressions that "revealed the exploration, experimentation, and transgression of meanings and values of colonial society."[80] On the broader subject of literature and colonialism, another important contribution is Priya Joshi's study of the English novel's reception in India, which studies the circulation of fiction in India with fine nuance to the historical and regional distinctions in what texts were read, in which languages, and by whom.[81]

This book's primary purpose, however, is to intervene in the historical field-formation of American literature, and to make the case for a new perspective on the ideological and geographical origins of the field. Given this necessarily limited scope, I have not been able to attend to the complexities of resistance with the detail that would otherwise have been possible. The point, however, is not to make U. S. hegemony appear seamless (which of course was not the case), but to locate the contradictions and constitutive tensions within the ideological outline of the program of literary humanism as a form of colonial tutelage itself. Humanism was formalized, as Lisa Lowe has demonstrated, in an "economy [that] civilizes and develops freedoms for 'man' in modern Europe, while relegating others to geographical and temporal spaces that are constituted as uncivilized and unfree."[82] *Empire's Proxy* seeks to show how American literature was one such site of reproduction for what Lowe demonstrates as the liberal humanist "violence of forgetting" the conditions of unfreedom for others, both in the United States and outside of it. Further studies, informed by the principles of subaltern historiography and focused on how Filipinos exploited those contradictions, are undoubtedly still necessary.

Empire's Proxy thus attempts to theorize the formation of American literary culture, and the national identity it worked to consolidate, as achieved in the global, transpacific articulation between the multiple publics in the United States and its colonial sites in the Philippines. Scholar C. J. Wan-ling Wee has reminded us that the lesson of Edward Said's *Orientalism* (1978), published some thirty years ago, is that the material and discursive creation of the colonial Other is not without its effects upon the cultural formation of the colonizers themselves.[83] With this in mind, the chapters that follow aim to show that the origins of American literature are both nationalist and necessarily international, found in the curricular reforms of New England but also in the ideological and practical administration of its Philippine colony. Chapters 1 and 2 address these questions most explicitly. Chapter 1, "The Alchemy of English," reads the archives of the U.S. civil government in the Philippines to trace the pedagogy of English in the islands. In particular, I detail how the English language was posited as the lingua franca of democracy in the Philippines precisely because of the symbolic capital attributed to American and English *literature* at the end of the nineteenth century in the United States, as the marker of education, taste, and elevated class status. Thus English was imposed upon the polyglot nation of the Philippines as a new language of dominance and a new signifying system, the language itself heralded as the "alchemy" that would transform resistant, racialized Filipino subjects into willing colonial subjects.

Chapter 2, "Empire's Proxy," turns to the instruction of American literature in both the United States and the Philippines. In the antebellum period, literature functioned as an agent in the extension and popularization of middle-class sentimentalism; I explore how, in the colonial context, it served as a privileged vehicle for the extension of that sensibility beyond the confines of the "domestic" and into the "foreign." Its crucial function, in this context, was to model this sensibility and teach its forms of self-discipline by making such discipline seem internal to the colonized subject herself. Literature, in that sense, became an apt proxy in the service of empire. In the absence of a white majority to survey, discipline, and reward the compliance of its colonial subjects to the norms of middle-class, white culture, the book became a powerful surrogate for communicating those values, transporting and enacting them in classrooms across the islands.

The ideological framework of colonial tutelage functioned not just as an institutionalized model of formal instruction, but as the guiding logic for the colonial project itself. Chapter 3, "Agents of Assimilation," explores the means through which the teacher-student relation provided a more general model for U.S.–Philippine relations, looking in particular at the gendered and racialized dynamics of tutelage as negotiated in the writings of American teachers recruited to work on the islands. To explore the representational and ideological nuances of this shift, this chapter focuses on the narratives of two teachers living and working in the Philippines: Mary Fee's *A Woman's Impressions of the Philippines* (1910) and William Freer's *The Philippine Experiences of an American Teacher* (1906). Within the mundane accounts of household management in the islands, these narratives offered a crucial vision of bourgeois respectability as it aligned with the imperial project, carrying abroad the logic of progressive reform and enacting the fantasy of benevolent assimilation through the perfected ordering of household and schoolhouse. At the same time, each illuminates the constitutive contradictions at the heart of the colonial enterprise, challenging those same notions of bourgeois domesticity through unconventional arrangements of dominance and desire made possible by the elasticity of the tutelary as a model of familial intimacy.

In reading the history of the U.S. colonial occupation in the Philippines, the question of resistance to American hegemony remains critical. Chapter 4, "The Performance of Patriotism," approaches the question of resistance through the prolific career of Carlos Bulosan, the Filipino American worker, activist, and poet whose collective autobiography, *America Is in the Heart* (1946), is considered a foundational text in Asian American literary studies. My interest in Bulosan stems from his own treatment as a "rediscovered" writer with a belated acceptance as a canonical author of American literature, and from his important role as a writer of the Philippine diaspora. Bulosan's own movement between the Philippines and the United States foregrounds the centrality of English literacy to his explorations of his transforming identities and his shifting relationship to the ideological power of the American dream. Examining the complexities of the text's regard for literary education and the utopian possibilities it holds for an inclusive public sphere, I argue that Bulosan's text exposes the complex intimacies of education and uplift in a narrative that charts, time and again, the social, political, and emotional costs of the exclusion of colonial subjects from the apparatus of progressive education that was the promise of the colonial occupation. In its formal complexities, nonlinear narrative, and nonsynchronous development, Bulosan establishes an epistemological break in which his readers find the traces of an imperial education, that knowledge project whose effect can only be such contradictions and logical incommensurabilities. As such, Bulosan forcefully contests the premise of American exceptionalism, illuminating the racialized and gendered hierarchies that have historically functioned to preserve the place of white masculinity at the center of the American imaginary.

Finally, in a brief conclusion, I address the legacy of U.S. educational imperialism in the Philippines by way of the continued valorization of literature in English. The conclusion, "An Empire of Letters," considers the distinction, made in 1900 by William Dean Howells, between an empire of and a republic of letters. Howells's view is that the republic of letters that is the publishing market of the United States guarantees, for a time at least, that the great power of the literary will have as much of a chance to do good as it will to do harm. As other critics have suggested, however, the enduring legacy of the U.S. educational system in the Philippines has been to enact a sort of empire of letters, a hierarchy of literary and cultural value that has historically privileged English and effaced the vibrant, revolutionary traditions of vernacular literatures. Such hierarchies of cultural value, I conclude, are not distinct from, but central to, the continued neocolonial exploitation of the Philippines for commercial and military purposes. This example points to the high stakes of educational "reconstruction" in Iraq. Despite more than $100 billion spent by U.S.-contracted private agencies to open schools and train teachers, there is little account of what has been accomplished. More pressing, those few reports that have been made available suggest a strong amount of U.S. censorship in the curriculum design and textbook writing. Such accounts serve as a reminder that the structures of educational imperialism continue to be mobilized in the interests of "rebuilding" occupied regions to make them hospitable for both U.S. military interests and multinational corporations with links to the U.S. government.

To be sure, instruction in American literature was only one part of the mechanism of U.S. rule in the Philippines. However, its importance as a model formation, as the embodiment of those values, morals, and ideals held to be particularly American, should not be underestimated. Similarly, the colonial use of American literature was only one part of the phase of the field's institutionalization in the United States in the early twentieth century. Certainly other aspects, including the rise of a professional managerial class, the expansion of access to the academy for new populations of students, and the concurrent institutionalization of other humanistic disciplines make the full breadth of that history beyond the scope of this study.

That said, the role of the colonial project in animating the consolidation of an American literary "canon" deserves further attention. In particular, this history illuminates not only the expanded international stakes behind the ongoing debates about the constitution and current value of that canon, but also demonstrates the incredible power of the literary in forging, shaping, and naming a national identity it claimed only to describe. It thus created the very national culture that the colonial project presupposed. Lastly, this history demonstrates how important the literary was in establishing the United States as a national player on the world imperial stage. Only through this evidence of its cultural achievements could the United States join Britain in exporting its brand of civilized Anglo-Saxonism and champion its culture as a gift to be bestowed upon those "persons sitting in darkness."[84] For those of us who currently teach, read, and write such literature, we ignore that history at our peril.

1

The Alchemy of English

Colonial State-Building and the Imperial
Origins of American Literary Study

What alchemy will change the oriental quality of their blood, in a
year, and set the self-governing currents of the American pouring
through their Malay veins?

—Senator Albert J. Beveridge, in a speech
delivered before the U. S. Congress, 1900

Our bayonets and rifle balls may force them into subjection but it
is left for our public schools to raise and elevate them and put them
upon the plane of thinking men and women, capable of governing
themselves wisely and well.

—Fred W. Atkinson, general superintendent of
public instruction of the Philippine Islands, 1902

This chapter tells one story, about the origins of the field of
English at the end of the nineteenth century, by way of three shorter stories, each a different episode in the history of English as a language, an
academic field, and a literature. Let me begin in August 1898, in Saratoga,
New York, where, at a meeting of the American Social Science Association
(ASSA), Dr. Holbrook Curtis put forth the idea of forming a special committee of men in literature and the arts. Curtis was not a professional literary man but a throat specialist from New York and an amateur of the arts;
approaching the ASSA president on a hotel veranda in upstate New York,
he proposed a new committee to assume a role like that of the Académie
Française, to stand as "an academic institution of unquestioned origin

and standard" that might recognize men of literary and artistic achievement and provide the occasion for their fraternity together.[1] The next February, in a ballroom rented from the Academy of Medicine in Manhattan, the first annual meeting of the National Institute of Arts and Letters was convened and its charter members selected. That year, the National Institute elected ninety members in literature, forty-five in art, and fourteen in music, and declared its official purpose: to provide for "the advancement of art and literature" and the revitalization of "the traditions of good literature," while remaining "hospitable to all discoverers of new worlds."[2]

The National Institute got off to a rocky start. The first president, Charles Dudley Warner, was so ill that he could not preside over the institute's inaugural meeting in February 1899, and instead had his paper read for him.[3] It soon recovered, however; under the tenure of its second president, William Dean Howells, at the height of his popularity as a novelist and editor, the National Institute began to assemble an impressive membership of literary figures like Henry Adams, Hamlin Garland, and Mark Twain. Within a few years, the membership of the National Institute stood at 150; a smaller, even more selective and elite group of 50 members, calling itself the American Academy of Arts and Sciences, had formed as a subgroup of the National Institute, with the self-appointed responsibility to "assist in securing just dignity and importance for refinement, culture, and creative imagination" and "advise the public on matters of taste regarding literature and the fine arts."[4] Its members included many, though not all, of the recognized authors of the time—all male, all white—as well as some "literary men" in politics: President Theodore Roosevelt and Secretary of State John Hay. While writers dominated its ranks, it was not exclusively a fraternity of authors but an assemblage of men with various connections to the literary—journalists, authors, editors, professors, and others. That is to say, it was elite not in the sense that each of its members was an established creative author, but that each was poised, by virtue of class and of cultural training, to recognize and appreciate "good" literature.

To some of its critics at the time, the National Institute, as well as the even more elite Academy, had little purpose beyond flattering the vanity of its members. William James declined membership in the Academy on the basis that he had a "lifelong practice of not letting [his] name figure where there [was] not some definite work doing in which [he] was willing to bear a share."[5] William Dean Howells betrayed similar fears in his presidential address before the Academy a few years later, when he opined that the American Academy of Arts and Letters could have neither the "authoritative structure" nor the "authoritative office" of Académie Française and its other European counterparts, but must instead content itself to offer merely the "affectionate recognition" of its own members.[6] Subsequent critics have similarly passed it off as an insignificant club with little initial literary or political effect.[7] Nevertheless, the founding of the National Institute bears witness to a cultural shift in the meaning and importance of the literary at the end of the century. Responding to the ready availability of cheap books for mass circulation and the changing material conditions of literary production, the goals of the group were emblematic of a trend that redefined the literary. No longer a broad category that would have included all printed books, "literature" was a concept in transition, coming to signify only creative works that embodied the imaginative genius of the artist and resisted, through the difficulty of language, form, and style, their commodification and mass circulation.[8] As more reading material became available to larger groups of people, the upper classes of the post–Civil War era retreated into what Richard Brodhead has called a "high literary zone" defined by literary magazines which targeted a highly educated audience, and a distinction in which popular writing was marked as "non-literary and unworthy of attention" while other writing was "identified as rare or select: in short, as 'literature.'"[9] The founding of the National Institute, with its goal of advancing the "traditions of good literature," was part of the redefining of the symbolic capital of the literary as a marker of education and elite class taste.[10] That it formed to guard these traditions suggests the sense of threat such men of letters felt from the changing nature of book publishing and of the reading public; that they assigned themselves the ability to confer the value of literariness to particular works and authors indicates the significant ideological value invested in the literary as a signifier of elite cultural status.[11]

As the literary elites of New England were convening to celebrate and safeguard the future of "traditions of good literature" at the "rather vulgarly fashionable spa" in Saratoga, there was quite another conflict playing out eight thousand miles away.[12] My next story begins in Manila that same August, as the United States engaged in a scramble for power in the Philippines. August 1898 witnessed a second project geared to celebrate and preserve a selected set of "American values," this time in the aftermath of the U. S. defeat of the Spanish forces in Manila. President William McKinley attempted to secure U. S. sovereignty in the islands by circulating instructions, translated into Spanish and Tagalog, in which he charged U. S.

commanders with the protection of Filipinos "in their homes, in their employments, and in their personal and religious rights."[13] Directed against the encroachment of British, French, German, and Japanese interests in the archipelago, McKinley's declaration ignored entirely the emergent Philippine Republic that had been established under the presidency of revolutionary leader Emilio Aguinaldo, as well as its subsequent infrastructural achievements: Aguinaldo's Declaration of Independence issued in June, the appointment of an executive cabinet, and the establishment of an official state press, *El Heraldo de la Revolución*.[14] Instead, McKinley's declaration signaled the start of a competitive state-building process in which the United States attempted to safeguard the Philippines as its war bounty by inventing and insisting upon a particular image of Filipinos as a "backward race," incapable of self-government and thus in need of the protectionist guidance of American sovereignty. Despite the fact that the United States had initially publicized its intervention as an effort to assist in Cuba's war for liberation against the "tyranny of Spanish rule," here the refusal to recognize Philippine independence was quickly reframed as a transfer from despotic rule to benevolent tutelage, as reflected in McKinley's "firm hope" that "all the inhabitants of the Philippine Islands may come to look back with gratitude to the day when God gave victory to American arms at Manila and set their land under the sovereignty and the protection of the people of the United States."[15]

Though members of the newly minted National Institute of Arts and Letters were almost certainly following newspaper accounts of the adventures of Commodore Dewey and his naval successes in the Philippines, it is doubtful that they perceived a connection between the institutional, literary flag-staking they had just performed and the expansionist maneuvers underway in the Philippines. In fact, most would have vociferously denied that any political intentions characterized the group, and the anti-imperialist views of several of its members, including Mark Twain, Hamlin Garland, and Howells himself, among others, would have made less likely the possibility that they would have seen their fraternity of letters in such a nationalist, pro-expansionist light. But by the National Institute's inaugural meeting in February 1899, the United States would be deeply embroiled in an imperialist venture in the Philippines, just one week into a new war against its erstwhile allies, the Filipino revolutionaries. While the members of the National Institute of Arts and Letters debated the future of American letters, the U.S. military government in Manila was ordering the reopening of schools, with mandated instruction in English, as the first step in establishing the sovereignty of the United States over its new territory. Thus as the future of American letters and the advancement of American cultural achievements were being promoted, defended, and worried over among the literary elite in New York and New England, a project of colonial domination was getting under way in the name of the very traditions the National Institute looked to uphold and defend. In fact, the National Institute's two aims—to secure the status of American literary traditions and to introduce the value of those traditions into the national consciousness—were so closely aligned with the self-described civilizing mission enacted in the Philippines that one might regard the two projects and their coincident development as unlikely twin births, emerging from the same body of cultural values and connected by a core set of values discernible to the careful eye.

These first two stories describe the political functions of English from different vantage points: one, from the elite circles of a narrowing sphere of literary production at the end of the century; the other, which I subsequently explore in more detail, from the schoolhouses in Manila where the imposition of English was regarded as the essential foundation for establishing the authority of United States rule. But there is a third site from which I want to tell this story, and that is in the academic institutions in which English became a defined and dominant field in the late 1890s. The National Institute of Arts and Letters was the professional society whose appearance coincided with the consolidation of the field of English at all levels of the curriculum, and the introduction of American literature as a field of study. Each of these developments was part of a late nineteenth-century process of redefining the literary, as an academic enterprise, a form of cultural capital, and a signifier of national identity.[16] Put together, these divergent histories ask us to reconceptualize the history of American letters and the field of English. More specifically, they suggest that the academic field of English must be conceived differently if the politics of English—its role as an instrument of power—were considered to be constitutive in its development as an academic discipline, and if that discipline were understood to be complicit in the public culture of English as an apparatus of social stratification, assimilation, and subjugation, not only in the United States but outside of it as well. What happens to the field of English, we might ask, when the schoolhouses in Manila, not the common schools of Massachusetts, are put at the center of its story of origin?

Standardization and the Field of English

The power of American literary study as an ideological force in the peda-gogical reproduction of the white middle class did not originate from no-where. Rather, it emerged in tandem with, and contributed to, the consoli-dation of the field of English and its dual mandates of language instruction at the elementary and secondary levels, and literary study in newly formed departments of English that were, by the turn of the twentieth century, beginning to offer defined curricula for American literary study at the un-dergraduate and graduate levels. Other scholars have usefully documented the historical process through which the field of English was consolidated; however, this scholarship has largely looked inward, defining the origins of the field within a national, or even regional, framework.[17] A review of how American literary study emerged as a field at the end of the 1890s will help to illuminate the stakes of the field, such that it was so instrumen-tal to the ideological and administrative tasks of colonial dominance and the paradigm of "benevolent assimilation." This is, then, a short history of how the field of English emerged and gained credibility, such that by the time of the U.S. occupation of the Philippines it had become a largely standardized field uniquely invested with specific cultural values and en-trusted with the function of mental and moral training. It will, as well, suggest how the new field of English, particularly at the secondary and university level in the United States, gained its animating force through its institutionalization as the capstone of the colonial project.

The origins of the study of American literature at the high-school and college level involved two developments: first, the institutionaliza-tion of literary study in the school through the consolidation of the field of English; second, the introduction of U.S. literature into the field, and the formalization of a list of standard American literary texts for regular study. Importantly, these developments occurred somewhat in tandem; that is, though we often think of American literature as the newcomer to the older field of English literary study, American texts found their way into the curriculum of English studies at the same time that the study of English literature began to replace that of Latin and Greek as the proper training ground for instructing the mental discipline of young minds. This is not to say that they carried the same cultural weight, however. As David Shumway has documented, late nineteenth-century efforts to define American literature encountered a difficult paradox. On the one hand, the ideological value of the literary meant that its association with the nation was an important source of pride; "Literature—especially poetry and drama—had long served to glorify England, "the land of poets" and home of Shakespeare."[18] Enthusiasts of American literature, like the *Atlantic Monthly* editor Horace Scudder, championed a national literature as the most effective source of "Americanism."[19] On the other hand, it was through its relation to English literature that American literature was originally attributed its high cultural value; many of its supporters emphasized the shared linguistic heritage of the two nations as a way of claiming for American culture the racial privilege of Anglo-Saxon superiority. As Nina Baym has demonstrated, literature textbooks "rather emphasized than played down the English origins of the American nation, thereby instructing classrooms of children of non-English ancestry to defer to the Anglo-Saxonism of their new country's heritage."[20] So, while the likes of Milton, Shakespeare, Chaucer, and Pope dominated the earliest courses in literary study, such courses integrated American authors like Nathaniel Hawthorne, Washington Irving, and Henry Wadsworth Longfellow.

These were seen as unique but not antithetical traditions, and the cultural value of American literature, as we shall see, derived in part from the ability of its field-practitioners to mark its distinctiveness from British literature and its role as a nationalist influence. Moreover, it is important to note how relatively quickly English was formalized in high-school and college curricula. In 1850, the field of English was nonexistent, and literary study in the classroom was largely limited to the use of excerpts for the study of grammar or rhetoric and oratory; by the mid-1890s, however, English was the only subject recommended for study in each of the four years of the standard high-school curriculum.[21] In a related development, in 1876, Francis James Child, of Harvard University, had the distinction of being named the first professor of English literature. Even as late as 1883, such positions were rare; among the twenty institutions represented at the first organizational meeting for the Modern Language Association, they could count only thirty-nine faculty in English.[22] By 1900, however, Berkeley, Stanford, Michigan, Chicago, Harvard, Yale, and Johns Hopkins were among the many universities across the country offering graduate degrees in English and courses in British and American literature.[23]

Arthur Applebee has described the rapid emergence of the field of English in the last quarter of the nineteenth century as rooted in two long-developing traditions around the function of literature and of American English. The first was an "ethical tradition" which had its roots in the connection between reading and religious instruction.[24] The second was a belief in the ennobling effects of the English language itself, and was marked by a desire for the standardization of an American idiom as both facilitator and guarantor of American democracy. On the side of the ethical, the roots of the field were manifested in the early primers that combined alphabet and verse with catechism and prayers. The most popular among these was *The New England Primer,* published around 1690 in Boston by Benjamin Harris and reputed to have sold 2 million copies during the eighteenth century; its success testifies to the popularity of this typical combination of moral and intellectual instruction, an important phase in the historical development through which reading instruction was linked, from the first, to concepts of moral uplift through religious salvation.[25]

The connection between reading and moral instruction shifted in the post–Revolutionary War period, which saw the proliferation of texts aimed not at religious instruction but patriotic pedagogy; here the primer took a foremost role in the cultivation of a common national culture, marked by texts that worked to formalize a common language that would transcend regional dialects, and to offer instruction in republican citizenship and self-government. Paradigmatic of this shift was Noah Webster's 1783 *American Spelling Book,* which offered, in addition to an alphabet and a reader, a speller that standardized the erstwhile erratic American spelling system.[26] He wrote that the "honor" of America "as an independent nation" required "a system of our own, in language as well as in government.[27] Instead, Webster imagined a specifically American idiom to be critical for the United States' independence from Britain on the one hand, and for the uniformity of its national identity on the other. Thus, he envisioned that "within a century and half, North America will be peopled with hundreds of millions of men all speaking the same language. [T]he consequence of this uniformity," he hypothesized, "will be an intimacy of social intercourse hitherto unknown, and a boundless diffusion of knowledge."[28]

Webster's *Speller* was significant not simply as a "declaration of linguistic independence" from both mother country and mother tongue. In championing the connection between American patriotism and American English, which he urged to be called by a new name, "Federal English" or, simply, "American,"[29] Webster sought to establish the primacy of English over the many other languages of the colonies and the continent. As Marc Shell has observed, "the revolutionary colonies were markedly polyglot."[30] One-quarter of the European settlers in the New World were non-English; German, Dutch, French, and Spanish all played an important role in the linguistic diversity of the colonies and of the new republic.[31] There were also numerous Native American languages spoken across the continent, and African languages that, while forbidden in the colonies, nevertheless constituted the mother tongues of one-fifth of the population.[32] The *American Spelling Book* effectively subsumed this heteroglossia into a new, nationalist understanding of American English as the unifying agent among the nation's varied populations.[33] Webster thus effectively rewrote the history of a polyglot continent by projecting its future as a monolingual nation, as one that was necessarily and uniformly English-speaking, all the while endowing English with an exemplary power for the "unification" of the nation's subjects—a clever euphemism for the submission of other cultures, languages, and peoples to the primacy of Anglo-American traditions. American English was thus poised to replace the old imperial language, British English, while fostering the building of a new American empire through the erasure or annihilation of linguistic and cultural difference under the uniformity of American English.[34]

This nationalist urge of the late seventeenth and early eighteenth centuries inspired one further shift of particular import, and this was the introduction of literature into the primary classroom. By the time of the formal disestablishment of the church in 1833, biblical selections in school readers had given way to secular selections aimed at cultivating patriotism and moral standards.[35] The McGuffey readers took over as the dominant texts of childhood learning, and, for the first time, offered excerpts from *literary* texts in order to stress the values of patriotism and Protestantism as companions to good reading habits. Literary work, in other words, replaced explicit religious doctrine, marking the literary as the secular replacement for biblical passages in the project of making moral citizens. What developed was a standardized format that aligned reading instruction with moral instruction.[36] Other American readers for the primary levels began, as early as the 1820s and 1830s, to include portions of work from the Romantics, reasoning that "our country both physically and morally has a character of its own. Should not something of that character be learned by its children while at school?"[37] This standardization, particularly among the literary selections in the McGuffey readers, was essential to the development of the idea that literature could furnish the ameliorative influence of moral instruction—a new function for literature that would prove essential to its role as proxy in the imperial mission.

Beyond the primary level, the landscape looked much different. Regular instruction in English at the collegiate level was rare.[38] Instead, the study of English in beyond primary school consisted largely of grammatical exercises aimed at aiding students in developing "mental discipline," while at the university level, rhetoric and oratory dominated, introducing the consideration of literature through lectures on texts translated from Latin and Greek, as well as those of English and French masters.[39] While the rhetoricians were not interested in the literary analysis of such pieces, it was through these courses that literary texts in English first made their way into the college classroom. The major impetus toward the professionalization of literary studies at the university came from philologists in the 1880s, whose etymological, bibliographical, and comparative work on languages required both formal training (first in Germany, and later in newly founded graduate schools like Johns Hopkins and Chicago) and texts through which to demonstrate the content of their research. Thus literature became an important object of study, not in its own right, but as it illuminated the linguistic principles of interest to the researcher. (Tellingly, the Modern Language Association was founded at Johns Hopkins University in 1883.)[40]

While the rigorous, "scientific" methodology of the philologists gave purchase to literary studies in the academy, it was this power "to move" and "to instruct" that provided the rationale for the field at the primary and secondary levels. It is on this level, that is to say, that literature became invested with an intrinsic moral and cultural value that made it a necessary part of a curriculum that was increasingly looking to expand as the basis of a homogeneous national culture. Certainly this notion of literature drew from the Romantic vision of art as a moral imperative, as necessary for life as food and water; as Shelley put it, "Poetry strengthens the faculty which is the organ of the moral nature of man, in the same manner as exercise strengthens a limb."[41] It also drew from Matthew Arnold's understanding of culture as "a study of perfection" that had "a weighty part to perform" against the spectre of class conflict he regarded as "anarchy."[42] His ideas contributed to a more general sense that literature could serve as an antidote for the cultural upheavals of the day by offering the Anglo-Saxon literary tradition as a representation of man's "best self," as the tutelary object to which all of the nation's subjects might aspire.[43]

Arnold's ideas, and those of his American contemporaries like Horace Scudder, were thus central as a motivating force in the valuation of literature both in institutions like the National Institute of Arts and Letters and in the curricular developments that began to use literature as a force of moral, cultural, and patriotic instruction. But its association with moral training needed the complement of mental rigor to become a "serious" subject. It was the confluence of philology's scientific methods of research with the standardization of grammar and a more general sense of culture as an ameliorative force that created the explicitly nationalist curriculum in which literary instruction was regarded at the end of the century as a necessary subject for all students. What this looked like was quite different across differently positioned social groups. At the elite level, this meant deciding on a standard body of texts that would constitute the core of a serious scholar's education. Yale University led the way in its standards for admission in 1894, when it specified that the object of study would be the "intrinsic importance" of the literary texts themselves, and not their utility for composition or philological study.[44] It thus had the distinction of being the first university to introduce questions that examined the knowledge of literary content.

This set of standards affected the high-school curriculum as well, where, as we have seen, English had only recently been recommended for inclusion in all four years of secondary study. As colleges issued their requirements for entrance, high schools adapted the curriculum to prepare students for such examinations. There was, however, no clear consensus at this point about which texts should be studied as a requirement for advanced study. The standardization of the entrance requirements was a principal step in forging such a canon, and this standardization came as the result of the National Conference on Uniform Entrance Requirements in English, which met in May 1894 and approved two lists of literary texts, one for "wide" and another for "deep" study.[45] Thereby appeasing both those who saw literary study as a means for mental discipline and those who favored literature as cultural appreciation, the function of the list is not to be underestimated in its work to make uniform and standardized the selection of certain texts as those most worthy of close study. Such evaluations also privileged particular texts above others as those whose literary merit was understood to offer the individual student the moral and intellectual improvement that classical literature had heretofore offered. Moreover, the very existence of such a list brought the field of English a new credibility at the high-school level, making explicit a particular set of classic texts to be taught with regularity. Implicit in this list was the assumption that such texts contained within them ideas and sentiments to which students should be exposed; thus Yale's claim to have based their list on the "intrinsic importance" of the works as well as their "probable attractiveness to the preparatory student" could be seen as indicative of the more general claims made about the import of the new field of English literary study.

By the end of the century, then, there was a field of English and a list of texts that students and schools alike could understand as representative of the best of the tradition of American letters. This list, of course, drew upon the list of books already being read and studied, taking its cues from the contents of popular anthologies and the text lists that universities like Harvard and Yale had begun to establish a few years earlier. With standardization, however, came a new kind of legitimacy and an important legibility for the field—the field was definable and clearly defined. It had not only a method, but also an object and, most importantly, a purpose.

But what of this purpose? Institutionally, this founding of the discipline preceded by only a small interval the institutional emergence of other fields of study as well, such as history and anthropology, which underwent similar shifts in methodology, training, and audience to become legitimated fields of study at the research-oriented university at the end of the nineteenth century. The American Historical Association was founded in 1895, followed by the *American Historical Review.* "By 1900," the historian Peter Novick writes, "the Ph.D. degree was a prerequisite for a professorial appointment at respectable colleges, and American universities had turned out more than two hundred doctorates in history."[46] By some measures, English developed its professional status a bit earlier than did history; by about 1900, 80 percent of the members of the Modern Language Association were college teachers, as compared to roughly 25 percent of the American Historical Association.[47] Anthropology emerged as a field of study through the more general professionalization of the social sciences in universities and in public perception. Harvard and the University of Pennsylvania appointed the first professors of "ethnology" in the late 1880s; by the mid-1880s, "anthropology" had replaced "ethnology" as the current name for the field. While many of the field's most respected practitioners were trained in other disciplines or lacked formal training altogether, the expectations for participation in the field had changed by the late 1890s, such that anthropologists could claim their role as "experts" in a field based on scientific knowledge. But the origins of these subjects have been to some degree more clearly implicated in the project of U.S. nationalism, their field-formation less ambiguous in its connections to the founding myths of American expansionism and exceptionalism. As Michael Elliott argues, "As they became recognized as arbiters of scientific knowledge, anthropologists would speak more frequently to non-scientific audiences as experts on questions relating to foreign peoples both at home and abroad: the indigenous populations living within the United States,

the increasing ranks of immigrants, and those brought under U.S. jurisdiction through the nation's imperial ventures."[48] In contradistinction, the
field of English marshaled its scientific knowledge toward the declaredly
apolitical realm of the text. In elite universities, and increasingly in primary and secondary schools across the nation, the consolidation of lists of
required texts for study (memorization and inculcation/absorption) was
executed without any reference to the world outside of Anglo-American
literary production. The point here is that it was precisely because English
was purported to be apolitical that it proved to be particularly efficacious
as a tool of colonial management.

Beyond these elite classrooms, the consolidation of English, while just
as sure, worked toward different aims. Its recently standardized format,
the drive toward "mental discipline," and the transformative potential of
literary study were all, in their turn, mobilized as strategies of containment and domination, manifest under the banner of tutelage as progressive education or enlightenment. Here, we note another, very concrete
utility of this formation of American letters:—even as the expansion of
public education was heralded as a service in the name of democratic governance, the consolidation of a collection of texts as representative of the
"best that has been thought and said" reaffirmed notions of the cultural
advancement of white American men even as it invented a literary tradition within which they could secure their place.[49] These were fabrications
of the past, mobilized to give weight to a particular cultural fable of the
present—one in which these texts represented the cultural heights toward
which the nation's Others might be brought.

English without Borders?

So far, I have drawn upon the resources of the field to retell, in condensed
form, the story of the New England origins of the discipline of English in
the United States. This part of the story is in keeping with the dominant
history of the field, which has largely seen the growth of English in the
United States as a national enterprise, contained within the ideological
and geographical space of the nation. There is another aspect to the consolidation of English in the late nineteenth century, however, that takes
us from the literary institutions of Massachusetts to the schoolhouses
of Manila. Here I begin in 1898, after the defeat of the Spanish by U.S.
naval forces under the leadership of Commodore George Dewey and the

collapse of Spanish colonial authority under pressure from Filipino rebels. The advent of U.S. rule on the islands precipitated the question of language, a matter of no small concern both to the American military officials engaged in the administration of the colonial state, and to the civil administrators whose authority was grounded in the claims to benevolent leadership for which the public school system in the Philippines was regarded as evidence.

The issue of formal English education was introduced by the First Philippine Commission, a five-member group sent by McKinley in March 1899 to evaluate the conditions on the islands and make recommendations for the establishment of the civil government. The Schurman Commission, as it was called, was headed by Cornell president Jacob Gould Schurman, who had been a professor of philosophy and English letters. When the Schurman Commission issued its report the following year, it was precise in its recommendations about the importance of education as part of the civil government, and about the immediate and complete dominance of English in the new colonial state. "It is evident," the report asserted, "that the fitness of any people to maintain a popular form of government must be closely dependent upon the prevalence of knowledge and enlightenment among the masses." A "clear understanding" of the "natural capacity" of Filipinos, as well as the opportunities for education under Spanish rule, was thus of "great importance."[50] After lamenting the "wretchedly inadequate provision" for education provided under Spanish rule, the commission praised the reopening of Manila schools in 1898 under the direction of the American military government. "The introduction of the teaching of English into these schools," the report assured, "was received with great satisfaction by the natives. The young Filipinos display a considerable aptitude for learning new tongues, and it is believed that, if this policy be followed out, English can within a short time be made the official language of the archipelago."[51] With regard to the radical departure that instruction in English would constitute, the report concluded that "the introduction of English, wherever made, had been hailed with delight by the people, who could hardly believe that they were to be encouraged to learn the language of those in authority over them."[52] The report's final recommendation was that English instruction be introduced at the primary level "as speedily as practicable," with the implication that this would establish its priority over Spanish, Tagalog, and other languages.

From the first, then, the imposition of English was justified as a democratizing measure, one that, in the case of the commission report, would

demonstrate the judicious authority of colonial rule. This point was reiterated by Capt. Albert Todd in a letter to Secretary of War Elihu Root.
Recently appointed to act as head of the Department of Public Instruction
while temporarily under military authority, Todd asserted that he could
"think of no expenditure which will have greater influence in developing
peace and progress in these islands than public schools. . . . The acquirement of the English tongue—to speak, read, and write it—will prevent
distrusts and misunderstandings, which must ever exist where the rulers
and the ruled have diverse speech."[53] Pointing at once to the dangerous
nature of colonial guardianship—the potential for "distrusts and misunderstandings"—Todd suggested that a common language would unite
ruler and ruled into common goals and understandings. He hinted as well
at the potentially ameliorative quality of English as the language of democracy—an association established, as we have seen, by Noah Webster,
and one increasingly insisted upon by American colonial officials in the
Philippines.

By the end of 1898, some public schools had been reopened in Manila,
all initially under military control, with soldiers recruited to work as
teachers.[54] That the public schools under military control had "little intrinsic utility" was admitted frankly, as when Captain Todd offered that the
department was "chiefly valuable as it shows the good will of our government in establishing or continuing schools for the natives."[55] Thus, while
U.S. soldiers continued to fight a protracted and brutal war against the
organized Filipino resistance across the islands, the occupying U.S. military government applauded its own quick work in reopening schools in
the "pacified areas" and assured the American people that this free, public education system would be the surest way not just to gain the trust of
Filipino civilians, but also to lead them toward gradual independence under the patient guidance of American soldiers.[56] General MacArthur concurred, asserting that "this appropriation (for schools) is recommended
primarily and exclusively as an adjunct to military operations calculated
to pacify the people and restore tranquility throughout the Archipelago."[57]

With the transfer of power from military to civil governments, the Bureau of Public Instruction was established in January 1901. The responsibility for establishing the hegemony of English rested with three political
figures: Bernard Moses, a member of the Second Philippine Commission,
was charged with the task of overseeing the work of the general superintendent of public instruction; Fred W. Atkinson, a former high-school
principal from Massachusetts, served as superintendent from 1900 to

1902; David P. Barrows, an anthropologist from California, was appointed superintendent in 1903, and held the post until 1909.⁵⁸ Moses was instrumental in establishing the English-language policy for the system of public education in the Philippines; Atkinson and Barrows were the earliest architects of the school curriculum and played a large role in the instruction in English and the selection of primers, readers, and literature that were adopted for use in the Philippines. Though each of these men was an educator, none of them was linked to the field of English, nor did any continue to work in the discipline after their time in the Philippines.

The hegemony of English on the islands was made official with Act 74, which called for mandatory instruction in English, requiring that "the English language shall, as soon as practicable, be made the basis of all public school instruction, and soldiers may be detailed as instructors until such time as they may be replaced by trained teachers."⁵⁹ This was in keeping with the practice already under way. In his instructions to the commission, President McKinley specified that "it will be the duty of the Commission to promote and extend, and, as they find occasion, to improve, the system of education already inaugurated by the military authorities"; he regarded it as "of first importance" to devise a system "which shall tend to fit the people for the duties of citizenship and for the ordinary avocations of a civilized community." As to the specifics of that task, McKinley stipulated that "in view of the great number of languages spoken by the different tribes, it is especially important to the prosperity of the Islands that a common medium of communication may be established, *and it is obviously desirable that this medium should be the English language*" (my italics).⁶⁰

It could be presumed that the "obviousness" of the desirability of English would have stemmed in part from the considerable practical difficulties to be faced in any attempt to provide instruction, as many of the Spanish friars had done, in the indigenous languages, or in the continued use of Spanish, which was the preferred language of the elite, educated class of *ilustrados*. The historian Glenn May is representative of the critical work on this point when he offers that "U.S. policy-makers could not, realistically, have chosen Spanish as the medium of instruction. It made no sense to reject English in favor of a language which only a small percentage of the population understood. What is more, it would have been too costly for the United States to hire enough qualified Spanish-speaking teachers to supervise the instruction."⁶¹ In this regard, however, May's analysis reiterates the dismissal of indigenous languages that is striking in its resemblance to the stance taken by both soldiers and teachers themselves. Advisors to the educational system insisted that the local languages were too dissimilar and were shared too infrequently among the population, so that a unified system of education in the native vernacular would be unworkable. "It would be impossible to get out some forty different sets of text-books, in the as many different Filipino languages," one officer coldly concluded. "The native dialects must therefore be abandoned as a basis of instruction."[62]

United States colonial officials were thus emphatic about the teaching of English, and dismissed the cultural import of indigenous languages with disdain. "All people would like their children taught their own dialect, I presume, as a matter of sentiment," one general concluded. "It is a practically unnecessary accomplishment, as scarcely any literature exists in those dialects and any communication by writing or printing will be better for the Government if done in English."[63] This discourse of practicality, however, is quickly revealed as an ideological construction in which English was necessary to bolster the presumed superiority of Anglo-American culture. Important here was the relentless insistence by American officials that the polyglot nature of the populace could only stand as evidence of the fundamentally uncivilized and utterly divided nature of the people. A chief proponent of this interpretation was the University of Michigan zoologist and member of the First Philippine Commission Dean C. Worcester, whose study entitled *The Philippine Islands and Their People* launched him as an "expert" on the question of Filipino character and Philippine sovereignty.[64] As one editorial reported, Worcester was "the highest authority we have on the condition of civilization, as well as on the natural history, of the archipelago," and thus "the testimony of such a man is worth a worldful of sentimental and academic literature and mere political talk."[65]

Worcester authored the commission's report entitled *The Native Peoples of the Philippines,* in which he proposed that the Philippine population consisted of "three sharply distinct races," the Negrito, the Malayan, and the Indonesian, which had reproduced and intermingled to produce no fewer than eighty-four separate "tribes, which often differ very greatly in language, manners, customs, and laws, as well as in degree of civilization."[66] By dividing the Philippine people into so grandiose a number of separate groups, Worcester was able to popularize the understanding that independence and self-government would be impossible for a population so fragmented; as the report concluded, "the Filipinos are not a nation, but a variegated assemblage of different tribes and peoples."[67] Moreover, his insistence on the strong tribal identity of the masses of "uncivilized" natives formed the backbone of the report's overall picture of the islands as a site in which the evolution from savagery to civilization was condensed; if the Philippines could not be conceived of as a nation, there could be no thought of self-government, and in the report's repeated claims that the islands were inhabited by a "multiplicity of tribes" in "multifarious phases of civilization—ranging all the way from the highest to the lowest," it found its most convincing justification for prolonged U.S. rule in the islands.[68]

These conclusions are particularly telling in light of the fact that the United States, at its origin, was a polyglot nation, and that this quality in no way preempted its capacity to declare independence from Britain. Indeed, as we have seen, many members of the new republic feared that the official continued use of English would only prolong the United States' dependence upon its former colonial authority, and thus they encouraged the use of another language or the invention of a new one. In other instances, bilingualism was tolerated or even encouraged; in Pennsylvania, where two-fifths of the population spoke German, Benjamin Franklin famously attempted to publish a newspaper in that language. California had also embraced bilingualism as one outcome of the Treaty of Guadalupe Hidalgo; the state declared in 1849 that all official documents would be published in both English and Spanish. It was not until nearly thirty years later, when the state constitution was amended in 1878, that it included a specific provision limiting official proceedings to English, making California the first state to establish an official "English-only" policy.[69] So while linguistic uniformity had its important supporters, it was not the only conceived way of achieving national identity.

Certainly cognizant of this history, American educators in the Philippines began to import and design textbooks based on the instruction of English as a conduit for Americanism.[70] Guides for teachers insisted that English be the sole language of instruction and conversation, and demanded that English lessons dominate the academic study of young children, to be supplemented by lessons in manners, hygiene, and civility.[71] Textbooks for the Philippines were selected by the general superintendent. In his notes to Commissioner Moses, Fred Atkinson notes that the military government had begun its work by requesting a series of Spanish-English reading books, but these were almost immediately replaced, after the passage of Act 74, according to the new philosophy of total English immersion. Filipino teachers were instructed to use English, and those American teachers who had some knowledge of Spanish, Tagalog, or other languages were directed not to use them, so as not to delay the entry of the Filipino child into the totality of English. By 1904, the system of public instruction was using a series of textbooks called the Philippine English series, written specifically for use in the islands. Based on the structure of the Baldwin and McGuffey readers, the Philippine English series aimed to replicate the pedagogical structure of those secular American texts while adapted to "the temperament and needs of the young Filipino boy and girl."[72]

One of the most striking distinctions in the materials prepared for Philippine schools is the extent to which these textbooks aimed to describe for Filipinos the conditions, history, and cultures of their would-be nation. It is no accident, then, that many of these books were written by American teachers or administrators who worked in the Philippines; the Philippine English series was authored by the division superintendent and a high-school teacher, both American, in Pangasinan; the other staple of primary English education was the Philippine Education series, of which the primary volume was penned by Mary Fee, whose memoir of teaching in the Philippines is the subject of chapter 3.[73] David Barrows, director of education, published *A History of the Philippines* in 1905, and the text was used almost exclusively in the public schools, with new editions as late as 1924, when it was replaced in 1926 by Conrado Benitez's *History of the Philippines*. As Ileto notes, Benitez himself was a product of the system of American education in the Philippines, and taught at both the Philippine Normal School and the University of the Philippines; as such, the same discourses of progress from the premodern to modernity dominate his narrative, as they do many of the textbooks penned by graduates of the American colonial system. A telling example is provided in the textbook on colonial history that reflects on the U. S. relocation and extermination of Native Americans as a process through which "barbarous tribes had been subjugated and brought into touch with the benefits of civilization"; the book's coordination with American interest on the islands was further evidenced by its own dismissal of Philippine independence: "Full civil liberty cannot be granted to a people who have had little or no experience in exercising such powers or enjoying such privileges and who are sometimes in revolt."[74]

To the degree that the English curriculum in the United States was adapted for the context of the Philippines, then, it appears that, at the primary level, such a curriculum differed quite little. Like their counterparts in the United States, these books focused on the U.S. history of white, European settlers and the literary productions of Anglo-American authors, with lessons designed to model the virtues of the Protestant work ethic: thrift, respect for authority, love of country, and mastery over nature, among others. As should be clear, however, this was an education in a particular version of American culture and identity. These were books aimed to form an implicit national identity through the inculcation of an exceptionalist story of American history, as cast into relief through short stories, tales of "great men," and literary pieces by American and English authors. What is not to be underestimated is the degree to which this story was calculated toward the deliberate refusal of Philippine nationalism and self-articulation, in the interests of the consolidation of American hegemony through the absolute erasure of Philippine national identity and claims to sovereignty, and through the rendering of all Filipinos as subject to the tutelary power of American cultural and political traditions.

Importantly, however, all this obvious cultural nationalism at work was justified in the name of *linguistic* uniformity. Against the unifying effects of English, the linguistic "chaos" was insisted upon as a sign that Philippine sovereignty would be an impossibility, since a nation of many languages, it was asserted, must be a divided nation. Such were the conclusions of naval officer Arthur Stanley Riggs, who also worked as a correspondent and editor of the *Manila Freedom*. Riggs interpreted Filipino linguistic plurality as the evident antithesis of national identity, and construed it as a "strange lack of cohesiveness" in Philippine society, which had no genuine national literature but only one that had been "singularly adulterated" by "foreign influences" of Spanish and Chinese.[75] Other commentators concurred; one editorialist for the *Philippine Teacher* argued: "Our school department was designed for the purpose of accomplishing the task of substituting a uniform language for the babel of dialects that at the present are a source of weakness and a power for disintegration in the islands." Entirely dismissing the creative import of the polyglot nation, the editorial insisted, tellingly, on the threat of difference to national unity: *"For with the uniformity of language will come logically a uniformity of mind habits, of ideas, of expression* (my italics). The source of information and knowledge will be simplified. Intercommunication will create common interests, and from a divided people this will become a sympathetic and united one, with common aims and common ideals."[76]

Passages such as this one demonstrate the incredible power invested, by architects of the colonial apparatus, in language as a transformative agent as well as an apparatus of social control. Like Noah Webster's assertions about the unifying force of English, they emphasize the linguistic as a marker of social and political power. Where conflict, difference, and division were imagined, a common language became the salve through which a "divided people" would become both a "sympathetic" and a "united" one. But, of course, it was not any language, but English, that was envisioned as the antidote for "disintegration" on the colonial terrain, and taken to be the cohesive agent to combat the chaos that is the "babel of dialects." In this way, racialized assumptions of Filipinos' lack of aptitude for self-government merged with a discourse of practicality that passed off as self-evident the efficacy of English as a pedagogical tool.

Assertions of the practicality and expediency of English belie the intense ideological force that the imposition of English would entail. Such assumptions underscored not just the proliferation of racialized assumptions about Filipinos, but about Americans as well, and here the force of this project was most clearly revealed as a tandem project of field-formation of English at home. For implicit in these assertions of the practical value of English was a companion logic of English as the bearer of cultural value and moral authority, the lingua franca of a democratic public sphere. And it should be clear that the imposition of English was understood to work seamlessly with the "advancement" of Filipinos from a state of "savagery" to civilization. As one civil service examiner put it: "In mastering the English language the Filipinos not only fill their minds with a knowledge of its literature, but are thus better prepared to appreciate the high aims and purposes of the present government."[77] Bernard Moses, for his part, imagined the language transmitting with it the moral values and political traditions of the entire Anglo-Saxon race; asserting that "the practical remedy adopted . . . was to give to the Islanders a knowledge of English," without which "they were doomed to remain in, or to drift toward, the stagnant state of isolated barbarians. . . . Knowledge of a European language, possessed by at least a considerable part of the inhabitants of the Islands, is thus essential to the progress of the Filipino people. Without it, their fate would be that of the Malay race generally, which, in none of its branches, without foreign assistance, has risen above a low stage of semi-civilization."[78] This depended on a complete identity between language, culture, and race, seeing in literature and in language the expression of the racial characteristics of a people. Working in precise tandem with American democracy, English became the embodied ideal not just of American cultural and political advancement, but of white racial superiority as well.

Alongside the assertion that English was the necessary language through which Filipinos would learn to think, speak, and write their own political destiny as a nation was the companion claim that Filipinos themselves desired English above all else, and that the United States was demonstrating its own exceptional national character in training its colonial subjects in the language of its own sovereignty. In their project of suppressing Filipino resistance to U.S. rule, it was necessary not only to impose English as the new language of authority, but also to assert that this was, in fact, the evident desire of Filipinos themselves. It was alleged that Filipinos would "cheerfully bear almost any burden of taxation" for the installment of a system of English education, and that there could be "no other object on which liberal expenditure could be made with such certainty of good returns."[79] Given the long resistance to U.S. rule that continued into the twentieth century, and the sustenance and shelter provided by Filipino civilians to the revolutionary forces during their guerrilla campaigns against the U.S. military, it is hard to interpret as anything but wishful thinking the claim, made in the report of the First Philippine Commission in 1900, that "the introduction of the teaching of English into [the] schools was received with great satisfaction by the natives."[80] Regardless, the supposed enthusiasm of Filipinos for a steady diet of English instruction was uniformly stressed by military and civilian officials alike. Fred Atkinson offered on several occasions that "the people are generally anxious to learn English" and that "the desire of the Filipinos to secure instruction, and above all to learn the English language, is general, hence the American teachers have been welcome everywhere as a means of enlightenment and progress."[81] Such was the opinion of Worcester, when he concluded: "The educational policy which the United States has adopted in dealing with the Filipinos is without a parallel in history. . . . Even now English is far more widely spoken in the Philippine Islands than Spanish ever was, and this is a boon the magnitude of which cannot be appreciated by those who have not had brought home to them by experience the disadvantages incident to the existence of very numerous dialects among the inhabitants of one country." That such disadvantages would go unnamed speaks to the extent to which both the uniformity of language and the superiority of English were insisted upon. David Barrows concurred when he asserted that "the desire of the Filipinos for the English language was, at the time the decision was made, strongly felt and earnestly pled for."[82]

Despite the repeated insistence that it was Filipinos themselves who "greatly desired English," the desirability of English would have been "obvious" only to the colonial administrators committed to a program of cultural domination enacted in no small part through the imposition of a foreign linguistic paradigm. There is little indication that the introduction of English and of American literature was done with any thought toward the desires or resistance of Filipinos themselves. While administrators and educators repeatedly invoked the notion of Filipinos' eagerness to learn English, there is no record of their consultation, either in the design of the system of public instruction or in the formalization of the curriculum there. Imposed upon a polyglot people, the supremacy of English was presumed not just to bring with it the promise of political legibility within an American political sphere, but also to unite a people through a common language, and within it, shared values, political aspirations, and moral ideals. Its work in consolidating the colonial state was marked explicitly by military officials who asserted that English would both establish the authority of the U.S. government as an occupying power and work toward bridging the gap between Filipino character and American national identity. "The problem of the amalgamation of the natives of the islands as American citizens can best be solved by promptly and properly taking hold of the work of educating the young," one lieutenant reported. "The problem of education can be solved by making English the only language taught in the schools."[83]

There should be no mistaking the fact, then, that the imposition of English was designed to support the consolidation of colonial rule among a population who continued to resist U.S. authority well beyond the declared end of military conflict. It was also aimed, in no uncertain terms, toward assuring the cultural dominance of American institutions and the suppression of indigenous languages and cultural practices. It was widely assumed that English, in the end, would transform the racial character of Filipino subjects, erasing what American colonizers understood to be the "deficiencies" of their "Oriental" character and replacing them with the independence and resourcefulness characteristic of true Americanism, which would include a new understanding of democratic self-government. Such a sentiment is reflected in the assertion of another soldier-teacher that "there seems to be no good reason why [Spanish] should be made by use the basis of instruction, and so "boosted" into a prominence which, after centuries, it has been unable to attain itself, and when our own language is better, is the one desired by the natives."[84] It was echoed in the words of the Filipino journalist Trinidad H. Pardo de Tavera, who was closely aligned with the Taft Commission and the U.S. occupation: "After peace is established all our efforts will be directed to Americanizing ourselves; to cause a knowledge of the English language to be extended and generalized in the Philippines, in order that through its agency the American spirit may take possession of us and that we may so adopt its principles, its political customs and its peculiar civilization that our redemption may be complete and radical."[85] Thus posited as the language of radical redemption, English carried with it the moral and ideological burdens of true Americanism—the seamless connection between language, race, and culture intended to inspire Filipinos' moral uplift and secure their submission to the righteousness of American sovereignty.

The Literary Imperative

Significantly, there was no single figure we might trace as notably important to the emergent field of American literary study and in the colonial project in the Philippines. In this way, however, English as a field was quite unlike some other contemporary fields, where key actors can be linked more closely to the professionalization of certain disciplines and the role those disciplines played in the forging of American empire. Franz Boas in anthropology and Isaiah Bowman in geography served as bridge figures, each helping to institutionalize the discipline in the academy while working centrally in popular or political venues to expand its influence.[86] In the case of the U.S.-occupied Philippines, there was no single individual who was active both in the academic field foundation of English in the United States and in the colonial project in the Philippines; most scholars of American literary study in the United States had little to say about the imperial project, and to my knowledge there is no archival record of any literary scholars having intervened directly in the policy or administration of the colonial school system.

My point is to suggest that the absence of key animating figures in the institutionalization of English in the Philippines and in the United States indicates instead the presence of a more general literary cultural force, or what I will call the *literary imperative*. By this, I refer to the complex of values and assumptions about literature, and its role in more general understandings of national culture, that factor into decisions about when and how the literary is introduced and what kinds of *political* work it is expected to do. I go into more detail in chapter 2 about how the literary object functioned, ideologically and politically, as a tool of colonial management in the Philippines. For now, I want to underscore the fact that the value of English as a colonial language depended upon its status as a literary language. Even in the earliest days of the public education project, when there was little possibility that Filipinos, newly introduced to English, would be reading or working with the literary texts themselves, the language itself was presumed to be able to convey the moral value of Anglo-Saxon traditions and to work its "civilizing magic" because of its connection to this literary corpus. English and American literary objects contained within them powers formerly invested in Latin and Greek: that is, the power to communicate the complexity of Anglo-Saxon culture, its morals, values, religious beliefs, political traditions, and most important, its superiority over other organizations of human life; in this way, American literature in particular, having newly made the shift from a literature of appreciation to a literature of study, became the cultural twin of the military project that heralded this moment as the United States' arrival on the world imperial stage. This moment marked a coming-of-age of sorts, an arrival of two fledgling forms of American dominance, one cultural, one military, through which the United States was presenting its intent to occupy its new role at the cusp of the "American century."[87]

Inasmuch as the link between literary pedagogy in the Philippines and literary study in the United States was formed less through the conscious policy decisions of educators and more through a political imperative of colonial management, the promotion of English, both language and literature, in the Philippines might be more closely aligned with the establishment of English literary study in India, where its adoption can be understood to be a political necessity more than a curricular one. As historians of the British empire have shown, the dominance of English in India was urged and determined in large part under the influence of Lord Thomas B. Macaulay, whose famous "Minute on Indian Education" argued, in 1835, for the legislative necessity for securing English as the language of the colonies. It asserted, too, the efficacy of English literature in inculcating the notion of British superiority, instilling the values of the English, and creating "a class of persons Indian in blood and colour, but English in tastes, in opinions, in morals, and in intellect," upon which the security of British hegemony would depend.[88] As Gauri Viswanathan has argued, English literature was introduced under British rule in India in order to mediate the conflict between the colonial government's increasing involvement in

Indian education and the policy of noninterference in religion. The British policy of religious neutrality, according to Viswanathan, created an impasse "by what was perceived to be the sustaining structure of error embedded in Hinduism, blocking instruction in modern science, history, and other empirical disciplines. Because the knowledge of the West could not be imparted directly without seeming to tamper with the fabric of indigenous religions, British administrators were virtually paralyzed from moving in either direction."[89] It was English literature that British legislators introduced to ease this tension. As a morally persuasive and righteous canon, English literature seemed to present the opportunity to secure the hegemony of the British by creating such a class as Macaulay described, without seeming to interfere with Indian cultural practices.

David Barrows echoed the language and the intent of Macaulay's "Minute" in the testimony he gave to the United States Senate Committee on the Philippines in early 1902, when he offered that "I think it is possible in a very few years to raise up an educated class there who will understand English, will understand ourselves, will know something of English literature, and who will form a large body of Filipino people, universally distributed, who can understand us and whom we can understand."[90] In words strikingly similar to Macaulay's reasoning, Barrows testified to the efficacy of the literary in securing U.S. interests by creating a large class, "universally distributed," of Filipinos who would have internalized American beliefs, values, and customs. The specific utility of American literature is made clear in a later part of that same testimony: "We hope that a thorough understanding of American literature will have a beneficial political effect; that is, the more they know of America and Americans and American institutions the more satisfied they will be under American rule."[91]

In the context of U.S. rule in the Philippines, the literary imperative worked to resolve or efface three constitutive tensions. The first concerned the material exploitation of the islands. While the consistent line of policy makers was to insist upon the benevolent motivations for the continued U.S. control of the islands, private correspondence and memos suggest a full awareness of the importance of the Philippines as a source of natural resources and labor, and highlight the potential of the islands for profit by U.S. corporations. This is something noted with particular frequency by David Barrows, who wrote to friends and colleagues with assurances that there were "fortunes to be made" by investment in infrastructure, agriculture, and land ownership in the Philippines. Fred Atkinson also wrote of the "ample returns" that would attend the "development of these islands" by American industry and commerce.[92] Thus, in at least some measure, the introduction of English and the paradigm of humanist education as a racialized program of uplift was designed to erase the evidence of material exploitation that the imperial occupation enabled.

While the literary served in the colonial context to ease the tension between material exploitation and benevolent guidance, it served another function, arguably more important, in broadcasting American cultural sophistication to the rest of the world. This second function of the literary was to mark the United States as a nation of sufficient sophistication and advancement, not just militarily but also culturally, to hold its place among European colonial powers. The status of the literary signaled the superiority of American intellectual and artistic traditions, marking the United States as a player in the Western philosophical and epistemological project of Enlightenment. The prominence of American superiority demanded the mobilization of a national literary tradition that was itself under construction at the moment of its deployment. The introduction of English and the curricular inclusion of American literature announced America's intellectual sophistication over Filipinos, and declared the superiority of their customs and culture. This is nowhere more clear than in the repeated rehearsals of the position that instruction in the native languages would be counterproductive, and that it must be in a language with a literature that would lead Filipinos on the path to progress and modernity. As Bernard Moses, the commissioner of education, insisted, "it would have remained questionable whether ability to read a language that has no literature is worth the trouble to learn to read."[93] He argued, as well, that "for the purposes of more advanced instruction all the native languages were defective" as "they had not the words to express the ideas it would be necessary to convey."[94] Fred Atkinson concurred: "Native dialects will continue to be spoken, but English will be the 'official language,' the medium for the transmission of modern currents of thought, in short, modern civilization . . . and herein lies the justification of the present educational movement: *a preparation both for the pursuit of practical life sustaining occupation and for the best of past and present civilization in literature, culture and art*" (my italics).[95]

To be clear, this was an argument about language as well as literature. The majority of Filipinos were not deemed likely to embark upon a course of advanced literary study; for the bulk of the colonial subjects, however, it was the proximity to the literary object that mattered. The sentiment was that native languages lacked both the sophistication and the capacity to communicate the elements of science, literature, and political democracy offered in English; having no vocabulary sufficient to refer to these Western intellectual achievements, the native languages, it was asserted, lacked the complexity to accommodate their concepts themselves. This sentiment was echoed on numerous occasions by Barrows, who argued: "If we are seeking the enlightenment of the population[,] the population would have to have some language and literature upon which to rest that."[96] Making the point more forcefully, he elaborated: "It would be impossible to translate any work in English, as it has been impossible to translate any work of Spanish, into a native dialect without using a great many European words—English words or Spanish words." Following up in his testimony, and responding to the further questions about the ambitions of English instruction in the islands, Barrows clarified that while English developed by incorporating the scientific and philosophical principles of Latin and Greek and adopting foreign words as English words to express these new ideas, "it would be impossible . . . to take one of the Filipino dialects, like the Tagalo [*sic*] for example, and develop it; that is, to carry it along, incorporating into it words and materials for which there is no Tagalo, and making it a language suitable for wide commercial use or for literature." Rather, English, he asserted, would be "of the greatest advantage" for the "preliminary steps toward the enlightenment and organization of those islands."[97]

To insist upon the civilizing power of the American cultural traditions by drawing upon the legacy of Anglo-Saxon literary production, however, was to closely align the U.S. expansionist project with the British empire. This risked exposing the ideological proximity between the American project of "benevolent assimilation" and the practices of European colonialism, which U.S. administrators had castigated as despotic and undemocratic. The imperialist venture thus challenged the exceptionalist paradigm of American nationalism even as it consolidated that nationalism on another level. Eager to ward off such criticisms, colonial administrators took great pains to distinguish the U.S. occupation of the Philippines from the exploitative or despotic imperial practices of its European counterparts. The third function of the literary was thus to mark out the distinctiveness of the American project and to insist upon its ultimate benevolence. Balancing the tension between civilized tradition and European tyranny, however, U.S. colonial administrators took great pains to distinguish their work from the British imperial project. Bernard

Moses, as the highest official directly involved in overseeing the education system, wrote exhaustively on this issue, losing almost no opportunity to make his case that "the educational policy of the government of the Philippine Islands differs from that followed by any other European nation in its Oriental dependencies."[98] He condemned the British and Dutch models of imperial rule for their unwillingness to educate their native colonial subjects in the language of the colonizer. For Moses, this was a question of a lack of democratic principle, marked by the exploitative nature of British and Dutch rule: "It was the policy of the Spaniards in the Philippines, and of the Dutch in Java, not to mention other nations, to discourage, if not to prohibit, the natives from acquiring and using the language of the dominant nation. By this policy a line of discrimination was drawn, and the native, confined to the use of his own uncultivated speech, was made to feel his inferiority."[99] This determination, according to Moses, was the result of the purely commercial intent of both the British and the Dutch regimes: "When the Dutch went to Java, and the English went to India, they went to trade with the inhabitants. They did not concern themselves with projects to change the social condition of those who became their dependents. They sought simply to obtain whatever advantage might be acquired through trade with them."[100] By contrast, Moses paints a picture of the American regime as a benevolent occupying force. Effacing the material and military gains that U.S. policy makers envisioned in the Philippines, Moses insisted upon the exceptional nature of the American occupation, marked most clearly by the ready investment in linguistic and literary education: "The determination of the United States not only to permit the Filipinos to use the English language, but also to provide for them the most ample facilities for learning it, was regarded as a concession in favor of equality, and helps to explain the remarkable zeal with which the youth turned to the study of English."[101]

The U.S. pedagogical project was thus designed to sustain the myth of American exceptionalism in the imperial context. Deploying the language of democracy to describe the system of forced colonial rule, colonial officials like Taft and Moses, as well as education administrators like Atkinson and Barrows, relied upon the pedagogical project and the status of literary study as a way of signaling the benevolence of the colonial government. When, in 1900, Fred Atkinson was appointed to the office of superintendent of public instruction, his formalized course of study, complete with Baldwin primers, Baldwin readers, and Spanish-English grammars (followed, for advanced students, by the guided study of Longfellow,

Irving, Hawthorne, and Lowell), put into formal curricular terms the assumptions of Western superiority and the ameliorative function of the literary that were already animating the project.[102] The literary was needed to address the central tension of American exceptionalism: that to enter the game of imperialism was to jeopardize the free republic, and to degrade America's reputation as that of a liberating force to that of a despotic tyrant. English was key to the project of benevolent assimilation; lest the demand for independence call to mind the violent military basis for colonial power and the threat of force behind the claims of U.S. sovereignty, the emphasis on literature worked as a sign of American intellectual, moral, and cultural superiority (and thus their right to rule) and as a signal of the generosity of the colonial mission. According to Moses, this policy of instruction constituted "a helping hand to lead [Filipinos] away from their traditions into the ways of modern civilization."[103]

Imperial Cultures of Letters

In the imposition of English as an apparatus of rule, the U.S. educational system in the Philippines was not dissimilar to its treatment of other colonized people under the jurisdiction of the United States. Between 1879 and 1902, the U.S. government built twenty-five boarding schools where Native American children would be "removed from the examples of their parents and the influence of the camps" so that they would no longer remain "destitute of all that constitutes civilization."[104] Boarding schools for Native Americans isolated the power of English to assimilate indigenous peoples and to break the bonds of tribal identity by routinely insisting upon English as both the spoken and written language of all residents, making it a harshly punishable offense for any student to be caught talking in his or her native language. Such was the official policy enacted by Secretary of the Interior Carl Schurz, who decreed in 1880 that "all instruction must be in English."[105] The commissioner of Indian Affairs, J. D. C. Atkins, followed suit by declaring in 1887 not only that English, "while good enough for a white man and a black man, ought to be good enough for the red man," but also that "teaching an Indian youth in his own barbarous dialect is a positive detriment to him. The first step to be taken toward civilization, toward teaching the Indians the mischief and folly of continuing in their barbarous practices, is to teach them the English language. The impracticability, if not impossibility, of civilizing the Indians of this country in any other tongue than our own would seem to be obvious."[106] In such circumstances, the assimilative force of English was multifold, as the historian Lonna M. Malmsheimer has explained; it involved not only "an education in white racial consciousness" through which "the children of culturally diverse tribes had to learn that they were Indians," but also the inculcation of white standards by which they were held to be "an inferior race."[107] As the historian Jay Reyhner has documented, the prohibition against speaking Native languages was both forceful and pointed, including food deprivation or a coup of the leather strap for each violation.[108]

The imposition of English in the education of Native Americans was part of the "civilizing mission" devised to effect the assimilation of Native Americans into the cultural values, social structures, and economic system of an expanding white America. But this is where the model of Native American education diverges from the colonial paradigm of the Philippines. What was extraordinary about the colonial apparatus in the Philippines was precisely that the assimilation of Filipinos into the American national body was neither imagined nor desired. Filipinos, like other Asians, were considered racially ineligible to naturalize in the United States; as "nationals" of the United States, they were not citizens.[109] The architects of the colonial project were clear in their intent to "govern [Filipinos] at arm's length." As Jacob G. Schurman, president of the First Philippine Commission, put it: "As it is the policy of our republic to maintain a national development unmixed with Asiatic immigrants, so it is to the interest of the Filipinos to have opportunity for a full and independent development of their own individual capacities, their own racial characteristics, and their own civilization. Their own organic life being thus recognized as self-contained and inviolable, when it reaches a degree of maturity qualifying them for independence, a new republic may arise in Asia without any shock to the United States of America."[110] English thus functioned in a purely idealist manner, providing not an assimilative function but an ameliorative one, assisting in Filipinos' growth from political "childhood" to "maturity." The implicit answer to the question posed by Indiana senator Albert J. Beveridge, "What alchemy will change the oriental quality of their blood, in a year, and set the self-governing currents of the American pouring through their Malay veins?"[111] was clear. It was English that was presumed to offer the ennobling influence through which Filipinos would climb the evolutionary scale from savagery to civilization and demonstrate that they had reached "maturity" sufficient for independence.

In this light, the desirability of English is revealed in its complicity with the racialized dominance of this particular population, neither foreign nor domestic, whose own demands for autonomy were suppressed under the weight of "benevolent assimilation." I would argue, however, that the academic study of English in the United States provided the ideological underpinning for the exceptionalist paradigm that invoked and justified this investment in English, as a language and a literature, as an ameliorative force. In the ideological functioning of English as an imperial force, the complicity between the various institutionalizations of English is revealed. Despite the assertions of members of the National Institute of Arts and Letters that their organization was hardly political, and despite the vociferous anti-imperialism of many of its members, the very cultural weight and symbolic value they attributed to the literary positioned it as the co-conspirator in the linguistic and cultural domination of a subject people. For what was this literature but the repeated and selective expression of the national culture that was itself under contestation in the United States, a national culture that colonial administrators wished to export in the service of empire through the efficient medium of the English language itself?

This chapter has told three different stories about the history of English at the end of the nineteenth century: the first, about the National Institute of Arts and Letters and its nationalist advancement of American literature; the second, on the field-formation of English as an academic subject and its investment in the ameliorative potential of literary study; and a third, about the colonial project of English-language education in the Philippines. These are stories about the field-formation of English, the cultural and political environment in which it took shape, and the historical contingencies and political exigencies of its coming into being. But they are not stories only about that. They are also stories about the political and cultural violence that is the history of English—as a language, a literature, and an academic field—in the U.S. political sphere. Really, they are one story—that is, they are all essential and interlocking parts of the politics of English at the end of the nineteenth century.

The National Institute looked to revitalize the "traditions of good literature" at the very moment that those traditions were being opened up to greater numbers of people in primary and secondary English courses across the United States, and as they were being imposed upon a resistant people in a new colony, as proof that Americans had "benevolent" intentions in asserting their political sovereignty in the islands, and had in their language and their literature a civilizing apparatus adequate to the task. The functions of literature in the academy, with its emphasis on moral training and mental discipline, provided the ideological apparatus through which the very language of English, as the language of this noble literature, would serve as the "alchemy" to transform the nation's racialized Others into willing subjects. The history of the field of English is thus inseparable from the project of colonial dominance. Field-formation is part of the empire-building process, not calculated exclusively for that purpose but rendered an efficient agent in the service of empire through its very imbrication in the racialization of language and the attribution of hierarchical and exclusionary cultural value to the literary.

We see, then, that the nascent appreciation for American literature as an institutional presence and as a sign of national culture—an appreciation reflected in the founding of fields of American literature at institutions like Yale, Harvard, and others, and in the National Institute of Arts and Letters—was integrally linked to the design of public instruction in the Philippines, and thus to the entire ideological project of colonial dominance in whose name that instruction was imposed. Put more simply, *even when the literary was not directly invoked*, its purported civilizing presence is everywhere felt in discussions about the efficacy of the English language as that "alchemy" through which a population of resistant, "savage" colonial subjects would be introduced to the achievements of Anglo-American culture and to the asserted superiority of its political traditions. As I discuss at greater length in the next chapter, it was the literary that was held up as proof of this superiority. For the majority of Filipinos, whose education was not anticipated to continue to the point of close literary study, it was the language itself, in its very connections to the literary and all of the traditions there implied, that was presumed/counted upon to do the "civilizing" work of the imperial project. That is, even where it could not be instructed, the presence of this literature was held up as the benevolent and justifying measure that made possible the whole myth of benevolent assimilation. That façade depended upon the literary as a mode of communication and a marker of distinction, signaling the superiority and nobility of Anglo-Saxon culture and presenting U.S. colonial rule as an ameliorative, even progressive, measure.

2

Empire's Proxy

Literary Study as Benevolent Discipline

Rizal was the apostle of evolution, not of revolution. . . . *Who will say
that looking into the great beyond he did not see his people reach the
wished for goal under a tutelage stronger, more powerful, and more
compelling than his own?*

—Gen. James F. Smith, secretary of public instruction
in the Philippines, December 30, 1905

On February 11, 1899, five days after the ratification of the
Treaty of Paris, the popular weekly satirical illustrated magazine *Judge*
published a political cartoon in which it offered a concise commentary on
the United States's new colonial acquisitions. Entitled "Our New Topsy,"
the cartoon drew on the overwhelming popularity of Harriet Beecher
Stowe's sentimental novel, *Uncle Tom's Cabin*, by reanimating Stowe's famous pair, the orphaned slave child Topsy and the prim Yankee aunt, Miss
Ophelia. Engaged in a new drama of racial dominance, the Filipino revolutionary leader Emilio Aguinaldo is recast as the defiant Topsy, dancing
with a wide grin while Uncle Sam plays a prim Miss Ophelia, watching
with hapless concern. Quoted directly from Stowe's novel, the caption has
Topsy confessing: "I's so awful wicked there cain't nobody do nothin' with
me. I keeps Miss Feely (Uncle Sam) a-swearin' at me half de time, 'cause I's
might wicked, I is."[1]

At the moment of its publication, "Our New Topsy" weighed in on
what was still a heated question about the future of the Philippine Islands, which Spain had ceded to the United States for the price of $20
million. Two days before the vote for ratification, tensions between the
occupying U. S. military and Filipino revolutionary forces reached their

Figure 2.1. "Our New Topsy." Topsy (Aguinaldo)—I's so awful wicked there cain't nobody do nothin' with me. I keeps Miss Feeley (Uncle Sam) a-swearin' at me half de time, 'cause I's might wicked, I is. (Courtesy of HATI-an Archives)

peak when an American soldier fired upon a Filipino sentry in Manila, thus marking the commencement of what would be more than a decade of determined resistance to U.S. rule.[2] Even beyond the undeniable opposition to American sovereignty on the islands, however, within the United States powerful questions emerged about the legitimacy and advisability of this new phase of expansion. While some supporters of the imperialist project, like Indiana senator Albert J. Beveridge, saw this new phase as the inevitable and righteous fulfillment of the promise of Anglo-Saxon civilization, others, like Mark Twain, decried it as the degradation of American principles and the defilement of the flag.[3] Still more urgent were legal questions about the citizenship status of Filipinos and their potential immigration to the United States: Samuel Gompers, founder of the American Federation of Labor, warned that Asian laborers would flood the United States and trigger another depression; others reacted to the fears of "yellow peril" and imagined Filipino immigration to pose a threat to Anglo-Saxon racial purity. As pressingly, the very status of the islands as foreign or domestic territory, and the applicability of the Constitution and the rights it conferred, remained points of contention.[4]

In the midst of such debates, "Our New Topsy" offered a striking vision for America's new role as a global colonial power. More particularly, it aimed to address anxieties about the future of Philippine-American relations by returning to the past and reanimating the antebellum relations of domestic slavery. Embodied in the figure of Aguinaldo as Stowe's rebellious "wild child" Topsy, here Filipino resistance to U.S. rule and to Anglo-Saxon hegemony is reframed as the willful rebellion of a child, one who, as readers of Stowe's novel would certainly have known, would eventually be domesticated by the love she is offered first by another child, the angelic Eva, and eventually by Ophelia herself. I will return to the racial dynamics of that triad in a moment. The point with which I want to begin is that the power of this cartoon, published exactly one week after the shot that began the Philippine-American War, relies heavily on the power of that novel, as well as the familiarity that late nineteenth-century readers would have had with the particular scenes of racialized domination and sentimental violence that characterize the scene referenced here, in which Topsy suggests that she be beaten as a consequence of her unwillingness to behave in accordance with Miss Ophelia's wishes. In other words, it counts on readers' familiarity with both the circumstances of Stowe's plot and the sentimental narratives of conversion and salvation it contained.

As *Uncle Tom's Cabin* was the most widely sold novel of the century, this would have been a fair bet.

What demands more attention, however, is why Stowe's sentimental novel would function so effectively at the end of the century, nearly fifty years after the original publication of the novel and in a social and economic climate far different from the antebellum context that is the novel's setting. So strategic and timely an appearance of Ophelia and Topsy, at the dawn of the United States's new imperial power, suggests something about the enduring cultural and political power of the sentimental novel. My contention here is twofold: first, that the reanimation of Stowe's famous pair illuminates in greater clarity the racial dynamic of the U.S. colonial occupation of the Philippines and the role of the sentimental as a domesticating force in the racial drama of empire. Second, the cultural reference to the popular sentimental novel registers the new power of the book—not just *Uncle Tom's Cabin*—as a mobile commodity form invested with cultural value, to work as an agent of empire. Thus to understand the cultural value of "Our Topsy," we must look to the novel itself, and beyond it. With this beginning, then, I mean to index something beyond the power of Stowe's novel and the salvific powers it intended, to explore the enduring legacy of the novel more generally as the agent of transformations not wholly unlike those Stowe imagined.

The Tale of Two Topsys

Perhaps more than any other novelistic scene in the nineteenth century, the death of Little Eva, the angelic child heroine of Harriet Beecher Stowe's *Uncle Tom's Cabin,* has been scripted time and again as the moment that renders readers completely, even unexpectedly, moved.[5] The scene's iconic status seemed unrivaled in the nineteenth century; the deaths of other child characters like Charles Dickens's Little Nell and Louisa May Alcott's Beth March demonstrated a particular preoccupation with dying children, but it was Little Eva's death that resonated, years beyond, both as the exemplary scene of the popular novel's soteriological framework and as evidence of the power of sentimental literature to reach and move its audiences.[6] George Sand, responding to unauthorized, serialized translations of the novel that appeared in *La Presse* in 1852, spoke for many in the novel's wide international audience when she lauded the dramatic scene of Little Eva's death as "so new, so beautiful, that one asks one's self in thinking of it whether the success which has attended the work is after all equal to the height of the conception."[7] The poignant demise of the young girl, "fading away through a mysterious malady which seems to be nothing but the wearing of pity in a nature too pure, too divine, to accept earthly law," was thus an iconic representation not just of death and loss, but of the salvific potential in such death.[8] As Stowe herself frames it, Eva's final moment, her face transformed by "a bright, a glorious smile," marks a new beginning, her passing "from death unto life" (257).

For contemporary critics, Little Eva's death has been no less important. Ann Douglas has described the death scene as "archetypal and archetypically satisfying," noting that despite what she regards as its "essentially decorative" function, it remained for her the most memorable of the domestic scenes from her childhood reading.[9] Countering many twentieth-century critics' disregard for this exemplary moment of Victorian sentimentalism, Jane Tompkins reads its captivating effect on nineteenth-century readers as indicative of Stowe's mastery of the ideological framework of Christian salvation through sacrifice.[10] Calling Stowe's novel "probably the most influential book ever written by an American," Tompkins reads the scene of Little Eva's death as the key site in which the novel's eschatological vision confirms the period's dominant belief structure in "the power of the dead or the dying to redeem the unregenerate."[11] Not simply drawing from the Bible, *Uncle Tom's Cabin,* in Tompkins's reading, "rewrites the Bible as the story of a Negro slave," thus "retell[ing] the culture's central religious myth, the story of the crucifixion, in terms of the nation's greatest political conflict—slavery—and of its most cherished social beliefs—the sanctity of motherhood and the family."[12] And in a powerful counter to Tompkins's reading, Hortense J. Spillers has read the death of Eva not as salvation and redemption through sacrifice, but as the retribution, within a patriarchal Calvinist tradition, of a vengeful God upon the "lush sensuality" of Eva and her desire for Tom, spoken pointedly at the moment when her father considers his purchase: "You have money enough, I know. *I want him*" (Spillers's italics).[13]

The critical work on Stowe's novel and on Little Evangeline St. Clare's important role as a nineteenth-century literary heroine has emphasized something to which the popularity of Eva and her death scene already attest: that powerful cultural work is done in this scene where the young child, with skin of "intense whiteness" and "large, soul-like eyes" sees into the next life, "O! love, —joy, —peace!" (250, 257). While the histrionics of Eva's illness and death scene have garnered extensive comment, it is important to note that the transformative effect of these plot twists, as Stowe imagines them, is not just on the novel's readers but on Topsy, who emerges by Eva's bedside after a tearful scene in which Eva has said good-bye to the family "servants" and distributed among them locks of her golden, curly hair, with the reminder, "If you want to be Christians, Jesus will help you. You must pray to him" (251). Moved to tears, Topsy implores of Eva, "O, Miss Eva, I've been a bad girl; but won't you give *me* one, too?" upon which moment she receives the "precious curl" with Eva's lesson: "every time you look at that, think that I love you, and wanted you to be a good girl."

Readers of Stowe's novel will remember that Topsy's role in *Uncle Tom's Cabin* is to play the wild child. Raised by speculators from so young an age that she carries no knowledge of mother, father, or God, Topsy claims adamantly that she "never was born" but simply "grow'd" (210). She enters the novel a resistant and unrepentant young girl, purchased by Eva's father, Augustine St. Clare, and given to Miss Ophelia as a test for the aunt's Yankee ideas about discipline and child rearing; it is soon revealed, however, that Topsy's steady diet of neglect and abuse has inoculated her against all of Miss Ophelia's attempts to reform her. It is this imperviousness to the corrective influence of Miss Ophelia's discipline that establishes her singularity in the novel. No stranger to conflict or to the harsh physical discipline of authority, Topsy reveals herself to be admirably adept at performing the detailed household tasks Ophelia requires of her, and equally uninspired to do them. Unburdened by the fear of punishment, Topsy declares, "I an't used to workin' unless I gets whipped," and revels in the distinction of being "the wickedest critter in the world" (217). Thus it remains for the space of the "year or two" in which Ophelia undertakes Topsy's "training" with the daily difficulty described as "a kind of chronic plague" (218).

Unlike the novel's eponymous hero, Topsy stages her noncompliance with the authority of white patriarchal racism by showing neither fear of its violent discipline nor faith in its prescriptions of righteousness. This is important, for it is all the more telling that even Topsy's authoritative indifference proves no match for Eva's sentimental power. Shortly after her introduction into the novel, she becomes the object of Eva's transformative attentions. It is the exclamation of Eva's affection, "O, Topsy, poor child, *I* love you," and the touch of her "thin, white hand on Topsy's shoulder" that initiates the young black girl into the realm of affection and, through this, of religious sentiment (245). That is, Eva's assurance that "Jesus loves all alike" elicits from Topsy her first sign of feeling, which is also a signal of subjection, of trying to "be good" though she "never did care nothin' about it before!" (246).

Returning to the site of Eva's deathbed, readers are able to appreciate the full effect of this transformation. Initially startled at Topsy's appearance, Eva asks where Topsy "start[ed] up from" (252). The question is purposeful; Stowe here revisits the story of Topsy's unknown origins but finds a new answer, this time, with Topsy's definitive statement of presence: "I was here." This affirmation locates Topsy's new origins within the St. Clare family, suggesting that her introduction into Eva's love constitutes a sort of rebirth. Indeed, it is this transformation that is the promise of Eva's death, its immediate purpose within the logic of evangelical Christian salvation. A few pages later, after her death, Eva's power is confirmed in the remarkable exchange between Topsy and Ophelia. The young girl lets out a "wild and bitter cry" by Eva's deathbed, and wishes for her own death because "there an't *nobody* left now" to love her; similarly transformed, Miss Ophelia responds, "I can love you; I do, and I'll try to help you to grow up a good Christian girl." Topsy's "wild and bitter cry" is duly tamed by Miss Ophelia's "honest tears" such that "from that hour, [Miss Ophelia] acquired an influence over the mind of the destitute child that she never lost" (259). Moreover, it is not just the unrelenting tutelage of Miss Ophelia that produces this striving, but Topsy's own capacity, awakened by Eva's love and consolidated by her loss, to *feel*. As St. Clare realizes, upon witnessing Topsy's continued mourning, "Any mind that is capable of *real sorrow* is capable of good" (267, my italics). Here Stowe directs her readers to the novel's critical function. Like Topsy, any reader who feels the sorrow of the novel's many tragedies must be "capable of good." The lesson of discipline through Christian love and sacrifice is enacted both on Topsy and on her newly benevolent mistress; whereas before Miss Ophelia avowedly "had a prejudice against negroes [*sic*]" and "never could bear to have [Topsy] touch [her]," Eva's "Christ-like" love "teach[es]" Miss Ophelia the lesson of benevolent authority, of mastery through love.

While it is the legacy of Eva's love that its influence can endure longer than the child herself, it is the imagined durability of the structure of conversion through sentiment, formed around the female triumvirate of Eva, Ophelia, and Topsy, upon which the efficacy of Stowe's novel rests. What "Our New Topsy" stages, then, is a revisiting of the scene of domestic slavery as a way of sorting through a number of crucial questions about the character and consequences of this new phase of U.S. expansion. In the midst of debates about the racial status of Filipinos and their eligibility for inclusion, legally or figuratively, into the national body, popular and political representations of the colonial Philippines typically made direct analogies between Filipinos and African Americans as subject and "inferior" peoples. It is no accident that Aguinaldo is pictured as a willful, unrelentingly "wicked" and orphaned slave child, as such a depiction brought together competing assertions about Filipinos' "childlike" character and their "savagery" into the familiar iconography of black-white domestic race relations.

To represent Aguinaldo through this famous caricature of black childhood brought into play a whole range of critical assumptions about race and gender to navigate this new encounter. The racialized social, domestic, and national formations naturalized in *Uncle Tom's Cabin* resurfaced in the context of U. S. expansion in a number of ways. Throughout the 1890s, race riots in New York, Nebraska, Louisiana, and North and South Carolina marked what Rayford Logan has called "the nadir of American race relations," in which white violence against African Americans reached a new height in the post-Reconstruction era.[14] Between 1899 and 1903, there were 543 reported lynchings; 95 percent of the victims were African Americans.[15] As U. S. aggression against Filipinos continued, representations of Filipinos coincided with racialized depictions of African Americans, thus drawing a parallel between the armed suppression of resistance in the Philippines and the racialized violence against African Americans at the end of the nineteenth century. The historian Richard Slotkin has traced the racialized analogies that fueled aggressions against Filipinos, noting that "the parallel between the logic of massacre in the Philippines and the lynching of Blacks in the South and Midwest was a fact of contemporary life and rhetoric. If 'Indian' was the racial epithet for Filipinos preferred by the high command, the second most popular—and the one preferred by the rank and file— was 'nigger.'"[16] These depictions abounded in letters sent home by U. S. military personnel fighting in the islands, in which soldiers refashioned the terms of racial conflict in the United States to fit the circumstances of fighting in the Philippines. As one soldier wrote home, "we commenced to chase niggers"; another reported that his division had "put the black rascals over the hills."[17] The production of a racialized enemy in these terms recast the U. S. military aggression in the Philippines as a race war like that being fought in cities across the United States.

But Topsy's sinister glee, and her admission that she is "might wicked" resonate on another level, as well. Despite the overwhelming number of

Filipino casualties in relation to the aggression of American soldiers, U.S. military officials insisted that it was the Filipino "insurgents" who were "savage" and lacked knowledge of or capacity for the civilized arts of both warfare and government. Indeed, the guerrilla strategy adopted by Filipino revolutionaries by 1899 initially proved so difficult for U.S. forces to counter that they railed against it as a violation of the codes of "civilized warfare" and held it up as further proof that Filipinos were racially unfit for independence.[18] These claims resurrected and recirculated arguments leveled against citizenship and voting rights for African Americans, maintaining Anglo hegemony by the logic of a racialized tautology where those historically denied sovereignty on the basis of race were subsequently deemed too "inexperienced" to participate in government and even basic individual acts of self-determination.

In bringing to mind the troubled history of U.S. slavery, Stowe's novel addressed yet another tension regarding the occupation of the Philippines, and that is the racialized character of freedom and the legal status of the islands and their inhabitants. This anxiety coalesced around two related questions. First, what would be the legal status of Filipinos with regard to United States citizenship and the Constitution? As Asians, Filipinos were considered racially ineligible for citizenship in the United States, and would instead occupy a liminal legal status as "nationals."[19] Legal challenges to antimiscegenation laws that prohibited marriage between Filipinos and white U.S. citizens continued to debate the racial status of Filipinos as "Malay" or "Mongolian," or, as one case put it, "yellow" or "brown," well into the twentieth century.[20] Further complicating this matter was the ambiguous status of the Asian laborer in the Americas. With the extensive importation of Chinese workers to replace African slave labor on Caribbean plantations after the end of slavery in the British empire, the figure of the "coolie" seemed to represent the successful end of slavery; at the same time, the deplorable conditions that surrounded the coolie figure—forced indentureship, hard labor, and no recourse to legal rights or freedom—made the system of coolie labor seem, simply, "a new system of slavery."[21]

In the United States, the ambiguous status of the "coolie" strained the distinction between free and unfree labor, and was vigorously debated by politicians on both ends of the political spectrum. As Moon-Ho Jung has argued, "'coolies' occupied the legal and cultural borderland between slavery and freedom"; by collapsing the Chinese immigrant with the "coolie," legislation to prohibit Chinese immigration in the late nineteenth century was enacted under the banner of preserving, not restricting, freedom in the United States.[22] With their much-debated racial and legal status, Filipinos pushed these ambiguities further, igniting fears about the consequences of the legal immigration of Asian workers into the United States. A third complicating factor concerned slavery in the Philippines. By mid-February 1899, information about the existence of slavery in the Philippines added to racialized assumptions about the "laziness" endemic to the tropics to further fan the fears that Filipinos represented the degradation of American liberty through the renewal of slavery. As Stanford president David Starr Jordan concluded, the Philippines were "not contiguous to any land of freedom" and "their population cannot be exterminated on the one hand, nor made economically potent on the other, except through slavery."[23]

Addressing the contradictory logic of racialized categories of free and unfree and the anxieties excited by the ambiguous status of Filipinos therein, "Our New Topsy" seeks to allay such anxieties by rehearsing the scene of a familiar spectacle of racial dominance. At the same time, the choice of Stowe's abolitionist novel indicates a deep desire to disavow the tenacious and resilient resistance on the part of Filipinos who opposed U.S. rule. Slavery, as Stowe's pen drew it, was capable of perpetrating great violence against the innocent. Its central crimes, however, were enacted against a pacified, submitting people who markedly did not resist. The Christianizing effect, in Stowe's vision, would save white slaveholders not only from themselves (by convincing them to confront and forsake their own capacity for cruelty) but also from the righteous resistance or revolt of the human beings to whom they laid claim as property. Despite the heightened tensions in the first half of the nineteenth century about the possibility of an outright slave rebellion, and despite the threatening spectre of the Haitian revolution, Stowe's novel shows little outward concern for such an uprising.[24] As many scholars have demonstrated, the congressional ban on the international slave trade, enacted in 1807, was a response to the uprising of slaves and free persons of color in the French colony of Saint Domingue, and the establishment of Haiti as a free, black republic strained to its ideological limits American slaveholders' arguments that people of African descent were incapable of citizenship, much less self-government.[25] The potential threat posed by the Haitian revolution to the order of the slaveholding South "redoubled [the] conviction of the need for a prudential ban on the importation of African or foreign slaves," and the immigration to Louisiana of thousands of slaves and free persons of color from Saint Domingue between the 1790s and 1810 indicated that the organized and vehement resistance to slavery could not be dismissed.[26]

Within the sentimental realm of Stowe's novel, however, resistance to slavery's violations is abandoned in favor of the deferred justice of heavenly reward. Thus not only does Tom submit to the physical violences and degradations that befall him, but he admonishes others for their resistance as well, insisting that "good never comes of wickedness" and urging others to "love our enemies" (344). Tom follows the lead of faith, replacing revolutionary action with forgiveness, submission, and patience. This establishes a pattern in which the righting of slavery's wrongs rests not with the forceful refusal and revolution of those violated by the institution, but through the knowing guidance of the faithful.[27] Within Stowe's view, the ameliorative effects of Christian salvation provide a far more efficacious route to slavery's end than armed resistance.

It is little wonder, then, that the cartoon features the leader of the Philippine revolution as a young slave girl who, readers of Stowe's novel would have known, would be duly tamed by the religious benevolence of her masters. The political work that the cartoon performs is thus multifold; it quickly announces the racial terms of the conflict, while seeking to assert the triumph of white hegemony as an inevitability. The popularity of the novel ensures that readers of this cartoon would well know that Miss Ophelia, in the end, prevails; this is not to say that she loves Topsy, but that she assumes, through her newly benevolent regard, "an influence over the mind of the destitute child that she never lost" (259). In addition, it looks to make assurances about the future: like Topsy, Aguinaldo and the revolution he represented could be domesticated. In other words, this image seeks to reassure its white audience, by making recourse to one of the most popular cultural texts available, of both the efficacy and the righteousness of its imperial expansion. Its metaphorics insist that the cultural power of white Christianity will prevail, and that it will do so in the name of love. Like Stowe's novel, this cartoon seeks to understand a political conflict in the social terms of the domestic novel; though Uncle Sam and Aguinaldo are pictured on the islands, the rendering of both figures as woman and girl-child renders playful the aggressively masculinist imperative in Anglo expansion.

"Our New Topsy" addresses such anxieties, but it cannot resolve them. One notes quickly that the vivaciousness of Aguinaldo's Topsy quite outdoes the wizened, harried-looking Ophelia, betraying a certain anxiety about whether the white matrons of the nation are up to the challenge of

holding dominion over this new population of imagined children. Likewise, the island setting of the scene has Miss Sam out of her element; looking pale and overdressed, she seems incapable of the energy or force that
Aguinaldo displays. Perhaps most tellingly, Little Eva, so crucial to the
transformations of both Miss Ophelia and Topsy, is absent from the cartoon—a gaping omission because, in the struggle to establish U.S. domination over the Philippines, there is no figure of pure love, no comparable
"Little Eva" to soften the hard blows through which the institutions of racial dominance are maintained. If Eva is the figure of perfect, and thus
impossible, benevolence in *Uncle Tom's Cabin,* here her absence marks the
inconceivability of any intimacy with the innocent, ghostly-white femininity she represents in this new scene of racial conflict. Topsy and Ophelia are left unreconciled as they confront each other across their mutual
disdain. It is the fear of this impasse, however, that the popular power of
Uncle Tom's Cabin is marshaled to address. Despite Aguinaldo-Topsy's assertion that "there cain't nobody do nothin' with me," Stowe's novel tells
us otherwise. We already know Topsy's fate and Miss Ophelia's, and thus,
we are told, will the nation be saved.

The Power of the Book

Just as Stowe's best-selling novel performed the delicate cultural work of
maintaining white American dominance in the form of a sentimental
novel, the cartoon drew upon the enormous power of the novel to tell its
readers something about the continuity of that dominance and the forms
it could take. But while the cartoon banked on the enormous social and
political influence of Stowe's novel, it also indicated something about the
political importance of the novel form more generally. In order to understand the social function of the cartoon's revision of Stowe's novel within
the project of racial dominance in the Philippines, it is necessary to look
more closely at the parameters of the occupying regime and the forms of
social control it authorized.

By the end of the nineteenth century, the production of sentimental
novels had slowed, and their enormous popularity faded somewhat in the
face of growing interest in literary realism, regionalism, and local-color
fiction as forms that addressed the new social order that attended the increasing urbanization and industrialization of the American populace. It
would be a mistake to assume that the ideological force of sentimentalism

had diminished, however. Rather, by the last decade of the nineteenth century, its codes, structures, and social norms had become culturally diffused, moving beyond the specificity of the middle-class home to constitute the generalized standard of a "civilized" America against which all classes and races would be compared. The late nineteenth century would thus be best understood as what Laura Wexler has called the "afterglow of sentimentalization" within which the "externalized aggression" of the sentimental, marked by its capacity to naturalize "the subjection of people of different classes and different races" and effect their dehumanization by making the white, middle-class home the center of civilized life, had spread beyond the pages of its novels to become the cultural standard by which members of that social group were deemed proper Americans and other groups were not.[28]

Detached from the interiors of the middle-class home, sentimentalism had thus become a crucial strategy aimed at the "rehabilitation" of the nation's imagined Others through the forcible interiorization of its values. Before its export to the American colonial Philippines, it was installed at the center of a number of late nineteenth-century social programs meant to "Americanize" immigrants and Native Americans and "uplift" African Americans and members of the working class, most notably in schools. The opening of schools like the Hampton Normal and Agricultural Institute in 1868 and the Carlisle Indian Industrial Training School in 1879 marked the institutionalization of the nineteenth-century faith in the domesticating function of the sentimental. At Hampton, newly emancipated African Americans were trained not just in teaching and in mechanical and agricultural trades, but also in the manners, moral values, and habits of middle-class domestic life. "Success," within the terms that Hampton founder and principal Samuel Chapman Armstrong delineated, meant adopting proper "habits of labor" while demonstrating fluency with the domestic arts.[29] Publicity photographs taken for the school featured before-and-after photo sequences that compared the modest surroundings of "old-time" African Americans next to the well-appointed dining rooms and impressively built homes of Hampton graduates, displayed in the photos as perfectly poised to illustrate the benefits of middle-class domesticity.[30] In re-creating such domestic scenes, Armstrong envisioned the structure of the domestic sphere to have a salvific force for a people he regarded as "a thousand years behind us in moral and mental development."[31]

With this belief in the rehabilitative potential of the domestic was paired a complementary belief in the moral necessity of labor. Thus industrial and domestic training were key elements in African Americans' immersion into the norms of middle-class domesticity, even while it taught them their specific, highly circumscribed role within that sphere. Convinced that an academic curriculum, including "reading and elocution, geography and mathematics, history, the sciences" would "exhaust the best powers of nineteen-twentieths of those who would for years come to the Institute," Armstrong eschewed the academic subjects for a more "practical" training, which he understood to be more "genuine" with respect to the futures that awaited graduates of the school.[32] Working from the "conviction of labor as a moral force," Armstrong and his successor, Hollis Burke Frisell, insisted upon the efficacy of instruction in industrial and "domestic arts" so as to evaluate the "moral worth" of students in addition to their intellectual achievement.[33] Through its emphasis on the industrial and domestic arts, Hampton was meant to constitute a "home" of its own, a "little world" in which, under the supervision of white teachers, morality, thrift, and responsibility would be modeled and taught.[34]

Harriet Beecher Stowe herself embraced the pedagogical power of the sentimental beyond the page as well. Some of the early royalties from *Uncle Tom's Cabin* were donated to schools for African Americans, where Stowe supported the expansion of education in the "domestic arts" as a means for African Americans to find their place in the social order.[35] Early in 1866, she began to contemplate a move to the South in order to participate in the work of Reconstruction on behalf of "that poor people whose course in words I have tried to plead and who now, ignorant and docile, are just in that formative state in which whoever seizes has them."[36] She opened a school for freedpeople outside of Jacksonville, Florida, in 1867, and enlisted the help of William Lloyd Garrison in raising funds to support her school and another in a settlement a few miles away.[37] Stowe wrote of her opinion that "all that is wanted to supply the South with a set of the most desirable skilled laborers" is industrial education for African American children. She added that "if the whites, who cannot bear tropical suns and fierce extremes, neglect to educate a docile race who both can and will bear it for them, they throw away their best chance of success in a most foolish manner."[38] Other educators throughout the South concurred, establishing a system of race-based discrimination through curricular design. University of Tennessee president Charles W. Dabney asserted that "the negro is a child race, at least two thousand years behind the Anglo-Saxon in its development," and concluded that "Nothing is more ridiculous than the programme of . . . teaching Latin, Greek, and philosophy to the negro boys"; the president of North Carolina's College of Agriculture and Mechanic Arts concurred, positing that "the Old South was overthrown not by Webster and Greeley and Lincoln, but by the industrial inefficiency of Negro slavery" and recommended that the Hampton-Tuskegee system be "duplicated in every southern state."[39]

Also in Florida, Stowe began to work as a volunteer teacher at a prison for Native American chiefs at Ft. Marion, in St. Augustine. What educators and reformers like Stowe deemed as the "success" in the reading instruction and military drill at Ft. Marion in "pacifying" the Native warriors enabled the prison commander, Richard Henry Pratt, to open a larger school for Native Americans in the old military barracks in Carlisle, Pennsylvania. The Carlisle School embraced the ethos of Americanization through the paradigm of sentimental education in more direct ways. The flagship school for Native American children, it was one of many residential schools where white men and women, employed as teachers, were also encouraged to usurp the role of parent while the children remained forcibly separated from their own families and communities, usually for years at a time. In some instances, Native children were compelled to call these teachers "mother" and "father," thus making explicit the domestic fantasy through which Carlisle and other residential schools attempted the cultural retraining of Native children. That acculturation through immersion was the explicit goal was made clear by founder and headmaster Richard Henry Pratt, who declared, "To civilize the Indian, get him to civilization. To keep him civilized, keep him there."[40]

While the Hampton Institute taught African American adults to recreate their own domestic scenes within their families at home, the Carlisle School attempted to Americanize its diverse population of Native American children by incorporating them into the national family, envisioning the extinction of the "Indian" through his or her inculcation into the norms of white domesticity. The falsity of this paradigm was revealed at multiple levels, however. Forced to endure harsh conditions, extreme food deprivation, demanding physical labor, and violent punishment for crimes like speaking in their native tongues, many children rebelled and fled; others died, either in trying to escape or from the sickness that resulted from such withering conditions.[41] The memoirs of those who survived attest to the rigorous system of military drill that organized the daily activities of boarding school students. "We marched to the dining room three times a day to band music. We rose to a bell and had a given time for making our beds, cleaning our rooms, and being ready for breakfast," one student reported; "Everything was done on schedule, and there was no time for idleness."[42] Within the purportedly benevolent design of domesticity was a sinister program of cultural annihilation, in which physical violence accompanied domestic tutelage in a prolonged effort to solve the "Indian question" by "civilizing" Native children.

In contrast to the example of institutions like Hampton and Carlisle, however, the educational program in the Philippines was not immediately designed around an industrial program, despite frequent lamentations by Armstrong and others that Filipinos failed to realize the "dignity" of manual labor. Instead, the choice between an industrial and an academic curriculum was the subject of considerable debate, revealing much about the stakes of the paradigm of cultural assimilation through education. Fred Atkinson, the first superintendent of instruction in the Philippines, had been a high-school principal in Springfield, Massachusetts, a state reputed to be the epicenter of curricular reform in the United States. As such, Atkinson was familiar with the growing trend in manual and industrial education, particularly as a standard of education for training African Americans and Native Americans in the norms of middle-class, white domesticity and for preparing them for occupations in service industries. In addition, Atkinson inaugurated his tenure over the public education system in the Philippines with a tour of the three flagship institutions of colonial education in the mainland United States. In May 1900, before his departure for the Philippines, he visited Hampton and Carlisle, as well as Booker T. Washington's Tuskegee Institute in Alabama.[43] Fresh from these visits, Atkinson initially proclaimed himself an advocate of industrial and vocational training for Filipinos, insisting: "In our system we must beware the possibility of overdoing the matter of higher education and unfitting the Filipino for practical work. We should heed the lesson taught us in our reconstruction period when we started to educate the negro [*sic*]. The education of the masses here must be an agricultural and industrial one, after the pattern of our Tuskegee Institute at home."[44] It's not difficult to speculate what the "lesson" of Reconstruction was, in Atkinson's view. Many African Americans were suspicious of the instruction in "domestic arts" that defined their access to "progressive education." As one critic put it, "If Negroes don't get any better education than Armstrong is giving them . . . [then] they may as well have stayed in slavery!"[45]

Atkinson seemed to have been eager to disavow Filipino resistance to U.S. authority, and his advocacy for industrial and domestic training everywhere evidenced an anxiety about containing that resistance through the quick absorption of Filipinos into the highly servile training modeled at Hampton. His admiration for Booker T. Washington, who was famous for his outward acquiescence to segregation and his opposition to African Americans who called for expanded political rights, emphasized this point; contacting Washington before his visit to Tuskegee, Atkinson wrote that "any suggestions from you and your work will be invaluable."[46] Further support for industrial education for Filipinos took similar routes in making analogies to the education of African Americans, clarifying the extent to which the project of Filipino education was from the start oriented toward training Filipinos as moral, racial, and intellectual inferiors. Comparisons between African Americans and Filipinos were quite explicit, as were appreciative accounts of Booker T. Washington's role in promoting industrial training, as instanced in a letter to William Howard Taft from his brother, Horace, in which he declared that Washington was "a rare man" and queried: "Won't you go in for industrial education in the Philippines? Certainly there is no other education for a race like the Negroes [sic] that compares with that in its effect upon character and race deficiency."[47] Just as programs like those at Hampton and Tuskegee reassured white businessmen, industrialists, and politicians that black militancy would be avoided, so did Atkinson aim to contain the spectre of Filipino resistance through the "tender violence" of colonial education.[48]

In one respect, the repeated insistence that Filipinos needed guidance, training, and education in order to be eligible for the responsibilities of citizenship and national autonomy was in keeping with the ideological purpose of industrial training. Such training was seen as that which would fit Filipinos for eventual autonomy through the civilizing effects of "honest labor" while instilling a strict limit on the kinds of knowledge they were deemed eligible to incorporate. A debate featured in the leading educational journal, the *Philippine Teacher,* put the matter bluntly by enumerating the possible negative effects of an academic curriculum on Filipino students. Regarding the curriculum best suited for a population characterized as "comparatively primitive," one contributor wrote: "Teaching men like those under consideration to speak Latin and English, to paint pictures and write poetry is all very well, but without a foundation of ability to earn a living such teaching is vanity and vexation of spirit. . . . The condition of the colored race in the South immediately after the war was similar to that of the Filipinos to-day, at least with respect to their industrial condition. . . . The man who shall convince the Tagal that skilled labor with the hands is a thing to be desired, even as Booker

T. Washington has taught the negroes, will be doing more to pacify these islands than many armies."[49] The casual dismissal of an academic curriculum, "Latin and English" as well as "pictures" and "poetry," is here justified on the grounds that Filipinos needed to learn the self-discipline of labor, not the mental discipline associated with training in classics. This, in these terms, was a moral issue that converged with an economic one. Clearly the spectre of slavery haunted this discussion; if, as Stanford president David Starr Jordan asserted, Filipinos could not be "made economically potent . . . except through slavery," then the pedagogical imperative to ingrain the desire for labor would solve the ethical and political problem posed by the principle of forced labor.[50] This philosophy was in keeping with Armstrong's, who insisted that Hampton students "can never become advanced enough . . . to be more than superficially acquainted with Latin and Greek; their knowledge would rather tend to cultivate their conceit than to fit them for faithful educators of their race."[51] But here the intent is rendered even more explicit. It is not the skills themselves but the acceptance of labor as "a thing to be desired" that is the object of this educational paradigm. In its presumed efficacy to teach all of the values implicit in the Protestant work ethic—industry, thrift, self-discipline, and moral righteousness—the function is not to uplift but to pacify, thus laying bare the coercive intent behind the educational paradigm as a more efficacious instrument of rule.

Importantly, however, there was another contingent, a significant network of educators and administrators who favored an academic curriculum over industrial training. This is particularly interesting given that the comparisons to African American and Native American education were so prevalent, and that belief in the positive results of industrial training were so widely accepted among white reformers like those who assembled annually at the Lake Mohonk Conference of Friends of the Indian and Other Dependent Races, as well as other benefactors of Native and African American education.[52] Such administrators insisted that the ennobling effects of a humanist education were needed for the social and moral training of Filipinos. That is, while no less quick to insist upon what they assumed to be the racial limitations of Filipinos, they saw a wholly different educational path leading toward the eventual enlightenment of this subject people. This is stated quite clearly in an article, again in the *Philippine Teacher*: "Youth form ideals; it is the ideal-forming period. It will be a daily study of the teacher to form just and noble ideals of life and conduct. Youth are constructing a philosophy of life. . . . The higher ends of existence must be presented. That one comes to school to get ready to work in a store or on the farm must be overcome by loftier considerations."[53] In the service of such "noble ideals" and "loftier considerations," "the arts," it was argued, "must be imparted to the pupil." This was a new function attributed to the arts as an academic subject, as we have seen, and arguments such as this one arose in tandem with the new reliance on the literary as a transformative enterprise. Such ideas drew from the work of the British poet, critic, and school inspector Matthew Arnold, who famously argued for the power of culture as "harmonious perfection," an ameliorative force against the threat of "anarchy" posed by the protests of the working classes in Britain. Arnold's vision, as Gauri Viswanathan has shown, was deeply embedded in a nineteenth-century Evangelical discourse, in which "an innately depraved self could hope for regeneration through the transformative, moral action of literary instruction."[54] Within this view, literary education modeled, even replaced, the function of religious salvation, in the "growing and becoming" toward, as Arnold saw it, "human perfection."[55]

The insistence that literature would provide the basis for Filipinos' instruction can be partially explained by the new role that literature was starting to play as a subject in children's education in the United States. The novelty of this new role is revealed in the works of one of its primary advocates, Horace Scudder, a teacher, editor, and author of readings for children. In an address entitled "The Place of Literature in Common School Education," which Scudder delivered before the National Education Association in 1888 (two years before taking the helm as editor in chief of the Boston-based literary magazine the *Atlantic Monthly*), he built the case for literature as a central part of the common school education by calling upon its function as a secular body that would elevate the spirit as well as form the character of young people. Making a direct comparison to the school's traditional emphasis on religious training, Scudder suggested that the new role of the school was not to train children to "fear God," but to "become good citizens."[56] The common school, for Scudder, was not simply an institution for the moral education of future citizens, but the site that produced children as citizens; inasmuch as common schools "epitomize the nation," they both "reflect the prevailing thought of the people" and "embody its ideal."[57] Here, literature was crucial.

To this end, Scudder proposed "the free, generous use of [our great authors] in the principal years of school life" when "their power is most profoundly needed and will be most strongly felt." Being released into the "power" of such authors, Scudder contended, would enable "instant and close connection with the highest manifestation of our national life."[58] Scudder emphasized the importance of the "unimpeded circulation of the spiritual life of the people," defined by "the sacrifices of the men and women who have made and preserved America from the days of Virginia and New England," and declared that "in literature, above all, is this spirit enshrined."[59]

Literature had thus a moral function and a national one—or rather, its national function was, for Scudder, a moral one. The urgency of American literature was in its role as the focal point of the school's mission to make "good citizens." As Scudder put it, "there is behind the facts of history and the methods of politics something more intangible, yet more vital to any large and lasting conception of Americanism" that is "expressed . . . mainly through the art of letters. It is literature, therefore, that holds in precipitation the genius of the country."[60] It was a genius of the spirit and passion as well as of the intellect, and one that Scudder raised to an issue of national security; that is, literature is nothing less than the "spiritual deposits of patriotism," through contact with which the love of country was "kept fresh and living in the hearts of the young."[61] Literature, he argued, provided "the strongest defense" of the nation, and was as urgent as the building of armies and the strengthening of more material defenses against attack. The "most admirable way" of cultivating a patriotic citizenry was thus, for Scudder, "a steady, unremitting attention to American classics."[62] After all, as schools became "more and more secularized," Scudder warned, "it is to literature that we must look for the substantial protection of the growing mind against all ignoble, material conception of life, and for the inspiring power which shall lift the nature into its rightful fellowship with whatsoever is noble, true, lovely, and of good report."[63]

Such conclusions were essential to the educational project, particularly as it served as the primary rationale for the continued U.S. presence on the islands. Through the colonial subject's introduction into the world of American literature, the unification, civilization, and collective uplift of the subject people was imagined, and the focus of this strategy extended well beyond the instruction of grammar and reading to constitute, even demand, the Filipino pupil's entrance into a new signifying system in which the linguistic held crucial keys to the racial, cultural, and gender hierarchies of the colonial paradigm. Let us consider how this worked by way of the paradigm explained by the secretary of public instruction,

Bernard Moses. I quote at some length here from his *First Annual Report* on the Philippine educational system in 1902:

> Elementary books might have been prepared and printed in the various dialects and made the basis of primary instruction. Pupils having passed over this stage of their cultivation by this means would have found only *a barren waste before them*. There is no great advantage in learning to read in a language which offers nothing worth reading to those who acquire the art. Children educated in the common schools with only such means . . . are shut out from the advantages enjoyed by their more fortunate fellow-countrymen who have had the means to enable them to acquire a language through which may be derived a knowledge of civilized society. *The boy who grows to manhood knowing only a language without a literature finds that as a result of his training in school he has not the means for increasing his knowledge, and he very readily falls back into the mental darkness of the semi-savage state.* The boy who in his school days has learned the language of a civilized nation, even if he has learned nothing else, has put himself *en rapport* with civilization.[64] (my italics)

As we have seen, such ideas were still very new in the United States; the coordination of the high-school curriculum and the steady inclusion of American literature as a field of study had only developed a few years before, and with little of the outright emphasis on, or even confidence in, its status as a marker of "civilized society" and its ability to lift the pupil from "the mental darkness of the semi-savage state." Even in 1901, while 73 percent of the high-school students in Massachusetts were enrolled in literature courses, in New York that percentage was as low as 32, and in Idaho, 22.[65] Clearly, the study of English and American literature had not yet found its place as an essential subject in the academic lives of most American children.

These questions of the tutelary function of literature took on a particular urgency in the context of the Philippines, however. If there is any doubt about the results of literary instruction in the Philippines, there can be no doubt as to its goals. An early reader in American poetry grandly embraced the task by introducing its selections with the assertion that:

> American literature includes all writings, whether prose or poetry, which have interpreted sympathetically, faithfully, and truly, American life, manners, customs, and habits of thought. . . . Every one of these poems is well

known, and no person's education is complete without a genuine knowledge of them. . . . The greatest benefit to be derived from the study of poetry
is the Inculcation of High Ideals—Love of Country, Self-Sacrifice, Devotion to Truth and Duty, and the Appreciation of the Beautiful. It should be
the aim, then, of the teacher to impress these upon the student.[66]

Here, then, the poetic served two functions, first in instilling these "high
ideals" and then in indicating the path toward their fulfillment. Just as advocates of manual education aimed to inspire the belief that labor was a
"thing to be desired," so now it rested on the literary to inspire the desire
for the noble ideals of self-sacrifice, patriotism, and duty.

The development of a literary curriculum thus stood in contradistinction to that developing in institutions like Carlisle and Hampton, which
were so often considered comparable in social aim and function. When
the *Course of Study for Indian Schools* was first published in 1901, it attempted to provide a unified curriculum for all Native schools by addressing "the peculiar circumstances of Indian life."[67] By "using the articles
of the Hampton creed," its recommendations focused on advancing the
Native American student's progress toward "usefulness and citizenship,"
arranged almost entirely around the functional training in basic agricultural and craft skills. The elaborate course in agriculture, cooking, dairy-
ing, and housekeeping was only briefly interrupted by sections that address reading and writing; in these, the recommendations include regular
review of the *Farm Journal* and *Poultry Magazine*. Such a curriculum,
clearly, was still primarily informed by the notion that the function of the
school would be to "domesticate" Native American children by readying
them for land ownership through agricultural training.

The issued played out quite differently in the Philippines. While early
courses were designed to include "body work" like weaving and other
crafts, from the first a steady, focused attention on reading dominated the
curriculum. In the early years, these purposes were served by the same
primers used in the United States, and the curriculum for primary schools
in the Philippines differed little from comparable schools in the United
States; as of January 1901, the textbooks received in the Philippines included 100,000 Baldwin's Primers and an additional 100,000 Baldwin's
First, Second, and Third Year Readers.[68] Supplementary materials included
10,000 *Fifty Famous Stories,* also collected and annotated by James Baldwin, and 40,000 editions of the Heart of Oak series, a collection of short
fiction, historical sketches, and poetry, edited by Charles Eliot Norton.[69]

The initial expectation was that Filipino children would begin their acquaintance with English through what Norton, in the Heart of Oak series, called "the masterpieces of the literature of the English-speaking race"—in the Baldwin readers, excerpts from Longfellow, Emerson, and American authors dominated, supplemented by American anthems by Francis Scott Key and Samuel F. Smith ("The Star-Spangled Banner" and "America"); in the Heart of Oak series, these American authors returned with supplements from Shakespeare, Blake, and Wordsworth, among others.[70]

By 1904, the first series of readers designed and printed for use in the U. S. schools in the Philippines were introduced; these had been commissioned by the Department of Public Instruction based on what Superintendent Fred Atkinson called the "undesirable" nature of American textbooks that featured "a different environment intended for children of another country." Words like "strawberry," "snow," "Jack Frost," and "fairy," he added, "possess little significance for the children of the Philippines.[71] In the first examples of these, the material seems to have gone only so far as to replace "Jack" and "Mary" with "Juan" and "Maria"; selections in more advanced books continued to present pieces like Longfellow's *Hiawatha* with selections from Benjamin Franklin, and short historical sketches with such titles as "The Discovery of America," "The Landing of the Mayflower," and "Captain Miles Standish and the Indians," thus pursuing in both narrative and poetry the exceptionalist story of American nationalism.[72] Despite the recurring refrain in the preface to most editions that "the temperament and experiences of the Filipino child have been carefully considered," even as late as 1925, the overviews of the Philippine educational system lament the *lack* of adaptation to what administrators deemed the "Filipino temperament," saying that "the text-books used are unsuited to the needs, attainments, and experiences of Filipino pupils. They were written for American children for whom English is the native tongue. . . . Moreover, the content of these books reflects American conditions, institutions, and ways of thinking."[73]

Of course, it was precisely these "ways of thinking" that were the intended lesson of the instruction in the Philippines; accordingly, the Philippine English series was only slightly adapted from the standard curriculum for American students in the United States. Like the Baldwin and the McGuffey readers, they outlined a progressive curriculum of reading aimed at the moral and cultural formation of the child; the Baldwin readers begin with a preface that announces the purpose of the selections to be "to cultivate a taste for the best style of literature," "to appeal to the pupil's sense of duty," and "to arouse patriotic feelings and a just pride in the achievements of our countrymen."[74] Also like those readers, they worked toward these parallel goals by placing great emphasis on the secular heroes of American nationalism: Abraham Lincoln, Benjamin Franklin, George Washington, Christopher Columbus. Whereas in the United States these stories are framed to inspire patriotism and national pride, in the Philippines they seem quite explicitly calculated to announce the moral and historical superiority of the colonial nation; emphasis is everywhere on the foresight of such men, often at odds with those around them, under whose leadership first Europe, then America, had moved upward along the scale of Progress. Such texts thus reiterated a narrative of historical progress that Reynaldo Ileto has charted, in which Filipinos were educated to think of themselves within a racialized narrative of historical development where the present in Philippine history was aligned with Europe's feudal or medieval past, and American colonial guidance would be necessary to lead Filipinos into the temporality of modernity.[75]

What differences are discernable in the Philippine English series appeared less in the content and more in the book's framing narrative. In the first edition of the Philippine English series, the primer announces in its preface: "the subject-matter has been selected after careful consideration of the temperament and needs of the young Filipino boy and girl," with the proviso that "where it seems advisable, a note has been placed at the bottom of the page for the benefit of the Filipino teacher."[76] More to the point, the authors suggest that in addition to the "explicit directions" in such notes, Filipino teachers will require that the books be taught *to them* during the annual summer Normal School institutes, remarking that "the primer has been written from two points of view which are never very far apart and which in the end become one—that of the Filipino child and that of the Filipino teacher." Thus is the Filipino child merged with the Filipino teacher-as-child through a dominating colonial logic of tutelage. The Philippine English series announces its role as a series of books for children, but each text also invests in a cultural and colonial logic in which all Filipinos were seen as children, or childlike wards, so that the pedagogical instruction of the teacher, too, becomes the necessary work of the text. The colonial school was the site for a much broader and more general instruction in colonial power, one that was further institutionalized by a hierarchy of labor in which Filipino teachers were hired to instruct only under the constant supervision of American teachers or divisional superintendents. The schools become an analogy to the political system in which American rulers were portrayed as necessary teachers of democracy, preparing the way for Filipinos toward eventual self-rule; likewise, the textbooks perpetuated the racialized hierarchy of tutelage in which American teachers "are here not to displace [Filipino teachers] but to prepare them to take charge of their own schools."[77]

Beyond the most primary levels, these readings were replaced by literary selections, including, for all students, a full year of "American classics" like Longfellow's *Evangeline* and Irving's *Tales of the Alhambra,* and a collection entitled *Selected Short Poems from American Authors,* in which were included William Cullen Bryant, Edgar Allan Poe, Ralph Waldo Emerson, Henry Wadsworth Longfellow, John Greenleaf Whittier, Oliver Wendell Holmes, James Russell Lowell, Walt Whitman, Sidney Lanier, and Eugene Field.[78] What is notable about the high-school curriculum is the extended study of short texts (one survey of the Philippine curriculum heaps criticism on the fact that a semester is spent entirely on *Evangeline*), and that English was substituted quite explicitly for Latin and Greek as the subject of advanced study for the purposes of humanist cultivation and mental discipline.[79] As David Barrows put it: "While in the United States we depend, in our training of the youth, upon Latin and Greek for giving breadth of mind and depth of intellectual and moral insight, here in the Philippines we must depend upon English literature for these same purposes. It is believed that English is adequate to impart these essentials of education, both in disciplinary and spiritual aspects."[80] It was thus the role of the literary to perform the twin functions of mental discipline (English is the new Latin) and emotional discipline, transforming Filipinos from recalcitrant, "savage," or resistant antagonists into colonial subjects imbued with the Protestant values of "Love of Country, Self-Sacrifice, Devotion to Truth and Duty, and the Appreciation of the Beautiful." The value of the literary was revealed to be its efficacy as a replacement for the strong arm of colonial authority.

But the enduring power of English was not left to the English classrooms alone. Another of its centers was the library system, which played no small role in determining the availability, access, and priority of literary and historical texts for a large amount of the English-educated population. The collections for the libraries of the public system relied on a blend of autobiography, fiction, and history to present a comprehensive picture of the achievements of Anglo-Americans and Western civilization more generally. Strikingly, there is no record of any book by any Filipino author listed among the approved acquisitions for the public school libraries. That is to say, not even José Rizal's work, which had been published in English translation in 1900, was included in the list of approved works, this despite the fact that colonial administrators had already begun a decided campaign to promote Rizal as a national hero, both as a means of deflecting criticism of American colonialism through Rizal's condemnations of the Spanish colonial regime, and by emphasizing what they saw as Rizal's reformist tendencies, rather than revolutionary ones.[81] The promotion of Rizal to the status of a recognized national hero was initially proposed by William Howard Taft; Acts 137, 243, and 345 of the Philippine Commission named a province after the writer, authorized the erection of a monument to Rizal, and made a day of observance on the anniversary of his death.[82] Civil Governor William Cameron Forbes advocated for the promotion of Rizal as a national hero on the basis that he "never advocated independence, nor did he advocate armed resistance to the government. He urged reform from within, by publicity, by public education, and appeal to the public conscience."[83]

Such a reading of Rizal was, in fact, a strategic misreading; E. San Juan Jr. suggests that the U.S. administrators' image of Rizal as "totally committed to Westernization" was a falsely constructed one, no less a forgery than the two documents (the Code of Maragtas and the Code of Kalantiaw) erroneously publicized as dating from the pre-Hispanic period and circulated as proof of the essential complicity of "native" Philippine culture with the Anglo-Puritan values of patience, industry, thrift, and submission to authority.[84] All the more striking, then, that Rizal's work was excluded from the library holdings and the literature curricula, replaced instead by a range of now-classic American and English texts like Benjamin Franklin's *Autobiography*, the poetry of Longfellow, Tennyson, Bryant, Whittier, and Lowell, Washington Irving's *Sketchbooks*, John S. C. Abbott's biographies of Napoleon Bonaparte, Julius Caesar, George Washington, and others.[85] Even sentimental tomes like Louisa May Alcott's *Little Women* and Harriet Beecher Stowe's *Uncle Tom's Cabin* were prioritized as "recommended for first purchase." Meanwhile, what information was to be had about the Philippines was offered in volumes written by American colonial administrators and soldiers themselves; among these were David Barrows's *History of the Philippines*; *Life of Rizal* by Austin Craig (a professor at the University of the Philippines), and *The Story of the Philippines,* by one of the original Thomasites, Adeline Knapp. Subsequent approval lists for public libraries made longer and more detailed collections in American literature collections, American poetry, American drama, American essays, oratory, and humor; by contrast, there is only one brief listing for Filipino literature, categorized under the heading "Literature of minor languages."[86]

In this vein, statements by Secretary of Public Instruction Bernard Moses present the perfect extension of the Arnoldian idea of cultural training, though Arnold's own work was the object of some disdain in the United States.[87] Clearly the "semi-savage state" Moses warns against was not altogether unlike the anarchy Arnold feared emerging from the calls for reform among the working classes in Britain. As Dean Worcester, member of the First Philippine Commission and reputed "expert" on the Philippines, had warned, "with their lack of education and experience, they are incapable of governing themselves"; any attempt to allow even a degree of independence, he continued, would result in a situation where "anarchy would soon follow."[88] Against anarchy, Moses heralded the enlightening effects of literature, or, that is, a literary language that would ensure the student's continued affiliation with and incorporation into the ideological framework of the colonial order and the hegemony of Anglo-American cultural values.

And it is this formulation that marked Moses's emphasis on literature as a new and historic one; unlike Scudder, for whom an education in the national literature was essential to the formation of a national identity among citizens, Moses articulated a role for literature in an expansionist project that would depend on the efficacy of this form in the formation of subjects—presumably, "good" subjects who would internalize the lessons of this new national literature and embody the moral codes it offered. Moses analogized from Horace Scudder's theories about the utility of literature in raising the nation's children to the Philippine context, imagining that these new subjects are the "wild children" that can be tamed by the force of the literary. Just as Topsy was "tamed" by the love emanating from the Book that Eva embodies, in this new context it is the love of books (and the literary) that would render docile and malleable these newest wards of the nation.

If the popularity of the novel in the antebellum period was the result, as Richard Brodhead has shown, of its ability to enact the very model of "disciplinary intimacy" (that is, the internalization of discipline as part of the self) that was central to the "organizing habits and concerns" of the expanding middle class, then the unprecedented importance of literature to the disciplinary apparatus of the colonial school suggests that this value of *Uncle Tom's Cabin* and other sentimental novels was not isolated from the academic institutionalization of the literary, however exclusively the literary might have been defined against such popular fiction.[89] While concerns with "the canonical presentation of artistic value" surely dominated the introduction and institutionalization of literature in the secondary school and at the university, its role as both a model and instrument of interiorized discipline proved crucial to the ideological presentation of the colonial encounter.[90]

Brodhead has argued that the enormous disciplinary function of the sentimental novel had faded by the end of the nineteenth century with the waning of the popularity of sentimental tales and the greater importance of "secular urbanity" and "the sacralization of high culture."[91] I might consider this from a different vantage point by asking the question in terms of the defining characteristics of the paradigm of colonial tutelage, through which the expansionist occupation was justified not only on the grounds that a "proper" education would be provided to the colonial subjects, but that the very contact with a "civilized" people and their cultural effects would produce an uplifting, even ennobling effect. The new, urgent question would be this: What is colonial tutelage but the desire to create "a more thorough order of subjugation" through the internalization of the norms, beliefs, and values of the colonizing force?[92] Thus while Brodhead marks the passing of this particular function of the sentimental novel within its enlarged middle-class readership by the postbellum period, I would add that it was not that the sentimental novel was divested of this function, but that its disciplinary properties were redirected toward another population, no longer the middle class but the "other" subjects who had by then, however uneasily, entered the body politic. This function of the novel did not counteract but instead supported the institutionalization of the other kind of novel, not popular and thus "literary," in the coordination of the field of American literature that was just beginning to emerge as the discipline in which a proper education would be gained.

To return to "Our New Topsy," as I noted previously, in this cartoon there is no Eva, just Ophelia and Topsy left to confront each other across their mutual disdain. I would argue, however, that it was the book that was imagined to function in the place of the absent angel-child-mother, the book that could save others by imparting its values by being read, absorbed, and internalized by this new generation of "wild children," acting as proxy for the agents of imperialism themselves. The example of education in the U.S.-occupied Philippines suggests that by the end of the nineteenth century, the ideological force of the sentimental novel, like

Uncle Tom's Cabin, had become diffused and invested with the persuasive, ameliorative power of good literature. "Good" literature, it was imagined, would teach others to *be* good. If the novel's function in the United States had changed by the end of the century, it nevertheless retained its power precisely because of its close association with white, middle-class domesticity and its uplifting function. This power situated literature as a representative of that sacred domestic sphere and bestowed upon it an ameliorative power, a lasting investment in reading as self-improvement. In the Philippines there were no Evas, but there were libraries, schools, and books meant not only to instruct but to transform, to "teach the alphabet of liberty" to a people regarded as wholly unfit to manage it themselves.[93] If the sentimental was discounted in academic circles because of its distance from the abstract value that came to be associated with the literary, it was central to the imperial cause precisely for that trait—that it could make others feel. Like St. Clare's assertion that "any mind that is capable of real sorrow is capable of good," the fantasy of the entire system of English education was that the otherwise innocuous, even frivolous entity of the book would transform through feeling. The book was thus an agent of colonial power and an embodiment of the "civilized" values to be imparted.

Evangeline *in the Tropics*

To fully appreciate the role of American literature as a colonial force in the American-occupied Philippines, I want to conclude with an example of how the literary might have functioned in this new scene of racial dominance. I have argued that the symbolic force of the cartoon "Our New Topsy" was not just to reimagine the colonial occupation of the Philippines within the familiar paradigm of domestic slavery, but also to offer an uncanny vision of the force of the literary in normalizing the violence that attended the imperial project. This refashioning of the extraordinarily popular *Uncle Tom's Cabin* points to the domesticating power of the sentimental, both as it was modeled by Little Eva in the book, and as it was detached from the antebellum home and made mobile in the material, pedagogical instrument of the book itself.

There is no record of *Uncle Tom's Cabin* being taught at any level of the English curriculum, in the United States or the Philippines. Its very reputation as a *popular* novel would have precluded its academic study, particularly in view of the highly restricted definition of the literary at the end of the nineteenth century.[94] This does not mean that its pedagogical functions were left to chance, however. These were delegated to other texts but remained the distinct work of books; as one teacher expressed it: "The greatest care should, I sincerely feel, be exercised that, while no peculiar religious teaching is given, children all be taught, as heretofore, to reverence God, to obey their parents and teachers, to lead pure and moral lives, etc. *I mean that this should be taught out of a book*"[95] (my italics). The lessons for leading "pure and moral lives" were very much at the center of the design of instruction in the Philippines, as the believed necessity of such lessons provided the basis for all claims to legitimacy for U.S. rule. Far from an arbitrary curriculum, the fundamental values of the sentimental drama—sacrifice, self-abnegation, and "discipline through love"— were transported to the Philippines through the required reading of every high-school student on the islands.

Among the most important of these was the story of another Eva: Henry Wadsworth Longfellow's *Evangeline,* an epic poem about the expulsion of the Acadians from Nova Scotia in 1755.[96] *Evangeline* tells the story of a young Acadian woman who, separated from her betrothed at the expulsion, spends the duration of her life in search of him, crossing the continent and narrowly missing him each step of the way. A widely appreciated poem in the United States, *Evangeline* was praised as "the most perfect of domestic epics, the Odyssey of the nineteenth century."[97] A sentimental tale of thwarted love, it features the patient, endless travels of its heroine as unfolding within a vividly depicted natural landscape that gives an evocative sense of the increasing size and grandeur of the country, causing many to categorize the poem as the first truly *American* epic. Meanwhile, the national success of the poem solidified Longfellow's status as the nation's first professional author and as the patriarch of American letters, making the "good gray poet" a beloved national figure.[98]

Despite its notable popular success, *Evangeline* was not a dominant text in the developing English curriculum in the United States.[99] It was introduced in the 1890s into the list of recommended readings for the Uniform Entrance Requirements for university study, and given the influence of such lists in the forming of classroom curricula, it is probable that it was regularly taught in many classrooms. While Longfellow's poetry was often included or excerpted in readers for American primary school students, *Evangeline* does not appear to have been accorded a special place in the curriculum, however; by the time such entries were surveyed, it was not included in the list of the most frequently taught pieces at the secondary level.[100] In the Philippines, however, *Evangeline* was promptly adopted as a required text at the high-school level, and it remained one of only two texts required for all high-school students regardless of academic "track" (the other was Washington Irving's *Tales of the Alhambra*). It was, from the inauguration of the high-school curriculum in 1904 until well beyond the "Filipinization" of the curriculum in the 1920s, a central text in the curriculum, one that required a full half-year's study and analysis.[101] How, then, might *Evangeline* have functioned in the colonial order, and what were the lessons it was supposed to teach?

As the story goes, the idea for *Evangeline* was furnished to Longfellow by his friend Nathaniel Hawthorne over dinner one night in 1835.[102] Drawn from the historical events of the French Acadians' expulsion from Nova Scotia by the British during the French and Indian War, *Evangeline* dramatizes this historical injustice through the persuasive codes of the sentimental tale. The poem's eponymous heroine is, at the story's opening, a youthful seventeen years old and newly betrothed to her beloved, Gabriel. Both Evangeline and Gabriel are from respected families, and the friendship between their fathers mirrors a larger sense of fraternity in their village of Grand-Pré, where all "dwelt together in love" (line 52) and "the richest was poor, and the poorest lived in abundance" (line 57).[103] This Edenic scene is disrupted violently when the townsmen are assembled and told that their belongings must be at once forfeited to the British Crown, and that they are to be evicted from the village. Cast into exile, the Acadians are thus dispersed, and in the confusion, Evangeline and Gabriel are separated; he departs on a boat with his father, and she is left waiting on shore with her dying father while the village burns in the background.

What is striking, given the poem's dominant place as a representative piece of American literature, is how centrally the codes of sentimentalism figure in this tale about the political injustice of British expansion. Written amid the patriotic fervor during the war with Mexico over the United States' expansion into northern Mexican territory, it illuminated the moral and national disgrace of such unlawful expansion by turning to an eighteenth-century conflict between British and French settlers in the New World. As Kirsten Silva Gruesz has shown in her critique of this imperial project, Longfellow "deploys the abolitionist's strategy of portraying a political problem as a domestic one," such that the cruelty and moral injustice that resulted from the unmitigated exercise of a nation's power are rendered legible through their effects on the family.[104] Much as Stowe used the domestic as a site within which the moral degradation of slavery could be rendered visible, Longfellow transferred the political crisis of imperial expansion and territorial displacement to the domestic, rendering its injustices explicit in terms of the violated sanctity of the family. Describing the forced departure of the Acadians from their idyllic Grand-Pré, Longfellow paints a pathetic scene,

> Wives were torn from their husbands, and mothers, too late, saw their
> children
> Left on the land, extending their arms, with wildest entreaties. (lines
> 570–71)

Such violations are rendered vivid precisely because they are enacted in the seemingly inviolable realm of the domestic. Families separated, children orphaned, houses aflame—Longfellow depicts the consequences of national aggression as a crime against nature itself.

Within the original Eden that is the Acadian countryside at the novel's opening, however, Evangeline is a model of idealized nineteenth-century white femininity. A "fair maiden" of unapproachable grace, she has all the desirable qualities of a sentimental heroine; beauty, obedience, gentleness, fidelity, and piety form the bounty of her character, and we are assured that

> Many a youth, as he knelt in the church and opened his missal,
> Fixed his eyes upon her as the saint of his deepest devotion; (lines 105–6)

Much like Little Eva, this Evangeline is rendered saintlike, an object of others' devotion. Thus deified, she becomes the conduit for others' belief, an important task, particularly in the process through which the civilizing mission was regarded as a Christianizing one.

Saintly Evangeline is also a model "angel of the house," though her poetic appearance preceded by a few years the poem that coined the phrase.[105] In contrast to the wanderings that would animate the whole of her adult life, it is the domestic that occupies Evangeline's talents in the beginning of the poem. Ever industrious, her leisure time is spent at the hearth spinning flax for her loom, and she consults with care her "precious dower" of "linens and woolen stuffs" that are the evidence of "her skill as a housewife" (lines 366–68). Above all, she is pious, and it is this quality that marks her as a deserving heroine. Though Catholic, she is well-versed in the Protestant moral code of self-sacrifice and heavenly reward.[106] Following the British edict forcing the removal of the Acadian settlers, the "deeper shadow" that falls upon her "spirit" is banished upon remembering "the tale she had heard of the justice of Heaven" (lines 499, 522). From "the fields of her soul" rise up not bitterness or rage, but "Charity, meekness, love, and hope, and forgiveness, and patience!" (lines 500–501). It is her willingness to accept, even exult, in the trials of justice deferred that renders Evangeline the powerful heroine within the pedagogical terms of the sentimental narrative. Like Tom and Little Eva in Stowe's famous novel, the lesson of the text favors duty over justice, patience over fulfilled hope, and submission to authority, both human and divine.

Though Longfellow's story gains its pathos from the political injustice of national expansion, his critique of the violent excess of national power is undercut by the glorification of Evangeline as a silent, suffering heroine. In the context of the Philippines, her power as a model of self-abnegation resonates profoundly, and it is hard not to see in its pedagogical function a sinister lesson about self-discipline and patience. Evangeline is three times admonished to accept the deferment of her desires with stoicism; first by the village priest, who assures her that her patience will render her heart more "god-like" and therefore "more worthy of heaven"; again, when she arrives among the resettled Acadians in Louisiana and finds that she has crossed Gabriel on her journey, and the very trees around her whisper "patience!" (line 1057); and a third time by the Jesuit priest she meets at a Shawnee mission, who counsels her, "Patience! . . . have faith and thy prayer will be answered!" (line 1216). Finally, it is she who embodies patience itself:

Patience and abnegation of self, and devotion to others,
This was the lesson a life of trial and sorrow had taught her. (lines 1282–83)

Rendered "all-forgetful of self" by the suffering of others, Evangeline's cultural and pedagogical value is that she unambiguously embodies the moral values of self-abnegation and discipline, thus functioning, like Stowe's Little Eva, as a model for others. This is nowhere more clear than in the final passages of the text when she is reunited with Gabriel almost forty years after their initial separation. No longer the "fair maiden" but "faded" and "old," Evangeline has become a Sister of Mercy, redirecting her faithful search for Gabriel to a new aim, "to follow, meekly, with reverent steps, the sacred feet of her Saviour" (line 1287). Finding her lover on his deathbed, Evangeline witnesses his death with the resignation characteristic of her irreproachable piety:

> All was ended now, the hope, and the fear, and the sorrow,
> All the aching of heart, the restless, unsatisfied longing,
> All the dull, deep pain, and constant anguish of patience!
> And, as she pressed once more the lifeless head to her bosom,
> Meekly she bowed her own, and murmured, "Father, I thank thee!" (lines
>   1376–80)

This concluding moment, in which gratitude replaces what might otherwise be disappointment or righteous rage, is magnificent in its efficiency. One of very few direct lines to issue from the mouth of Evangeline herself, this single speech act renders her waiting heavenly, and banishes her desire into the infinite of total impossibility. Not the fulfillment of her longing but the knowledge that its fulfillment will be impossible—this is her reward. The heavenly refusal is the replacement for the fulfillment of her wish. Her exile is not avenged, the home is not reconstituted; all that is celebrated in this final moment is the total rejection of self-interest, the endurance of silent suffering through the refusal of woman's emotional and physical desire.

Evangeline thus prefigures a heroine like Little Eva, who would appear just five years later, in the lesson of self-deferment and heavenly reward. As the personal here stands in for the political problem of expansion, however, the lesson of the poem can be extended to read as the deferment of political sovereignty, particularly in the context of its circulation in the Philippines. Within the paradigm of benevolent assimilation, the promise of political independence for the Philippines was continually deferred into the imagined future; "patience," then, describes so aptly the admonition given, time and again, to those who agitated for political rights and national autonomy. To read *Evangeline* as an allegory about the reconstitution of the natal community—the reconstitution of the nation—the lesson is be patient, and then, be thankful.

In the end, the choice of Longfellow's poem seems hauntingly strategic. Who better to personify the benevolent address of white patriarchal nationalism than the "great gray poet" himself, particularly as his reputation was so firmly established as a writer of the established literary elite; his Cambridge address, his institutional status at Harvard, his friendships with Hawthorne and others of the New England literary elite: all these rendered him a perfect patriarch of American letters. Even more suitable, his disregard for activity in politics could give *Evangeline* an aura of timelessness (in the forests primeval) that undercut, or even disavowed, its position in the political fray and its role in instructing a particular "patience" with the crimes and excesses of national pride. As one Filipino student avowed, "the exposure of the Filipinos to the democratic virtues was made easier, not by Burke and Tom Paine and Jefferson and the authors of the Federalist Papers, but by a man of avuncular disposition by the name of Longfellow."[107] In this regard, Longfellow's personal opposition to political activity and his contention that he "c[ould] not for a moment think of entering the political arena" contributed to his malleability as a representative of American empire even as he disagreed strongly with its aims.[108]

Despite Longfellow's disavowal of the political, *Evangeline* perfectly embodies the disciplinary functions of the literary as an instrument of colonial rule in the Philippines. In its sentimental structure of love and loss, desire forever deferred, it presents the model subject as an infinitely patient one, wholly compliant with her subjection to the authority, both divine and human, that reigns over her. In her tale there is something of a guide to the domestic model that would be so important a marker of Filipinos' achieved civilization. This aim was spoken no more clearly than in an article penned by Dean Worcester only months after the arrival of the U.S. naval forces on the islands, when he underscored the importance of establishing civil rule as the outgrowth of domestic harmony characterized by "orderly children, respected parents, women subject but not oppressed, men ruling but not despotic, reverence with kindness, obedience in affection."[109] How closely, then, does this describe the actual picture that American colonial administrators told themselves about their own rule over these subjects whom they regarded, in many cases, as children? If, in *Uncle Tom's Cabin,* the achievement of the benevolent self-discipline mastered by Miss Ophelia was that she gained "an influence over the mind [of Topsy] that she never lost," the project of such mastery and influence would have needed, in the American colonial Philippines, to be assured by other means. Far from the actual domestic structures of the U.S. middle-class home, this was something that only the literary could provide.

3

Agents of Assimilation

Female Authority, Male Domesticity, and the Familial Dramas of Colonial Tutelage

In the late morning of July 23, 1901, crowds of people gathered at Pier 12 of the San Francisco wharf to bid farewell to the U.S. transport ship the *Thomas*. Among the ship's passengers were 509 American teachers on their way to the Philippines, enlisted to work in the fledgling public school system instituted during the U.S. occupation of the islands.[1] The Thomasites, as the teachers came to be called, were not the first envoy of Americans recruited to teach in the Philippines; the *Sheridan* had arrived a month earlier, bringing with it forty-eight teachers, and more were to arrive during the following year, such that, by 1902, there were more than a thousand Americans teaching in Philippine schools. This was the largest cohort, however, and as such, the departure of the *Thomas* represented a significant moment in colonial occupation of the Philippines and in the establishment of colonial dominance through President William McKinley's program of "benevolent assimilation."

Significantly, this was not the *Thomas*'s first trip on this imperial route. The ship, originally named the *Persia*, was constructed by Irish shipbuilders in 1893; after serving as a commercial transport under British and American commercial lines, the U.S. government purchased the *Persia* from the British in July 1898. Renamed the *Thomas*, the transport had first carried soldiers and supplies between Cuba and Puerto Rico, then expanded its imperial route to include the Philippines. This was its seventh trip between Manila and San Francisco, previously carrying soldiers as reinforcements for what Secretary of State John Hay called the "splendid little war" against Spain. Essentially a ship of imperial conquest, the *Thomas* was this time carrying a new battalion, what one passenger, the journalist and teacher Adeline Knapp, called "an army, not of conquest, but of education."[2] As a transport for teachers, the *Thomas* was refitted to mark a new phase in the colonial strategy in the Philippines, timed to combat the growing unpopularity of the U. S. intervention in the Philippines and to mask the growing brutality of the U. S. military's campaign to crush Philippine resistance to continued colonial rule.

The launch of the *Thomas* was part of a larger public-relations display. Three weeks before, on July 4, U. S. colonial administrators had declared the end of the war in the Philippines and celebrated the inauguration of a new civil government under the leadership of William Howard Taft, despite continued widespread resistance to the U. S. presence on the islands.[3] Against a backdrop of parades, balloons, and balls, Taft's inauguration as civil governor on the United States' Independence Day marked an ideological shift in the colonial strategy. The festivities of Independence Day in 1901 could hardly herald the success of the United States Army in securing the consent of Filipinos to U. S. governance on the islands; the continued guerrilla strategy of resistance on the part of Filipino revolutionaries wreaked havoc on the U. S. military's claims for peaceful control of the islands, and the hollowness of such claims were made increasingly evident by the brutality of the United States' maneuvers for military control, such as the forcible relocation of Filipino civilians into "reconcentration" camps and the deliberate destruction of land, villages, and crops.

Furthermore, Americans at home had begun to perceive the human cost of the continued conflict, as well as its moral and ideological complications. William Howard Taft made light of the conduct of American troops by asserting that "there never was a war conducted, whether against inferior races or not, in which there was more compassion and more restraint and more generosity."[4] Soldiers' letters told another story, however. Correspondence sent home and circulated by organizations such as the Anti-Imperialist League depicted a brutal war in which whole towns were razed and civilians killed; they described in detail the "water cure" and other acts of torture used against Filipino soldiers or civilians suspected of collaborating with the "insurgents."[5] Such testimony made fictions of a peaceful or willing adaptation to U. S. colonial rule, rendering the façade of benevolence an insufficient antidote for the contradictions between the language of benevolent uplift and the practice of violent subjection in securing the colonial order.

It is precisely such a contradiction that rendered this voyage of the

Thomas so crucial. With its cargo of white American teachers recruited to participate in the "pacification" of the islands, the *Thomas*'s move from soldier to teacher transport offered a persuasive image of the shift from armed conflict to civil occupation, suggesting the cessation of armed conflict and successful establishment of U.S. rule following Taft's Independence Day inauguration. A highly performative gesture, the arrival of this "educational army" eclipsed Filipinos' continued struggle for independence against the United States by announcing the finality of American sovereignty in the islands and adopting as charges America's new "little brown brothers." Knapp's depiction of the transport, as a "white speck lifting and ascending in mid-ocean" with "her forefoot set toward the Philippines, her deck thronged with young men and women actuated for the most part by high ideals and a genuine desire to be helpful," is a good indicator of the racial and national assumptions undergirding the optimism of this imperial mission, for it was precisely within the logic of "helpfulness" that the violence of the colonial project was disavowed as a necessary strategy of uplift.[6]

This "army of instruction" represented a new phase in U.S.–Philippine relations, one in which the civilian project of uplift would be intertwined with the brutish suppression of Filipino resistance. American teachers stood at the forefront of U.S. colonial policy, meant to smooth over the contradictions between the fantasy of democratic self-rule and silencing of calls for independence. In this chapter, I explore the nature of such contradictions, and illuminate the gendered and racialized constructions of teacher and student, master and pupil, that subtended the colonial administration. In particular, I delve more deeply into the function of teachers as representatives of the colonial state, into their deployment as a performative gesture of benevolent domination, and into their participation in what Ann Stoler has called the "intimate frontiers of empire."[7] I'm particularly interested in the symbolic and iconographic function of white, middle-class womanhood as it came to represent the benevolent character of American imperialism. The arrival of white American women at the forefront of the colonial project produced a *highly gendered representational* shift; the move from military occupation to peaceful collaboration was signified by the iconographic shift from white male soldier to white woman teacher. Despite the actual numerical insignificance of white women on the islands, the "army of instruction" was quite consciously constructed as a highly feminized one, and white women approached the islands as "bearers of benevolence," bringing what Laura Wexler has called "the resources of their gender" to resolve the vexed question of American imperialism.[8]

Critical scholarship has recently begun to take into account how the domestic worked as a paradigm of empire, contributing ideologically and practically to the process of United States expansion.[9] Remarkable work has traced how British colonial rule in India depended upon conventions of bourgeois white femininity to "domesticate" the empire, at the same time that it constituted those conventions. Rosemary Marangoly George has demonstrated how participation in the colonial project was "one of the primary arenas in which English women first achieved the kind of authoritative self associated with the modern female subject" and thus serves as "a crucial chapter in the history of the formations that we know today as Western feminism."[10] In the context of U. S. empire, Amy Kaplan has shown that the project of national expansion relied upon notions of the domestic as counterbalance to the "male activity of conquest," even as it allowed women's direct participation in the imperial project. "Domesticity," she argues, "monitors the borders between the civilized and the savage as it regulates the traces of savagery within its purview." The notion of "separate spheres" thus effaced the powerful role of the domestic as a "mobile and mobilizing outpost that transformed conquered lands into the domestic sphere of family and nation."[11] Looking specifically at the context of white American women's writing in the Philippines, Vicente Rafael has explored how the paradigm of benevolent assimilation constituted "a sentimental reworking of manifest destiny," promising the domestication of Filipino subjects through "sentimental affiliation or 'special relation' between colonizer and colonized." Euro-American women, he argues, refashioned the relations of domesticity in the tropics as a mechanism for "rehearsing and containing the quotidian crisis of empire" in the Philippines.[12]

Building on the work of these critics and others, this chapter moves to the schoolhouse as a midway point between public and private spheres, to consider the gendered politics of empire. In particular, I argue that the model of tutelage enabled articulations of white femininity and masculinity that were incommensurate with dominant models of the bourgeois nuclear family. Crucially, the paradigm of benevolent assimilation initiated a colonial relationship of tutelage that extended beyond the classroom, functioning instead as "an idealized partnership of Americans and Filipinos within the teleology of progress" such that the teacher-student relation became a powerful model for American-Filipino relations more generally.[13] The tutelary model, I argue, made possible particular domestic formations and fantasies that the middle-class American familial model did not. In so doing, however, it expanded the practical possibilities for participation in the domestic sphere even as these narratives tried to foreclose on those possibilities ideologically.

This chapter reads narratives by U.S. teachers participating and writing about their work in the settlement of what they frequently called the "new frontier."[14] Such narratives drew on the conventions of popular literary forms like dialect literature, local-color writing, and ethnography, all of which shared in the belief that "through the appropriate methodology, crucial group-based differences could be rendered upon the page."[15] By considering the specificity of how white women and white men functioned differently as representatives of the colonial state, this chapter brings together the domestic and the foreign as they collapsed in the form of the colonial teacher as the signifier of benevolent rule. In so doing, it explores two constitutive contradictions in the tutelary model of colonial rule. The first has to do with a crucial linking of femininity and patriotism, during a period in which women in the United States were struggling for legislative recognition of their own status as citizens of the republic. The chance to set up house in the Philippines afforded many women teachers a position of authority that was both materially and ideologically unavailable to them in the United States; with this independence, however, emerged questions of political power and sexual autonomy that fit uneasily with the model of bourgeois domesticity that underpinned the whole tutelary project. Not full citizens themselves, white women nevertheless were instrumental in the program to train Filipinos for self-government, thus bearing witness to the very limitations of the political model in whose name they worked. Within the domestic sphere of the nation, women suffragists addressed their not-fully-citizen status by investing in the civic optimism of the vote as a way of glossing over the structural violence of which limitations on suffrage were a part. Similarly, the exported domesticity that was the legacy of the white woman teacher in the colonial territories covers over other kinds of violence that are not commensurate with disenfranchisement, but whose forms merit elaboration. The iconographic status of white womanhood was premised upon an articulation between white femininity and Americanness that was quite distinct from the ideals of bourgeois womanhood at play in the United States, particularly at a time of great unrest as to the question of women's role in the public sphere and political world. Away from the domestic space of the nation, these colonial workers constructed a romantic patriotism fashioned to facilitate the strategic forgetting of the masculine excesses of imperial expansion, and of the lingering fact of racial and gender inequality at home.

A second concern of this chapter is to examine how the tutelary model offered a challenge to the martial masculinity that featured strongly in the jingoism of the Spanish-American War. Against the example of Teddy Roosevelt's Rough Riders, the white male teacher occupied a more contradictory place, one that reveals central tensions between the mandate of the civilizing mission and the gender conventions presumed to embody those visions of the civilized. While participation in the colonial enterprise offered white men the chance to participate in the militaristic masculinity of colonial adventure without being a soldier, the tutelary model established a racialized hierarchy across which were revealed powerful fantasies of desire and discipline, public and private, enabled by the domestic work of empire.

Great Armies of Instruction

The close relationship between soldiering and teaching was at once vociferously disavowed and publicly celebrated by the defenders of the United States' imperial expansion. While teachers were understood to embody the benevolent principles of American intervention and thus serve as the antidote to accusations of violent excess on the part of American soldiers, at the same time the teaching force was favorably compared, as we have seen, to an occupying army, itself charged with managing, leading, and at times disciplining an unruly population of "tender young Tagalogs" who were understood to be "orphans" newly "adopted" by "Uncle Sam."[16] Adeline Knapp, a committed suffragist and prolific journalist writing aboard the *Thomas* in 1901, pledged that as "a people who neither know nor understand the underlying principles of our civilization," Filipinos must be offered fellowship in the form of a "great army of instruction" whose "soldiers" would each "carry into his work in the wilderness the spirit of love, of loyalty, and faith."[17] The connection was in fact quite literal; the first American schools in the Philippines were opened by soldiers serving on the islands, when, in early 1900, General Otis established a Department of Public Instruction founded with the goals of compulsory attendance and English-language instruction. Of the crew on the *Thomas,* at least ten had already served as teachers during their enlistment as soldiers (though, tellingly, 107 of them had no experience in teaching, and 31 had only high-school diplomas themselves).[18] This overlap between military and civilian control was lauded as proof that even the most violent of military acts was intended to secure the best ends for Filipinos themselves; this sentiment was echoed in later praise of the U.S. colonial enterprise as a "great experiment in education" by the likes of school and government officials who asserted that the American soldiers were the first "conquering people" to initiate a system of education as a primary step in its occupation, such that "quickly, soldiers became teachers" and offered the "friendly guidance" of colonial education.[19]

It was precisely the role of the recruited teachers to suture together the seemingly opposing principles of democratic civilization and imperial aggression, becoming the visible sign of colonial benevolence, the material signifier of this new civilized order. The logic of colonial tutelage marked a shift from military to civil rule that was precarious at best. For one thing, civilian officials arriving in the Philippines ready to take the reins of colonial rule found an occupying military resistant to ceding control; this was demonstrated most tellingly by the scorn with which General MacArthur greeted William Howard Taft upon his arrival with the Second Philippine Commission. Helen Taft recalled that MacArthur seemed "personally humiliated" by the transfer of power to the civil government, despite the fact that he remained "still in command of about seventy thousand men and had the general executive control of a large civil force."[20]

Taft's recollections notwithstanding, the U.S. military's repression of independence of the islands continued in full force well beyond the transfer of authority from military to civil government in 1901, thus making unclear the status of the so-called postwar state. The particular brutality of the reconcentration policy, introduced in 1901, marked the violent means through which the United States was determined to secure the compliance of its colonial subjects. President McKinley had condemned such policies when enacted under Spanish colonial authority; he famously declared that the Spanish strategies of waging war against rural Cuban populations and forcing civilians into cramped concentration camps with insufficient food or supplies were not "civilized warfare" but "extermination."[21] U.S. military officials adopted the policy in the Philippines after 1900, once the success of the Filipino resistance in guerrilla warfare proved difficult for U.S. military strategists; U.S. forces began a campaign of deliberate destruction of the rural economy, the forced relocation of civilians into "reconcentration camps," the burning of villages and crops, and the killing of all remaining living people and animals.[22] Recognizing the exorbitant cost in civilian lives that such a policy would constitute, Gen. James Bell, an American proponent responsible for executing the re-concentration strategy in Batangas in November 1901, remarked that the brutality of such a measure was preferable to "a benevolent war indefinitely prolonged."[23] He added further justification for the severity of this strategy by asserting that "it is an inevitable consequence of war that the innocent must generally suffer with the guilty," but that "military necessity frequently precludes the possibility of making discriminations."[24]

While the war raged on, American teachers settling in the islands bore the ideological burden of marking the declared end of military conflict and demonstrating the professed good intentions of the U.S. government toward its empire. Gender was key here, as the very presence of white women, as teachers, army wives, nurses, and wives of civilian officials, signaled a distinction between military and civilian rule. White femininity, in other words, stood as a signifier of benevolent rule, bringing with it a paradigm of imperial domesticity meant to eclipse the military conflict as a family drama of errant children and benevolent mothers. In this role, white women teachers drew upon the gendered global force of Christian missionaries. Between 1890 and 1905, the global missionary force doubled; as of 1890, the United States was the largest source of Protestant missionaries in the world, and the majority of these missionaries were women.[25] In the age of social Darwinism, evolutionary biologism, and Protestant sentimentalism, white women were regarded as particularly strong players in the imperial mission, with the potent combination of their superior genetic inheritance and enhanced moral compass. In the United States and around the world, elite white women emerged as a class of "civilization workers" who served as representatives of social progress and Christian salvation.[26] In the context of the Philippines, the history of religious conversion under Spanish colonialism compelled U.S. administrators to stress the uniquely secular character of American authority. White women *teachers* thus played a singular role as secular missionaries, signifiers of the benevolent rule of the U.S. government and agents of its authority. The symbolic and iconographic importance of white women teachers was profound as the expression of an imagined transformed relationship between Filipino subject and American citizen, from conflict to tutelage, from enemy to brother.

The gender politics here are telling, because white women were, at all times, a significant minority on the island. According to the 1905 census of the islands, whites composed only one-fifth of 1 percent of the total population of the islands; of this number, 14 percent were women. In a total island population of 7.6 million, only 1,215 were white women. This means that American men in the islands outnumbered women by a ration of seven to one. Even among teachers, women were the distinct minority; there were more than double the number of male teachers than female. This was in keeping with the official policy of the Bureau of Education in the Philippines, which regarded the largely remote areas of most schools out of bounds for women teachers and insisted that "this is work which can obviously be accomplished only by a man. For this reason, the great majority of the teaching force is composed of men."[27] Nevertheless, the image of the white woman teacher became synonymous with colonial tutelage, in a racialized logic of colonial domesticity that idealized white women as mothers to Filipino citizens, figured as orphaned children in need of the guidance of the white family. This relation drew upon and reinforced a racialized teleology which placed Filipinos on a developmental path far behind Anglo-Saxon civilization; presenting Filipino subjects as mischievous children, moreover, enabled the erasure of Filipino resistance to U.S. rule, rewriting acts of resistance as the unknowing mischief of children and justifying the violent maneuvers of U.S. soldiers as the necessary discipline of parenting.

In relying upon the symbolic force of white women as mothers to the colony, the imperial project in the Philippines was imagined as the drama of the colonial family, essentially making moot all questions as to whether or not to "hold" the colonies or to incorporate them by extending the constitution there, since as children they were fit neither for independence nor for participation in the republic. One telling image from the January 31, 1900, issue of the satirical weekly U.S. magazine *Puck* renders the visibility of gender difference as a key marker of the tenuous distinction between armed force and benevolent uplift as tandem parts of the imperial project. In the foreground stands a proud and erect Uncle Sam who addresses a watchful, curious group of Filipinos by saying, "You have seen what my sons can do in battle;—now see what my daughters can do in peace" (fig. 3.1). On the left, even lines of white, armed male soldiers, rifles and flags held high, retreat toward a naval ship waiting in the background; meanwhile, a group of white women eagerly advances with a suggestive assortment of accoutrements; armed with schoolbooks, cooking implements, nurse's bonnet, typewriter, and spectacles, these new imperial workers are poised to advance the cause of civilization with all the resources of white,

Figure 3.1. "If They'll Only Be Good." Uncle Sam.—You have seen what my sons can do in battle; —now see what my daughters can do in peace. (Courtesy of HATI-an Archives)

middle-class womanhood. As if to leave no doubt about the status of the Filipino natives who watch the women's approach, all are pictured seated, kneeling, or sufficiently diminished in stature so as to be gazing upward at these new arrivals. Looming largest in the frame, with his palms directed outward to indicate the even balance between these two sides of the imperial apparatus, Uncle Sam's wish, "If They'll Only Be Good," reads also as a threat, demonstrating with succinct precision the logical system through which Filipinos' behavior will be read as "good" or "bad" and the ready consequences of each. The cartoon thus renders the distinction between military and civil dominance as primarily legible through the axis of gender, making visible through gender the transition between force and education as guiding principles of colonial rule. At the same time, the visual arrangement of the image makes explicit the alignment of male soldiers and female teachers; both are assembled in military formation, one bearing rifles, the other schoolbooks, at once undermining the very distinction between force and suasion even while it attempts to impose such a distinction through the visual signifiers of gender difference and the seemingly natural distinctions thus embedded.

The interconnectedness between armed force and education as tools of colonial dominance presented a contradiction in colonial rule not simple to resolve. In one sense, the geographical proximity between "pacified" and "unpacified" regions was the cause of concern expressed by civilians living in the islands; in 1901, 25 percent of archipelago remained in a state of war, concentrated largely in the regions of Luzon, the Visayas, and Mindanao.[28] Reflecting on such proximity, American teacher Harry Cole, newly arrived on the islands with his wife, Mary, wrote home: "Probably while we were on the boat or perhaps a little later in the day, only six or seven miles away across the water, between forty and fifty of our men were being slaughtered. The company was surprised while at dinner, and nearly every one was killed. Now the next thing the Americans do is to send over a number of soldiers with orders to burn the towns, destroy everything which can sustain life, and kill every living thing, man, woman, child, and domestic animal."[29] Cole's letter, describing an attack led by General Vicente Lukban on Company C of the United States Ninth Infantry in Balangiga, makes a surprisingly casual reference to the brutality of this conflict. Forty-five of the seventy-four soldiers in Company C were killed in the fight; in the U.S. infantry company's retaliation, the Samareño town of Balangiga was destroyed and thousands of Filipino civilians killed.[30]

Perhaps more tellingly, in subsequent letter to her mother, written in the aftermath of the U.S. infantry company's devastating retaliation, Mary Cole wrote that her situation is "very peaceful and quiet," adding, "I am not afraid over here and don't worry about us. We're all right."[31] Despite such assurances, however, the Coles bore witness to the violent means through which U.S. forces attempted to elicit the submission of the colonized, and as such, demonstrated their uneasy complicity with the colonial project and the failures of the ideology of benevolent uplift. The U.S. military's retaliation in Samar was categorically brutal, executed under Gen. Jacob H. Smith's orders, in October 1901, to "kill and burn," with the intent to turn Samar into "a howling wilderness!"[32] As Mary Cole wrote in another letter to her mother, she had witnessed the treatment of a Filipino prisoner whose body was covered in "great sores" and who had withstood myriad acts of torture from American soldiers, who beat and starved him, "cut the chord under his tongue," and "tied his hands and feet, then filled him with water and then jumped on him."[33] Demonstrating her own sympathy for the mistreated prisoner, she asked, finally, "Wouldn't such treatment make insurrectos of anybody;" however, Mary Cole's position in the colonial project linked her with such acts of torture, revealing the extent to which her own role in the colonial order and her very presence in the Philippines placed her within uneasy ideological proximity to the U.S. military's campaigns of terror and destruction, a proximity that she could only recognize as geographic: "although the soldiers are still fighting in Samar it affects Leyte very little."[34]

Such proximity rendered material the contradiction between armed colonial domination and benevolent uplift, giving the lie to colonial officials' ready assurances about the righteousness of the U.S. colonial occupation. This was a central anxiety that American teachers were meant to assuage by serving as embodied proof of the efficiency and adaptability of progressive ideals of reform and uplift through colonial tutelage. There was another source of uneasiness as well, which undermined the illusion of peaceful, seamless American control on the islands. Gen. "Howlin" Jacob Smith, chief architect of the brutal campaign in Samar, stated the problem in stark terms: "Every native, whether in arms or living in the pueblos and barrios, will be regarded and treated as an enemy until he has conclusively shown that he is a friend."[35] But the question remained: How could such an allegiance to the military occupation be "conclusively shown," when the distinction between civilian and *insurrecto* was neither visually legible nor consistent? This problem loomed large, particularly because U.S. soldiers were largely dependent upon Filipino guides for direction, translation, and other practical support. This was yet another vulnerability in U.S. authority, a daily practical, essential dependence upon Filipino assistance that was disavowed by insisting on Filipinos' racial inferiority and "childlike" dependence upon American righteousness and might.

Against the ambiguity between friend and foe among Filipinos, the United States tried to present the choice between resistance and submission in the clearest of terms. This illusion of choice is most clearly illustrated in a political cartoon that appeared in *Puck* in November 1901, just three months after the arrival of the Thomasites in the Philippines and one month into the U.S. military's aggressive reconcentration project. Facing a small crowd of Filipinos, a looming Uncle Sam holds out each hand, on one a white soldier holding a rifle, on the other a white woman teacher with three schoolbooks (fig. 3.2). Presenting his hands like a scale, Uncle Sam seems to be weighing the balance between them; importantly, teacher and soldier measure up equally. While Uncle Sam and the soldier look directly at the deliberating Filipinos, who themselves look back, apparently with concern, the teacher's eyes are harder to follow, seeming to look above the heads of her audience to the distance beyond them. While

Figure 3.2. "It's 'Up to' Them." Uncle Sam (to Filipinos)—You can take your choice;—I have plenty of both! (Courtesy of HATI-an Archives)

the caption reads, "Uncle Sam (to Filipinos)—You can take your choice;—I have plenty of both!" the title of the image, "It's 'Up to' Them," clearly instructs the reader to identify with Uncle Sam and the choice he offers, asking the reader to consider the question and identify which choice might be the correct one. Working as both assurance and threat, Sam's claim to have "plenty of both" suggested a limitless force behind the American mission to "educate, civilize, and uplift," whether by force or by consent. Most tellingly, the choice is a distinctly gendered one; while male teachers outnumbered women by a ratio of two to one among the American population, the vision of conquest is divided into a gendered spectacle of domination, with force and tutelage offered male and female roles. The spectacle, then, comes to look much like a vision of an extended colonial family, with the disciplining father and instructive mother literally watching over their newly adopted charges. In this sense, the title, "It's 'Up to' Them," reiterates the certainty of success, naturalizing the relation of domination and subjection through the "natural" ordering of the nuclear family.

All in the Family

It is to the particular ordering of that family that I turn now, by looking at the construction of the imperial as domestic in the memoirs of two teachers working in the Philippines: Mary Fee's *A Woman's Impressions of the Philippines* (1910), and William Freer's *The Philippine Experiences of an American Teacher* (1906).[36] In so doing, I aim to build on work by Amy Kaplan and Vicente Rafael on the crucial workings of domesticity in the management of empire. In particular, Rafael has demonstrated how, in the context of the U.S.-occupied Philippines, McKinley's political paradigm of benevolent assimilation amounted to "a sentimental reworking of manifest destiny," in which the relationship between colonizer and colonized was rescripted as "the bond between parent and child."[37] As the principal agents in this paradigm, white teachers on the islands bore a large share of the ideological weight of the colonial project. At the same time, their writings expose some of its central contradictions, revealing constitutive tensions within the colonial project. For Fee, the export of the domestic in the Philippines exposed the contradictions in the ideology of separate spheres; as an independent white woman working alone, Fee comes paradoxically to stand in for the authority of the colonial state—a position of public authority that would have been unavailable to her in the United States, where it would have violated the boundaries of the domestic as woman's righteous sphere of influence. For Freer, the work in the Philippines becomes a place to enact his own centrality in the domestic sphere, creating a paradigm of male domesticity quite at odds with the militaristic masculinity through which the imperial conquest was sold to a public "at home" in the United States. Thus, while the expansion of U.S. sovereignty was represented by U.S. administrators as a romantic extension of the national family, the domestic became a complex site of negotiation for the teachers themselves, many of whom traveled to the Philippines because the luxuries of middle-class domesticity were unavailable to them in the United States.[38] Such memoirs allow us to consider how the tensions between domination and persuasion, force and uplift, were carefully managed through these textual depictions of the daily intimacies of colonial contact. These narratives, read together, demonstrate the stark differences between men's and women's participation in the colonial project, while providing a compelling insight into the fraught nature of the pedagogical as an idiom of colonial order.

I begin with Fee's narrative because of its singularity as a full-length work by a woman teacher in the Philippines. Memoirs written by women who had traveled to the Philippines, as army wives or wives of civil authorities were popular, written as firsthand accounts from a place that, it was rumored, even President McKinley had trouble finding on the map.[39] Often composed upon the woman's return from the islands and collected directly from letters sent home during her stay in the Philippines, these narratives by no means disrupt the fantasy of colonial contact as the careful ordering of an unruly family. However, Fee's firsthand account displays a curious sense of ambivalence around the question of home, both in the immediate sense of her domestic situation and as a dominant metaphor for the nation. As precisely one of those participants poised to reconcile the stark disjunctures between the harmonious family unit and the violent resistance to empire, Fee's narrative betrays a sense of the irreconcilability between the ideals of domestic leisure and her own laborious work in the remote villages of the empire, as well as between the ideals of nation-building in the Philippines and the deferment of political recognition for American women (like Fee) at home.

What is striking at first about Fee's narrative is the carefully balanced tone. She begins by borrowing the popular style of travel writing, detailing her departure from the port of San Francisco, the trip to Honolulu, and her eventual arrival in Manila. Her opening speech sets the scene of adventure; mounting the gangway, she describes: "To me the occasion was momentous. I was going to see the world, and I was one of an army of enthusiasts enlisted to instruct *our little brown brother*, and to pass the torch of Occidental knowledge several degrees east of the international date line" (12). Boldly setting forth as part of this "army of enthusiasts," Fee introduces the gendered tension of her task. Entering an "army" to instruct the "little brown brother," she marks the colonial environment as a masculine one, a space of military authority and racialized fraternity. This tension about what her role will be and what authority she will exercise manifests across her narrative. Here, Fee is quick to deflect her own authorial power in these opening passages. Though a teacher herself, from the start, her narrative enacts a story of her own education; the opening scene describes the size and decoration of the ship, whose signifying decorations she claims she "was not at that time sufficiently educated enough to read" (11). Such moments are common in the text, in which Fee describes her transformation from a position of naïveté to worldliness in her encounters with new people, climate, food, and custom.

Kamala Visweswaran has elaborated on the paradox through which women anthropologists at the end of the nineteenth century worked to adapt the trope of "white women in peril," even as that trope's persistence helped to popularize their writing and lend them professional legibility.[40] Fee's narrative displays a similar tension between her epistemological authority as a white American, and the limitations of that authority due to her status as an unmarried woman traveling alone. As such, much of the book reads like the work of women anthropologists who were Fee's contemporaries, carving out a place for women's knowledge as "observation" in short, anecdotally arranged chapters titled "Weddings in Town and Country," "Sickbeds and Funerals," "Children's Games," and "Sports and Amusements." Ever the energetic ethnologist, Fee relates each encounter with an attention to detail that indicates the seriousness of her endeavor, despite her frequent dismissal of her own authority on such matters. That is to say, Fee mobilizes a gendered narrative style, at once disclaiming her authority, even as she claims the right to see, record, and describe in relation to the "exotic" experiences of her travels. This is a tense and tenuous fault line between knower and known, one that continues to trouble Fee's text, marking the unstable positions of power open to women in the imperial order.

Such instability is marked early on by Fee's anxiety about her place in the hierarchy of colonial authority. As I have noted, Fee's very presence on the islands conferred on her a particular kind of power that inhered in the privilege of her race and her status as a representative of the colonial government. At the same time, this is a position compromised by both her gender and her class. Accompanying Fee to aid in "passing the torch of Occidental knowledge" are a host of other teachers, comprised mostly of middle-aged, middle-class women who fit the type Fee herself describes as "old maid" (30), with the exception of two young women who quickly attract her attention. These are the "Radcliffe girls," two women, younger than Fee, who are acknowledged primarily for their access to an academic professionalization that Fee did not have. Her scorn for the "Radcliffe girls" is made evident by her references to them as women of "evil genius," which becomes our first indication of Fee's own anxieties about her place in the colonial hierarchy. The teaching profession was at this point undergoing rapid professionalization on the one hand, and increasing gender segregation on the other. Earlier in nineteenth century, as men moved out of the classroom and into supervisory roles, the teaching profession began to lose its prestige as a middle-class profession; by the end of the century, the role of teacher had become both overwhelmingly coded as a woman's role and highly professionalized, with the growth of normal schools and certificating bodies for the profession. This gendered split was no less the case in the Philippines, where men were typically assigned to supervisory positions, and women to work as classroom teachers.[41] For Fee, the Radcliffe girls, as younger women with more formal training, pose a threat to what authority she might garner as a teacher, and represent her place at the crossroads of the changing nature of the profession.

While Fee betrays, in her mode of address, some ambivalence about her role as expert in relation to her middle-class American readers, she demonstrates no such uncertainty about her relation to her Filipino students or servants. Full chapters are dedicated to topics like "An Analysis of Filipino Character" and "Filipino Youths and Maidens," in which Fee details the perceived deficiencies of the Filipino populace, burdened as they are, in her view, with the unfortunate traits of being both docile and obstinate, ignorant and opinionated, imitative and superstitious. She attributes these qualities to the "natural backwardness" of the population and their stagnation under Spanish colonialism. Such is the very core of the problem, which Fee is poised to ameliorate with what she describes as a particularly maternal touch. Explicitly positioning herself as a mother raising young, willful children, Fee doles out advice in a narrative voice that echoes the era's many advice manuals, demonstrating her facility with this familiar idiom of female didacticism.[42] Attempting humor as a way to address the considerable difficulties and estrangements of her task, Fee elaborates on the trials of this new adventure in domestic life, touching on an endless array of subjects, like why not to convert Filipinos to her own religion of Protestantism (advice: it's too abstract); how to treat Filipino servants (advice: be stern), and whether literature is an appropriate field of study for Filipino children (advice: no, as it inspires too much of what she calls "unrealistic thinking").

My point is not to mock Fee's racial prejudices as much as to mine them for their implications for early twentieth-century understandings of woman's place in a highly racialized domestic sphere, a realm that must also be understood as a very public endeavor. It is precisely the difficulty of this position that Fee's narrative betrays, and in so doing, she points to the constitutive contradictions of the colonial paradigm of benevolent assimilation and its dominating familial metaphors. Another example bears this out more clearly. En route to Manila, Fee observes a telling interaction between a group of teachers and a "shrewd, kindly, gray-haired Yankee" who leads them on a sightseeing trip in Honolulu: "He did not say anything about old maids, but the air was surcharged with his unexpressed convictions, so that all of our cohort who were over thirty-five were reduced to a kind of abject contrition for having been born, and for having continued to live after it was assured that we were destined to remain incomplete" (30). This passage is the first in which Fee moves from the jocular and observant to a more defensive narrative posture. Lauren Berlant has noted that "jokes and lightness of speech are central rhetorical forms of female complaint" in late nineteenth-century advice manuals and citizenship guides.[43] Here Fee's "lightness of speech" takes on more weight; citing this "abject contrition," it is not hard to read both defiance and doubt in Fee's ironic tone. Of course, it is she who articulates the critical title "old maid"; the man himself remains silent. And yet we sense in this passage the trace of an anxiety that runs throughout the narrative, in which Fee herself has difficulty finding her own place, both in the structure of colonial authority and narrative authority. This passage illuminates her situation in a place of contradiction; as a white woman colonialist, she holds a considerable representational and practical power on the islands. At the same time, the very notion of civilized culture that justified her presence on the islands and that was her mission to instill, depended upon the ideology of separate spheres and the notion that woman's hallowed place was in the home. As Louise Newman has argued, "Evolutionist theories linked sexual differences with racial progress . . . the more civilized the race, the more the men and women of that race had to differ from one another."[44] Fee's presence on the islands, unaccompanied by a male "protector," thus troubles the whole ideological paradigm that brought her there, making what authority she has a tricky, contradictory thing to manage.

It is likely that the scorn she reads in the "surcharged" air is also that which she anticipates from readers in the United States. Thus Fee attempts to resolve this tension by adapting her unmarried, and thus unvalued, status to the domestic work of empire. That is to say, it is her imperial family to which she must devote her feminine skills. The head of her own household, Fee is free to adopt all of her Filipino charges as her children. Unmarried and without children, she becomes both surrogate mother and motherland for America's newly incorporated subjects. And it is this arrangement of her domestic life that not only affords Fee a particular domestic comfort, but also legitimates her to weigh in on political questions beyond the domestic sphere. Discussing the matter of self-government for the Philippines, Fee writes: "The Filipino is like an orphan baby, not allowed to have his cramps and colic and cut his teeth in the decent retirement of the parental nursery, but dragged out instead to distressing publicity.... Naturally he is self-conscious, and—let us be truthful—not having been a very promising baby from the beginning, both he and his nurses have had a hard time" (96). In this passage, Fee likens the call for independence and self-government on the part of Filipino statesmen and populace to a misguided childish ambition. Within this developmental narrative, progress toward self-government is deferred to some future time, and the difficulties of nation-building become a mother's difficulties with a "not very promising baby." Fee thus echoes the sentiments of Fred Atkinson, the first U.S.-appointed general superintendent of education in the Philippines, who averred: "The Filipino people, taken as a body, are children, and childlike, do not know what is best for them.... In the ideal spirit of preparing them for the work of governing themselves finally, their American guardianship has begun.... By the very fact of our superiority of civilization and our greater capacity for industrial activity we are bound to exercise over them a profound social influence."[45] Such statements rested upon teleological understandings of racialized developmental path from savagery to civilization, positioning Anglo-Saxons at the highest point in the progression. Inserting herself into the powerful position of imperial mother, Fee demonstrates a fluency with the racialized hierarchy of colonial dominance and with the progressive belief in rationalized management that situated the American teacher as the exemplary representative of Anglo-Saxon civilization.

Making equivalences between nation-building and household management, Fee's account of her own household carries special weight in the text, as her example at the helm of her own domestic sphere is displayed for the admiration of readers who might wonder about the respectability of a middle-class woman setting up house "alone" in a remote country. As she observes:

> The Philippines are no place for women or men who cannot thrive and be happy on plain food, plenty of work, and isolation.... [Married women who are unemployed] break down under it very quickly; they lose appetite and flesh and grow fretful or melancholy. But to a woman who loves her home and is employed, provincial life here is a boon. Remember that for an expenditure of forty or fifty dollars a month the single woman can maintain an establishment of her own—a genuine home—where after a day's toil she can find order and peace and idleness waiting for her. Filipino servants are not ideal, but any woman with a capacity for organization can

soon train them into keeping her house in the outward semblance at least
of order and cleanliness. (246)

In this account, Fee finds her independence in the Philippines, to a far
greater degree than would be possible in the United States. Not only would
she lack the material resources for "a genuine home" of her own, but she
would be deterred on a number of other levels as well. She describes, for
example, a brief visit to Chicago in which the "joys of civilization" that
greet her amount to the threat of theft and murder at the hands of criminal
city-dwellers, as well as the insolent treatment from an African American
porter who, "with a confidence born of democracy," invites himself to sit
and speak with her. No such fear, either of violence or of insolence, clouds
her recollections of the Philippines, where "[she had] never heard of indig-
nity or disrespect shown to American women" (247).

Fee's valorization of the Philippines as the site of white women's freedom depends, importantly, on the unfreedom of others; likewise, the condition of her own independence in the Philippines is the denial of Philippine independence. Her "clean and orderly" household depends upon
the difficult, daily labor of Filipino servants, whose work she describes as
suitable for a people who "prefer routine work to variety" (92), who aspire
to attach themselves "like slaves" to wealthier masters, and whose condition of poverty does not render them unhappy because "[they have] not
developed enough to achieve either self-pity or self-analysis" (236). In this
way, Fee attempts to secure her own independence by obscuring her own
dependence on the Filipino servants, guides, and workers around her, and
rescripting the violence of the colonial project as the harmonious housekeeping of an efficiently managed household. Here we see perhaps the
most telling omission of all, which is Fee's disavowal of the potential identification with the Filipino laborers upon whom she depends. In a remark-
ably suggestive passage about the ideals of Filipino writers and politicians
toward national independence, Fee writes: "It seems as great a perversion
of abstract justice, to a Filipino, that an alien nation should administer his
[*sic*] Government, as it seems to a hard-working American woman that
she should toil all her life, contributing her utmost to the world's progress
and the common burden of humanity, while her more fortunate sisters,
by the mere accident of birth, spend their lives in idleness and frivolity,
enriched by the toil of a really useful element in society. But to most Filipinos, as to most American women, the contemplation of the elemental
injustice of life does not bring pangs sufficient to drive them into overt

action to right the injustice" (135). Here the comparison between Filipino nationalists and American woman resonates with earlier passages in the text, in which Fee describes the "femininity of the race" through what she reads as vanity and naïve self-assurance. Unlike these earlier castigations, however, in this passage we see a strain of indignation, calling to mind Fee's own earlier chagrin at the reminders of her "old-maid" status, as well as her explanation that life and work in the Philippines afford the industrious single woman a domestic life that would be unattainable in the United States. Within this context, Fee's comparison suggests the potential for a strategic identification between Filipino citizen and working-class American woman, each wielding the insights of a life of labor for others' benefit to see with great clarity the injustice behind the unequal distribution of wealth and the uneven distribution of political sovereignty.

As in her earlier castigation of the "Radcliffe girls," Fee rejects the possibility of identification or solidarity with Filipinos, thus reinforcing the gender, race, and class hierarchies that contribute to her sense of isolation. Perhaps, however, the antagonism runs deeper for other reasons as well. Despite its widely proclaimed intention to bring democracy to the Philippines, the U.S. civil government limited voting rights among Filipinos to English- or Spanish-speaking, landholding men; the practical result of this limitation was that few Filipinos enjoyed the right to vote, and elections of local and provincial governments, while supposedly in Filipino hands, worked largely to further consolidate power among elite Filipinos who supported the American occupation. Filipino women were denied suffrage altogether. Though Fee does not mention the question of the vote as it pertained to American women, the timing of Fee's text places her narrative within the lively and impassioned debate around woman suffrage; by her publication date in 1910, some women had secured voting rights in some local and state elections in the United States, and the debate about woman suffrage on a national scale was in full force. Many made explicit connections between political access for women at home, and political sovereignty for Filipinos abroad. One suffragist, speaking at the New England Anti-Imperialist League in 1903, declared that American women were "as badly off as the Filipinos" and needed themselves the same rights that anti-imperialists were advocating for the Philippines.[46] Others supported the United States' imperial expansion in the Philippines in an attempt to further the cause of woman suffrage by proving their patriotism. Elizabeth Cady Stanton declared herself "strongly in favor of this new departure in American foreign policy," for, as she put it, "What would this continent have been if left to the Indians?"[47] Others decried the perceived injustice of Filipinos being granted the civic right of the vote, which white women did not yet enjoy. Whether they advocated that women's energies should be mobilized in the global politics of uplift and religious conversion, or directed against the expansion of the United States' own barbaric policies abroad, both camps counted on women's privileged role as a civilizing force in the new world order.

Fee tellingly brings up these pressing questions of sovereignty, autonomy, and suffrage, only to deflect them onto foreign terrain, and thus avoids confronting the contradiction between the ideological promise of American citizenship and the nation's history of selective disenfranchisement and exclusion. This is a striking move, particularly in the sense that it was the United States' contention that it treated women properly that condoned its intervention in the Philippines as an effort to, to borrow from Gayatri Spivak, "save brown women from brown men."[48] Confronting this contradiction, Fee takes solace in silence. More specifically, she calls upon women's silence as proof that American gender relations were the most progressive and best suited to maintaining a woman's "high and noble" virtue, and she understands the American woman to have advantage over "her dusky sister" through the very freedom she enjoys in her daily life. It is this public freedom, with which comes a public caution around frankness in matters of love or sex, that gives an American woman strength in her "tenacity to her own ideal of chastity" (126): "Our prudery of speech is the natural result of the liberty permitted to women. When the protection of an older woman or of a male relative is done way with, and a girl is permitted to go about quite unattended, the best and the surest protection that she can have is the kind of modesty that takes fright at even a bare mention, a bare allusion, to certain ordinarily ignored facts of life" (126). This natural independence for women is thus the cause and the effect of their own natural prudery, a chaste ideal that cannot be hoped for among Filipino women, who "regard [their] virtue as something foreign to [themselves], a property to be guarded by her relatives" (126). Not owning her own virtue, and by extension, her own body, the Filipino woman, for Fee, can only be understood as at the mercy of the protection of the men around her. This, then, demonstrates the necessity of American intervention, for in their dependence upon American protection, paradoxically, Filipino women find their own independence. As Fee relates, it is "no uncommon thing" to see daughters of the Filipino elite riding trolley cars and "enjoying their liberty" when "ten years ago [they] would have been huddled into a quilez and guarded by an elderly woman servant" (128). Liberated from the confines of a crowded horse-drawn cart and the surveilling eyes of her elders, under the guidance of American tutelage Filipino women find the protection that inheres in the timidity and prudery that Fee deems natural to women.

Fee's concern is to introduce Filipino women into more "modern" codes of behavior and comportment, codes that, interestingly, draw from the standards of the New Woman as well as the ideals of Victorian womanhood. That is, while Fee's own narrative suggest disdain for the social freedoms of the New Woman (witness her disapproval of the "Radcliffe girls"), she nonetheless imagines the United States as the site where women's political emancipation has already been fully effected. Ignoring not simply the contemporary resistance to U.S. hegemony on the part of Filipinos, Fee erases the divisive debates over women's access to the political sphere in the United States as well, recuperating the potential for women's public political participation into the domestic management in the imperial outposts.

Men Gone Wild

While white femininity in the colonial context required an explicit connection to the nation as family and the colonized subject as adopted orphan, the masculine imperatives of colonialism, superficially at least, had little to do with the codes of domesticity. Indeed, much of the prelude to the U.S. entry into the war with Spain focused on the necessity of defending the nation's honor, a category explicitly invested with the qualities of masculine bravery and loyalty to nation. As Representative James R. Mann put it, "We do not fight for a fancied slight . . . we fight because it has become necessary to fight if we would uphold our manhood."[49] Debating the appropriate response to the suspected Spanish involvement in the sinking of the U.S. battleship *Maine*, members of Congress represented the event and the possible responses as a gauge of the vitality of the nation's masculinity. Senator Richard R. Kenney put it in starkly gendered terms by arguing that "American manhood and American chivalry give back the answer that innocent blood shall be avenged, starvation and crime shall cease, Cuba shall be free. For such reasons, for such causes, American can and will fight. For such causes and for such reasons we should have war."[50] As a new frontier upon which to try their might, the Philippines seemed to beckon as a site for the regeneration of white American masculinity.[51] The ideals of rugged masculinity had much to do with the search for new terrains upon which white American men could play "cowboys and Indians," and it is no coincidence that many of the generals at the head of the U.S. military administration in the Philippines had begun their careers in the "Indian Wars" of the nineteenth century.[52]

Feminist historians have traced the evolution of a martial ideal of American masculinity as an animating force in the Spanish-American War, and this ideal is suggestively embodied in figures such as the uber-aggressive, warmongering figure of Theodore Roosevelt.[53] While President McKinley argued at first against involvement in the Cuban and Philippine revolutions, his choice of Theodore Roosevelt as vice president in his 1900 reelection campaign signaled an acceptance of a newly emergent martial ideal of masculine citizenship upon which Roosevelt had based his political career. The most vigorous proponent of involvement against Spain, Teddy Roosevelt had grown up being characterized as an effeminate rich boy, mocked as a "Jane-Dandy," and a "Punkin-Lily." Reporters openly accused him of being gay; some referred to him as a "friend of Oscar Wilde's" and a "cock-smoker," and another condemned Roosevelt's privileged status by writing that Roosevelt was "given to sucking the knob of an ivory cane."[54] In the face of such insults, Roosevelt reinvented himself as a cowboy by buying a South Dakota ranch and publishing a four-volume celebration of Manifest Destiny called *The Winning of the West*. Once war was declared, Roosevelt led a volunteer cavalry unit called the Rough Riders, whose fighting in Cuba he rendered legendary by publishing his war adventures serially (by 1899). He continued to obsess about the physical atrophy of American masculinity, popularized in his famous essay "The Strenuous Life" (1899). Here Roosevelt proposed "manly virtue, masculine violence, and white American racial supremacy" as the "antithesis of over-civilized decadence."[55] Castigating "the timid man, the lazy man, the man who distrusts his country," Roosevelt's most vociferous condemnation was for the "overcivilized man" who, instead of taming the frontier, had been tamed by the city, rendered domesticated by the comfort of hearth and home, and no longer capable of "feeling the mighty lift that thrills stern men with empires in their brains."[56] Roosevelt's enthusiasm for war was unabashed; he claimed that the United States needed a war, and that "any war would do." Under such terms, the war with Spain appeared to be an available antidote not just to the anxieties over modernization and the potential "overcivilization" of American men, but also the spectre of same-sex desire that had newly become the subject of scholarship, analysis, and spectacle.[57]

When French colonial functionaries warned that "a man remains a man as long as he stays under the gaze of a woman of his race," they pointed to the dual anxieties of miscegenation and same-sex desire within the colonial frame, and this is no less true within the largely male corps of soldiers and civil servants in the U.S.-occupied Philippines.[58] With the low ratio of white women on the islands, so great was the worry about the potential coupling of white men with Filipino women or, worse, other men, that the U.S. civil government encouraged a regulated system of prostitution. Unlike the British colonies, which had "Contagious Diseases" ordinances that mandated the medical inspection and incarceration of prostitutes, the U.S. colonial government established no such official practices, instead preferring to allow the widespread growth of prostitution as a temporary stopgap for the threatening possibilities that attended the arrival of thousands of young white men to the islands. When the United States established its dominion over the Philippines by occupying Manila and blocking the entrance of Philippine revolutionary forces, it permitted hundreds of prostitutes to enter the city, establishing Manila as a new center for what one reporter called a "cosmopolitan harlotry."[59] Such was the widespread availability of prostitution that "Rough Riders," popularly a name for the cowboy masculinity that Roosevelt made famous, was resignified as a nickname given to soldiers who contracted venereal disease in the islands. "The joke," as the historian Paul Kramer points out, "turned potential emasculation by disease into a marker of masculinity" through the allusion to rough sex, thus linking sexuality and empire through the figure of the dominant and aggressively sexual white man.[60]

These celebrations of rugged masculinity evoked powerful anxieties as well, particularly about the character of the U.S. military as an occupying presence and as an example of Anglo-Saxon civilization. One letter from a brigadier general serving in Iloilo protested against the plan of having soldiers tutor Filipino boys in English by embedding these boys in the military companies, saying that the soldiers themselves "employ a language that is not English," but rather laden with such obscenity "that the most fertile imagination could not produce."[61] Another lamented the negative instruction that contact with soldiers provided, saying that "as so often happened among a company of men some one would teach [young Filipinos] to swear or say some vile thing."[62] Against such examples of militaristic manhood gone awry, white male teachers occupied a strange status between the feminized path of uplift and the masculine drive toward violent, racialized dominance.

The additional threat seen to plague white men in the islands was the possibility of tropical degeneracy. Multiple colonial authorities cited the hot, tropical environment as the cause of Filipinos' inferiority to white civilization. By 1915, Ellsworth Huntington had published his "climate hypothesis of civilization," which asserted that life in the tropics resulted in a "weakness of will" that "enfeebled" white men's self-control and resulted in a "lack of industry, an irascible temper, drunkenness, and sexual indulgence."[63] Much of this work, however, was built upon the research of medical staff in the Philippines who were charting the emergence of what Louis Fales called "tropical neurasthenia," a general fatigue, irritability, and weakness that seemed to clear up upon leaving the islands.[64] Worries about the effects of the tropical climate on white men in particular abounded; Bernard Moses, commissioner of education, worried about the long-term effects of island life on Anglo-Saxon men who were little-suited to enjoy "all the blessings of savagism," and Civil Governor William Cameron Forbes noted in his memoirs that some men in the civil government found the hot, lush environment ill-suited for the strict and righteous pieties of Anglo-American imperial culture, adding that "ill-health and other natural causes constantly depleted the number of American teachers in the Islands.[65] More strikingly, David Barrows, in letters to colleagues in the United States, wrote that he was "ashamed to tell of the hardships to which [his] this life subject[ed] [his] wife" and worried that his "family [was] too large and [his] life too slenderly insured . . . to keep it up much longer."[66] Regardless of his concerns for her frailty, it was Barrows himself who confided that he was "consistently not in good health" and plagued by "a nervousness that assails me at work and sometimes makes clear thinking and expression impossible."[67] The *New York Times* reported that Civil Governor William Cameron Forbes was "suffering from breakdown due to overwork in the islands" and had been confined to his bed with a case of "brain fag," a result of "too high a tension in a climate where we Americans cannot work as we can at home."[68] As Warwick Anderson has suggested, the "tropical neurasthenia" suffered by colonial authorities in the islands "came to represent the true, protracted weight of the white man's burden," and aligned "civilized" white men with the symptoms of what was in the United States largely considered a white women's disease.[69] What was feared as a racial slippage of white men in the tropics, from civilized to savage, was also the threat of sexual slippage from a position of masculine authority to feminized weakness.[70]

With this in mind, William Freer's account of his experiences as a secondary and normal school teacher marks a delicate balancing act. Not a soldier but a teacher, Freer could participate only obliquely in the militaristic resuscitation of white, middle-class American masculinity. At the same time, his very presence on the islands and the interest in the memoir he later published was motivated by shame for the atrocities that such masculinity had committed. Freer's position was a complicated one, marking a new construction of imperial masculinity not associated with physical force but with firm, patriarchal authority. Not surprisingly, then, *Philippine Experiences* marks its ideological project as early and explicitly as its opening dedication, where Freer makes the narrative an offering to honor "those Americans, who, by noble example, by benevolent ministration and by unselfish labor under trying conditions, are teaching the best Americanism to the Filipinos." He continues, in the foreword, to announce his intention that the book offer "a better appreciation of some desirable traits of Filipino character" so as to inspire, in his American readers, "a stronger conviction of the unwisdom of granting, at this time, any greater degree of self-government than the Filipinos already possess." It is the job of the school, in Freer's opinion, to compensate for this deficit in Filipino subjects' capacity for self-rule, and the entire raison d'être of the school can be no better judged than as an "attempt to fit the people for the eventual exercise of complete autonomy." Thus it is that the school stands as both instrument for English education and medium for Americanization, by which Freer means to indicate a broad range of ideological and practical lessons, including not only literature and geography but civics, hygiene, sport, and song.

The school stands at the center of the imagined reorganization of Filipino life, particularly in the provinces, where the authority of the U.S. colonial administration continued to be challenged. The looming presence of military conflict is cause for frequent but casual comment in Freer's narrative, as when he describes his journey to his post in Solano as one made dangerous by his route through "unpacified" regions and the required journey of "a week's constant traveling through an unsettled country inhabited by Igorrote head-hunters" (15). As a teacher assigned to supervise Filipino instructors in the barrio schools, Freer's job required his frequent travel through the provinces, journeys that required the accompaniment of a "big army revolver in leather holster" as a measure to

"retain the respect of possible head-hunters" (114), and his "faithful Domingo," an Igorot servant whose protection and fidelity he likens to that
of a "great, good Newfoundland dog" (115). While Domingo worries over
the safety of such travel, warning Freer of the dangers of a possible attack
by the "wild men" of the mountains, Freer asserts his casual indifference
to such threats, reveling in a jovial ignorance, remarking that "as we tra-
versed those four miles, Domingo continually looked toward the range of
forest-clad hills to the east, for it was thence that a descent of the dread
head-hunters might be expected. Fortunately for us, but unfortunately for
my tale, nothing of the kind occurred" (120). In such moments, Freer likens his story to an adventure narrative, mixing the genres of travel guide
and western frontier novel to entice his readers into ready participation
in the colonial adventure of expansion. Remarking that "a free hospitality
exists on the frontier, whether it be in Montana or the Philippines." Freer
situates himself within the familiar drama of westward expansion, rendering the Philippines the newest outpost in the march of Manifest Destiny (55).

The practical conventions of the travel guide appear in the interpella-
tive form of direct narrative address, as when Freer arrives in Manila, and
beholds the "varied oriental life which is so intensely interesting to the
Westerner upon first acquaintance" (5). Describing a span of early days
in which he "looked and lingered, and looked again, held by a fascination
[he] could not resist," Freer enjoins the reader to accompany him on a trip
up the Pásig River, inviting his readers to "see that woman masticating her
buyo, the while she arranges her cards and nurses her child," and noting,
"Here we see a huge pile of cocoa-nuts; there a bamboo cage containing
half a dozen monkeys. . . . [H]ere comes a *pudiente* who is about to breakfast, good-naturedly picking his way among the masses on the deck."
Among such observations, Freer offers his interpretive expertise, asserting that "the very infants absorb the love of gambling with their mothers'
milk" (6–7). Guiding his readers through the scene, Freer is careful to distinguish his own authority, asserting that "no one who has not traveled in
the Orient can conceive of the noise and confusion" upon such a journey.
As our expert witness and guide, then, Freer introduces his narrative, his
adventure, finally, as a drama between known and unknowable, marking
the Philippines as exotic Other that defies translation or representation;
"words fail utterly to describe it" (8).

To mark the colonial stage as that which defies or exceeds description
is to invoke the awe and terror of the sublime; it is also, however, to both

engage and manage that terror through narrative, and indeed one of the primary motivating anxieties of Freer's memoir revolves around accounting for the very difference that he relentlessly, tirelessly describes. In this sense, in exploring and detailing the minutiae of the islands and its inhabitants, Freer attempts to contain the spectre of a difference otherwise beyond language, a difference marked as untranslatable and thus unable to be mastered. Such is the function of the colonial memoir, situating the threat of that difference in a properly ordered framework and giving motivation to the design of the story, which charts Freer's time in the Philippines as a sort of "education" in the ways of the "Orient." Viewing all with the "unaccustomed eyes" of an "American newly arrived . . . to observe the native in his own environment" (8), Freer begins as an American everyman, guiding his readers into knowing acquaintance with the exotic spoils of territorial conquest. At the same time, his position as a supervisor of native teachers places him as a highly ranked administrator within the U.S. civil government, a position recognized at the outset by an American journalist who, returning from the "remote section" to which Freer has been assigned, congratulates Freer by offering: "it is a golden opportunity for you. Why, man, you may be governor some day" (15). Demonstrating the overlap between academic and political power, this comment serves to demonstrate the school's importance as an institution of political authority; it serves as well as a refusal of Filipino sovereignty, marking the Philippines as a site of political advancement for white men. Here, institutional power overlaps with visions of political authority to keep at bay the threatening proximity of the colonial Other, allowing Freer to disavow the very anxiety aroused by racial and cultural difference by rendering such difference containable through the authorizing gaze of the white American subject.

Freer's stance toward his own political authority is thus vexed by the ever-present threat of his powerlessness, as a white man and a teacher, indicated by the myriad ways in which he is dependent upon Filipino neighbors, as guides, translators, servants, friends, and protectors. This dependence, while most pronounced in passages like that above, when he looks to Domingo for protection from his "wild neighbors," is in no way limited to such encounters. In fact, Freer's narrative is everywhere populated by nameless figures who provide assistance in large and small ways, through small tokens and large gifts of food and housing, company and direction. As the only white man in the region for some time, Freer was, in fact, entirely outnumbered by those subjects over whom he claimed such clear authority. Rather than acknowledge the dynamic of dependency, however, Freer insists upon a strict demarcation between helper and helped, insisting upon his own place as benefactor and moral guide even as his safety and sustenance depends upon the benevolent acceptance of those he has come to "uplift." Freer's position as newcomer to the islands, and the potential crisis in authority provoked by his own ignorance about the land, customs, and vernacular languages is thus dismissed as trivial in the face of the noble purpose and high example that he embodies. The role of teacher, in Freer's view, is that of an American exemplar, defining through his or her own character the standards of civilized personhood so that his Filipino neighbors may, by his very presence, absorb and emulate such conduct; as Freer defines it, the teacher must understand "the high moral obligation of conducting himself so that he might be for his community an exemplar of that which is best in American civilization" (98). In this way, the American teacher is, even outside of the classroom, a teacher still, regarding all Filipinos as students in need of such fundamental guidance. His role, however, exceeds that even of teacher, or rather, elevates the calling of the profession beyond the confines of the classroom. As "the quiet mediator of modern ideas," the teacher has, in Freer's estimation, "far from transcended the role of mere pedagogue. He has won the affection and respect of the Filipino people as, from the nature of their callings, the soldier and the merchant could not do" (100).

To claim a privileged role of teacher over soldier and merchant as representative Americans is to disavow the violence of the colonial project, its physical and economic devastation, and to embrace the fantasy of affection as the guiding principle of U. S.–Philippine relations. This is what Vicente Rafael has called the fantasy of "white love," a "civilizing love" that "effaces the violence of conquest by construing colonial rule as the most precious gift that 'the most civilized people' can render to those still caught in a state of barbarous disorder."[71] Indeed, it is precisely as a gift that Freer conceives of his own work in the islands, a gift given of generosity and sympathy rather than desire for adventure or personal gain. What surprises him, however, is his own attachment in the exchange: "The American who has any sympathetic feeling whatever for children soon feels strangely drawn toward [Filipino children]; their docility, gentleness, and the sense of their dependence appeal to him, and before he realizes it he forgets altogether the difference in race and recognizes only the kinship of humanity when he looks into their trusting faces; and 'little brown brothers' they are to him more truly than he thought they could ever become" (277). Here the paradigm of benevolent colonialism morphs into a fantasy of undiluted affection, a love between colonizer and colonized in which racial difference is forgotten in the glow of shared affection. For, as Freer insists, the feeling is mutual: "They, too, feel the relationship, in evidence of which Josefa presents her teacher with a *lukban*, Santos brings some blossoms of the *ilang-ilang*, and Miguel draws from his pocket and offers an egg of doubtful quality" (277–78). It is a relation of uneven reciprocity, then, that marks the distinction between colonizer and colonized—the gift of perfect civilization given and acknowledged by the "doubtful quality" but willing and good intentions of its recipients.

It is through the fantasy of mutual affection that Freer attempts to resolve the contradiction between the United States' exceptionalist status as a democratic nation and its violent repression of Filipino nationalism. It indicated other desires, as well. Freer's notable investment in the domestic romance of the "wild savage" manifests in terms of a fantasy of the domestic that Freer establishes for himself. He begins by detailing the process of establishing his own household, noting that while "Americans find themselves harassed by the general unreliability of native help," he found "excellent servants" in employing Igorots from nearby villages (59). Testifying to the "obedient and reliable" qualities of the "wild men" he employs, Freer writes: "Although there was not a lock in the house, I left it and my possessions for a day at a time, and once for a week, it being understood that one of the men should always be there. Though the temptation would have been too great for the average civilized Filipino servant to withstand, these faithful savages proved themselves absolutely honest; for they never appropriated even the most insignificant article" (61). In contrast to the weakness of the "average civilized Filipino," Freer brags of the loyal fortitude with which "faithful savages" regard their benevolent masters, again invoking the fantasy of fidelity and affection as the terms of colonial contact. In what he interprets as the willing loyalty of his employees, Freer supposes the men's complicity with their subjugation as the natural consequence of his own effective authority. Interestingly, in these men so uncorrupted by civilization, Freer articulates his own romantic attachment to the "wild" state they embody, an attachment that can only be nostalgic for that which he aims to destroy by his very presence.[72]

The tension between dominance and desire is laid bare when Freer describes his initial encounter with Domingo; here I quote at length:

Most housekeeping Americans find themselves harassed by the general unreliability of the native help. For me the solution of the problem was easy,
for the town lies close to the rancherias of the Igorrotes, who make excellent servants. I employed as cook one-eyed Clemente, who had lived in the
valley long enough to acquire a Christian name and learn to write. He wore
ordinary Philippine clothing, except on wash-days, when he was obliged to
go back to the breech-clout. He cooked fairly well in the Spanish style, and
readily adopted what changes I suggested from time to time, such as using
less garlic with the fried chicken and cooking the rice a little more thoroughly. . . . He brought me for a man-of-all-work a "new-caught" Igorrote
from the mountains, a lithe young fellow about twenty years old, who, having adopted the name Domingo for the occasion, presented himself to me
for service. He appeared somewhat abashed, not because his sole raiment
consisted of a "gee-string," but because this was his first encounter with a
white man. My eyes ran over his satiny, chocolate-colored skin, and then
met his own; and I engaged him then and there. . . . Thus was my family
rounded out to three. (59–60)

Freer unwittingly reveals the layers of fantasy and desire that compose the
ideological project of colonial dominance. His lingering gaze on the Filipino body betrays the fantasy of affiliation and dominance, the desire to
"engage," to possess the colonial Other and to rewrite the violent process
of submission as the composition of family. First, there is the delight that
Freer takes in describing his household. Involved in the cooking, the management of servants, and the other domestic tasks, Freer plays the proud
little wife, and the point is not lost that this, for him, is a "perfect little
family of three." Then there is also Domingo's shy regard, his gee-string,
his "satiny, chocolate-colored skin." Freer here participates in a racialized
voyeurism with regard to the so-called "wild men" of the mountains; unlike the Christianized Filipinos who formed the majority of the population,
the Igorot men were the subject of great fascination as the embodiment of
a savage, racialized Other. They were first featured in an extensive *National
Geographic* spread shortly after the start of the U. S. occupation, and such
was their importance to the spectacle of the "civilizing mission" that they
were featured at the center of the Philippine Exhibit at the St. Louis World's
Fair in 1904. These men were shipped to the United States and placed on
display, in gee-string and tribal dress, for the fascination and fantasy of
American spectators. But Freer's display is somewhat different. Certainly
the racialized voyeurism is part of this, but running his eyes over the man,

"engaging him," and thus appropriating him into his imagined "family" suggests an intimacy and desire as well.

Moments such as this punctuate Freer's text, as Domingo becomes his "constant companion," and he lauds the devotion of the "faithful savage" in ways that move inconsistently between a relationship of lovers and that of father and child. Or rather, within the power arrangements of his colonial household, these relationships meld, so that Domingo can at once be Freer's protector and the object of Freer's protection, a "wild-man" and "faithful savage," a desired Other and domesticated child. Laying bare his voyeuristic fascination with the manservant presented to him, Freer unwittingly casts light on the spectre of sexual desire within this all-male "family" he has created in the tropics. As we have seen, it was in the service of a militaristic masculinity that the Spanish-American War was enthusiastically embraced. The threat it meant to address was that of the emasculation of white men. Such a threat was posed not just by the feared emasculation of white men as the bearers of civilization, but also by the increasingly visible subcultures of male same-sex sociality and desire in urban areas across the United States. In one report of 1889, one observer noted the existence "in every community of any size a colony of male sexual perverts . . . [who] are usually known to each other and are likely to congregate together." By 1892, the *New York Herald* and other newspapers were actively engaged in campaigns against "public immorality" that functioned as much to spectacularize male same-sex desire as to police it.[73] Thus, across the United States, the "fairy" had become a well-known figure of male effeminacy and sexual "degeneracy," and visiting the gay enclaves in such cities, or "going slumming," provided an arena in which middle-class men could "cultivate and explore sexual fantasies by opening up to them a subordinate social world in which they felt fewer constraints on their behavior" and could "engage in ribald behavior inconceivable in their own social worlds."[74]

Freer's narrative points to the role that such desire played in the "domestication" of the "wilds" of the Philippines. At once anxious to rewrite his own role as that of the adventurer or imperial cowboy, Freer also plays the adept manager of the home, making for himself a domestic space where his involvement and management is quite unlike that assigned to middle-class white men in the United States. This, I would argue, is a version of same-sex familial relations that is normalized by the tutelary model. A crucial conundrum of the colonial paradigm was that in civilizing the natives, the colonial authority himself risks exposing himself as overcivilized and thus feminized, particularly in relation to the overly sexualized "savage" masculinity he is entrusted to tame. Freer's narrative is a search for an articulation of a position of colonial masculinity that is civilized but not feminized—a contradiction managed by the tutelary model that insisted upon white men's authority over Filipino "children" while exorcising the spectre of pederasty or same-sex desire by making this an asymmetrical relation that, in the end, was not a familial one.[75] While Freer occupies a paternal role, he is not "father" but teacher, and this, crucially, opens up more room for both desire and discipline to inform his regard for the Filipinos over whom he regards himself as master. The tutelary model recoups the power and authority of Anglo-American teacher even as it allows for the structural space for those persons to indulge in or realize fantasies of gender and sexual difference for which the bourgeois heteronormative family model left little space.

In his imperial composition of the family, Freer imagines his own dominance as a paternal one, even as he betrays the desire for the colonial Other that must be integrated into the domestic dynamic of his authority. Finally, however, this desire for the colonial subject becomes, for Freer, a desire to incorporate that subject, as indicated when Freer calls upon his readers to "imagine a man once white but now bronzed by the sun stepping briskly along a dusty tropical road in the fresh morning air" (114). Here Freer offers the picture of himself as native, replacing his own white skin with brown, navigating adeptly through the terrain once foreign to him. In the end, despite his professed desire to "educate, uplift, and civilize the natives," it is Freer's own transformation that the narrative most joyfully announces, marking the colonial space as the site where he, too, can find a freedom not available at home.

As we have seen, despite the vociferous insistence that the U.S. occupation of the Philippines was a benevolent measure undertaken for the eventual freedom of Filipinos themselves, it was the liberty of the colonizer that was the outcome of the deal. It will be no surprise, of course, that the declarations of benevolent intervention rang hollow in the face of the violence enacted against a Filipino population that continued to fight for independence. More surprising, perhaps, is the extent to which the contradictions inherent in that very civilization deemed worthy of empire were the developments that caused those like Mary Fee and William Freer to leave the domestic space of the nation to discover their own liberty in the foreign space of the colony. Such narratives demonstrate how the domestic is a compromised site of political engagement, not divorced from but refashioned in the context of imperial expansion. They suggest, as well, that the paradigm of colonial tutelage, in its imagined reciprocity between Americans as teachers and Filipinos as students, was one that attempted to contain the violent excesses of empire while marking the failures of the nation's benevolent embrace.

4

The Performance of Patriotism

Ironic Affiliations and Literary Disruptions in
Carlos Bulosan's America

In late 1902, the adjutant general of the Insular Bureau of the U.S. War Department received a letter from Lt. Col. Richard Pratt, headmaster of the Indian Industrial Training School in Carlisle, Pennsylvania, on the subject of the education of Filipinos. Pratt's purpose in the letter was to propose the Carlisle plan as a method of educating young Filipino men and women; such a plan, sketched broadly, was to bring Filipinos "in as great numbers as practicable" to the United States to live among and be educated by "good Americans" for, as Pratt asserted, "It will hardly be disputed that the best way to make an alien American is to let him associate with Americans, nor that to make him a good American it is essential that he associate with good Americans."[1] Recommending the establishment of schools in the United States solely for the purpose of training Filipino students, Pratt reasoned that separating students from their homes was the surest way to offer them "our education, the language, industries, and other useful qualities of our American life." The results, he boasted, were "as uniformly successful as any work of its kind among our own people."[2]

Pratt was not alone in his concern about the educational potential for assimilating Filipino subjects. The Insular Bureau received dozens of letters regarding the possibility of educating select Filipino students in the United States. Most of these were from American educators eager to enlist their schools in the imperial project; a few were from soldiers returning home who assumed that the Filipino children they left behind would languish in the absence of their example.[3] Pratt's vision was unique, however. He was not concerned with educating individuals, but with inaugurating a system for the large-scale Americanization of the new colonial subjects;

he imagined that the success of a first group of fifty Filipino students would eventually lead to more schools and thousands of students who, once transformed into "good Americans," would carry forward the "civilizing mission" on their own. Suggesting that the "establishment in America of schools for the benefit of Filipino youth" be an immediate priority, he argued that the Carlisle plan was ideal for ensuring the "extraordinary benefit" that the influence of "fifteen hundred young Filipinos returning to their homes after being educated and living in America under the influences of our American system of education, training, and industries" would have in "Americanizing the islands." As further proof of the expediency of his proposal, Pratt offered the successful Americanization of forty-six Puerto Rican students who had been enrolled at Carlisle, beginning in 1899. Remarking that the Puerto Rican students' "superior intelligence" and "ready use" of Spanish made them "rather more of a problem in anglicizing than the Indians," Pratt claimed that "these students from our island dependency" have exhibited "extraordinary progress in English speaking and in the acquirement of a knowledge of our American ways and civilization and a complete readiness to conform to and adapt themselves to it."[4]

Here, Pratt articulated a significant connection between the treatment of Native Americans and of Filipinos, both of whom he considered to be morally and intellectually inferior populations who required the disciplined guidance of Anglo-Saxon teachers. In so doing, he offered a vision of Filipino Americanization based on a theory of cultural assimilation through immersion in American life. Of course, the American life he envisioned did not include the indigenous peoples of the Americas at its center. Rather, his plan was to mold Native Americans and Filipinos into a particular vision of middle-class American culture, indoctrinating students into the Protestant cultural norms of thrift, property ownership, submission to authority, and patriarchal domestic life. In the heavily controlled, surveilled, and regimented atmosphere of residential schools, he hoped to reinforce the dominance of Anglo-Saxon culture by marking Native Americans' and Filipinos' distance from its central traditions and their inferiority to its organizing power.

Pratt's proposal came at the end of a challenging year for the U.S. occupation of the Philippines. President Theodore Roosevelt had declared the end of the war in the Philippines on July 4, 1902, proclaiming the final pacification of the islands and the triumph of U.S. sovereignty. In the United States, however, the revelation of violent excesses of the U.S.

military was receiving widespread attention, giving reason to doubt the success indicated in such a moment. Throughout 1902, American citizens heard accounts of testimony offered in congressional hearings called to investigate allegations of atrocities inflicted by U.S. soldiers on Filipino citizens and captives. In front of the decidedly pro-imperialist committee, chaired by Senator Henry Cabot Lodge, witness after witness detailed the extraordinary violence that characterized the military's "pacification" project. Such testimony challenged the official reports of pro-imperialist politicians, giving the lie to assurances like that from Secretary of War Elihu Root, who praised U.S. troops for their "self-control, patience, [and] magnanimity."[5] By the time the Lodge Commission's report was published in August 1902, the cumulative effect of months of graphic testimony and years of continued conflict resulted in an American public increasingly skeptical about the success of the civilizing mission and wary of its great costs.

Writing four months after the publication of the Lodge report, Pratt's suggestion hinted at an anxiety about the efficacy of the project of benevolent assimilation and the nature of the civilizing nation behind it. In the midst of these national concerns about the picture of civilization the U.S. occupation presented, as well as those about the violent acts it enacted against a Filipino population characterized as "childlike," Pratt offered the assurance that the controlled environment of the residential school would atone for such excesses, again by comparing the fate of Filipinos to that of Native Americans:

> The vast amount of civilization and American life and inducement to higher and better things that has gone back to the tribes as a result of the training of these young people at Carlisle and returning many to their homes, is beyond all computation. Had there been no non-reservation schools and no opportunities of this kind during the past twenty-four years our Indians would today still be largely in the hands of designing white interpreters and manipulators of their interests on the reservations, and incomparably more helpless and useless than they are now.[6]

The passage is striking for a number of reasons. As late as 1902, decades after Carlisle opened its doors as a residential school for Native Americans, Pratt's justification of the project resonated in profoundly pessimistic terms, characterizing his students not as successful, but as only less "helpless" and "useless" than they would otherwise be. But the reason he regarded their education as necessary is even more telling; here, he made no grand gesture toward the benefits of Anglo-Saxon civilization, but deployed a protectionist rationale in which he deemed it necessary to bring these new wards, first Native, then Filipino, under the controlled supervision of selected white men so that they would not fall prey to the "manipulators" and unscrupulous interests of *other* white men. In a fascinating and contradictory turn, Pratt fashioned a vision of colonial tutelage as the process of good white men protecting colonial subjects from bad white men; good civilization, in other words, as the antidote for the corruption, greed, and violence that characterized the scarcely hidden underside of colonial expansion.

Pratt sent another letter a few weeks later, specifically requesting that Carlisle might host fifty Filipino students, selected "from the various tribes and peoples on the different islands," without need for any further appropriations from Congress.[7] Despite his persistence, however, the education of Filipinos according to the Carlisle plan was not realized. His designs were put to rest once and for all when the U.S. House of Representatives defeated a proposal to fund the education of Filipino and Puerto Rican students at Carlisle. Holding forth on the House floor, Representative Joe Cannon, a Republican from Illinois who served as chair of the Appropriations Committee and would later that year become Speaker of the House, insisted that it would be "an outrage" to allocate public funds for educating Filipino children who, he insisted, could not be educated "above the sentiment of the people from whom they sprang and with whom they must live."[8] Cannon thus refused the notion of Filipino education and Filipino immigration, insisting on an absolute difference that was at once biological ("the people from whom they sprang") and cultural ("with whom they must live"). Despite Cannon's refusal, however, by 1903 Filipinos did begin to travel to the United States, reversing the unidirectional path in which Americans traveled, lived, and worked in the Philippines, and wrote back of their experiences. Starting that year, the *pensionado* program began to select children of elite Filipino families for enrollment in U.S. colleges and universities. Several hundred Filipino students were brought to the United States through the program; they were required to return to the Philippines to work for five years, thus constituting a fully Americanized governing class, loyal to U.S. interests. Others, who were not part of the program but whose families had the financial means to send them, enrolled in U.S. schools as well, testifying to the powerful ideological force with which America was promoted, during the occupation, as a land of possibility and upward mobility.[9]

Some Filipinos thus came as students drawn by repeated promises of opportunity in the United States and favorable government jobs upon their return to the Philippines. Many more were recruited as laborers, however, first in Hawaii, and later to work in farms all along the west coast, and in canneries in Alaska. Filipinos in the United States occupied a liminal legal status as "nationals." Like other Asian immigrants, they were unable to naturalize; unlike other Asians, they could immigrate to the United States without restriction. Between 1920 and 1930, more than 31,000 Filipinos immigrated through ports in San Francisco and Los Angeles; between 1910 and 1930, the Filipino population in California alone increased from five thousand to more than thirty thousand.[10] Lisa Lowe has demonstrated how the United States has profited from the "'flexible' racialization of Asian labor," benefiting from the presence of a racialized labor force while preventing these laborers, through their selective disenfranchisement and exclusion, from capital accumulation.[11] Capital's need for "abstract labor," Lowe explains, finds itself at odds with the nation's drive toward a racially homogeneous, unified citizenry. In the United States, this contradiction has been resolved through the selective exclusion of different racialized groups who are at once essential to the material progress of the state but rendered "alien" to the nation.[12] This is particularly true of the history of Filipino immigrants to the United States, who were recruited energetically in the early twentieth century. Especially after the Immigration Act of 1924, which excluded "aliens not eligible for citizenship," Filipinos were regarded as an indispensable labor force, such that between 1923 and 1930, more than 4,100 Filipinos immigrated annually; by 1930, there were 108,260 Filipinos working across the United States, most as farmworkers on the west coast.[13] With the passage of the Tydings-McDuffie Act in 1934, deep in the midst of the Great Depression, Filipinos, too, became the object of exclusionary provisions, and the number of Filipinos annually permitted into the United States was limited to fifty; an exemption was granted for Hawaii, where the Hawaii Sugar Planters' Association continued to be permitted to recruit Filipinos as laborers. This uneven history of immigration, wage labor, disenfranchisement, and legal exclusion comprises what Yen Le Espiritu has called a system of "differential inclusion," in which Filipinos have been integral to the U.S. nation-state's economy, culture, and consciousness, but only by nature of their subordinate standing.[14] Like the histories of other racialized, exploited, and excluded populations, the history of Filipinos in the United States gives the lie to the ideology of benevolence that attended the civilizing mission of the colonial occupation, opening the way for questions about the ruptures, contradictions, and impossibilities that such an ideology attempted to smooth over.

Realizing the complexity and the legacy of the U.S. colonial state in the Philippines means recognizing the history of Filipino immigration to the United States, and this racialization, disenfranchisement, and exclusion as necessary parts of the colonial project. Filipino cultural production bears witness to the force of the educational apparatus, in particular, as an instrument of colonial rule. In contrast to the narratives of Americans who envisioned their travel to the Philippines as an exotic adventure, and part of a benevolent mission that reflected the altruistic nature of the Anglo-Saxon race, the stories of those who came to the United States hoping to fulfill the promise of those ideals espoused by the American colonial teachers and the books they brought with them tell another tale. I turn now to one of these, which serves as a haunting testimony to both the failed promises of benevolent assimilation and duplicitous nature of the expansionist project. Carlos Bulosan's *America Is in the Heart* speaks to the cognitive dissonance inspired by the contradiction between the America presented by its canonical literary texts and the experience of Filipino immigrants to the United States. Virtually forgotten after its initial success in 1946, *America Is in the Heart* has been a staple text in the body of American and Asian American literary study since Bulosan's "rediscovery" by students, workers, and activists in the 1960s and the republication of the text in 1972. Bulosan is just one among many important Filipino and Filipino American writers, of course; authors like Bienvenido Santos, N. V. M. Gonzales and Jose Garcia Villa, each quite differently situated in relation to their engagements with the politics of diaspora, have participated in alternate ways with the possibilities of the literary object as tool for managing the conflicting demands of American imperialism and Filipino nationalism; I address those concerns, as part of the politics of the production and circulation of Philippine literature in English, in the final chapter.[15] Here, I devote singular attention to Bulosan because of the way his work has been positioned by critics as the *porte-parole* for a generation of Filipino immigrant workers to the United States, and for the clarity and decisiveness he brings to his depictions of the disruptions that both provoked and resulted from these migrations.[16] More than that of any of his peers, Bulosan's work foregrounds the complexities of education as a central tool in the alienation of the colonial subject and in the promise of his or her assimilation into the American body. *America Is in the Heart* speaks also to the profound place of the literary as the bearer of those promises and the site for recuperating from their failure. Envisioned as both personal history and collective autobiography, this narrative challenges the central promises of the American occupation, rendering clear the contradictions implicit in the project of benevolent assimilation and the stark exploitation of Filipinos as alien to the national body but essential to national progress.

Bulosan and the Politics of the Literary

Two-thirds of the way into *America Is in the Heart*, the reader is confronted with a strikingly self-conscious passage describing the social and political utility of literature. Faced with the task of rallying support for a new literary magazine, our narrator, Carlos, listens as his brother Macario argues persuasively for a literary component to the workers' struggle: "It has fallen upon us to inspire a united front among our people. . . . We must achieve articulation of social ideas, not only for some kind of economic security but also to help culture bloom as it should in our time. We are approaching what will be the greatest achievement of our generation: the discovery of a new vista of literature, that is, to speak to the people and to be understood by them. . . . This is the greatest responsibility of literature: to find in our struggle that which has a future." Macario's words, delivered as part of a long speech that "seiz[es]" Carlos's imagination, rest imprinted there until "years afterward," when he is able to transcribe them into the text of *America*.[17] Situated in the final pages of part 2 of the novel, the passage offers conceptual closure to the section of the narrative that is most concerned with Carlos's arrival in the United States and his repeated exposure to violence, injustice, and exploitation across innumerable cities, towns, and states. In literature, Macario insists, Carlos and his compatriots will find the meaning and purpose of such experiences. Literature, as a "living and growing thing," not only *recounts* such experiences, but *defines* them, and in so doing, gives meaning to the past and form to the future.

What is striking about this passage, for Bulosan's readers, is the central role given to literary production in making sense of the immense contradictions that Carlos has faced. In a phrase that resonates as a foundational moment in the narrative, Macario echoes the title of the text, offering that "America is in the hearts of men that died for freedom; it is also in the eyes of men that are building a new world" (189). Thus gesturing faithfully to the idealist narrative of inclusive democracy, Macario insists that they "must live in America where there is freedom for all regardless of color, station, and beliefs," continuing to claim that "the old world is dying, but a new world is being born" (189). Here, for Macario, the literary represents the means toward that new world, providing the tools to "look for the mainspring of democracy" whose promise brought Macario, Carlos, and their compatriots to the United States.

Quickly, however, Macario's celebration of the liberatory potential of literature takes a sharp turn. The remainder of his speech goes to great lengths to detail the oppressions facing Filipino and other immigrants who come to the United States looking for opportunity. Cleverly juxtaposing that ideal of America as the site of racial harmony with a long lineage of those disenfranchised in the process of the settlement and expansion of the United States, Macario elaborates:

> It is but fair to say that America is not a land of one race or one class of men. We are all Americans that have toiled and suffered and known oppression and defeat, from the first Indian that offered peace in Manhattan to the last Filipino pea pickers. . . . America is also the nameless foreigner, the homeless refugee, the hungry boy begging for a job and the black body dangling on a tree. . . . We are all that nameless foreigner, that homeless refugee, that hungry boy, that illiterate immigrant and that lynched black body. All of us, from the first Adams to the last Filipino, native born or alien, educated or illiterate—*We are America!* (189, my italics)

In one sense, the speech contributes to what has been read as the assimilationist drive of the text, its triumphant refrain that "We are America!" confirming the identity between self and nation that marks the height of the inclusive discourse of liberal democracy.[18] At the same time, its linking of distinct episodes of racist violence in the United States powerfully undercuts the embrace that such inclusion would suggest. Moreover, at this crucial juncture, the text offers its own critique of that ideal by transcribing the speech within a narrative sequence that neither supports nor sustains such conclusions. The whirlwind of violent encounters, narrow escapes, and brutal confrontations overlap with moments of sacrifice, friendship, and devotion to provide a contradictory narrative that defies mapping and undercuts any teleological progress toward the realization of the ideals Macario articulates. As Sau-ling Wong notes, "through the formal unintelligibility of the professed transformation, the narrator/protagonist Carlos's experiences belie his passionate tribute to American ideals" (133). This is most notable in the abrupt end to Macario's speech, which fades to a close with the line, "The old world will die so that the new world will be born with less sacrifice and agony on the living" (189). As such, the speech's failed resolution—literally, its lack of closure marked by the trailing off of the final sentence—leaves the reader to continue pondering precisely that "sacrifice and agony" that is the center of the book's narrative.

Macario's words are remarkable in their rehearsal of the foundational contradictions of the novel; left formally as well as conceptually unresolved, Macario's speech points toward the contradictory narrative logic behind *America*'s own story. As importantly, however, it links literary production to the illumination and resolution of this contradiction, thus providing some clues as to the critical role of the novel itself. The function of literature is a primary focus of Bulosan's text, and one that displays an ambivalence characteristic of the novel more generally. By introducing the centrality of the literary, I look to think more critically about the ways in which Bulosan presents both the strengths and the limits of literary representation—limits often enacted through but not fully comprehended by Carlos, the narrator. Most often categorized as Bulosan's "personal history," as the text itself declares, *America* has been more recently received as a *collective* autobiography, a testimony to the trials and endurance of Filipino immigrants in the United States. It is a novel of the emergence of working-class consciousness, as it is inextricably linked, for Bulosan, to anticolonial, antiracist struggles for justice. Most significantly, however, it is a text that exhibits a profound ambivalence regarding the promise of "America" and the historical treatment of Filipino immigrants to the United States, seeming to vacillate between the opposite poles of hope and desperation, faith and renunciation with regard to the collective project of U.S. democracy.[19] Strikingly, it is the literary that mediates this ambivalence and illuminates the valences of these complex and contradictory formations.

Much critical evaluation has commented on the absence of an explicit, unambiguous critique of U.S. imperialism, citing instead Macario's refrain, "We are America!" as one of many examples of Carlos's professed attachment to America as the site of racial equality and personal advancement. Herein lies the tension behind the contradictory impulses of the novel, as the text seems to criticize the exclusionary promise of the American Dream while at the same time aspiring to achieve that myth's fulfillment. E. San Juan Jr., for example, introduces his critical interrogation of the novel with the question of how to reconcile "this stark discrepancy between reality and thought, between fact (the social wasteland called 'United States') and ideal ('America,' land of equality and prosperity)."[20] Similarly, Jae H. Roe notes the implausibility of the text's idyllic representation of the promise of inclusion in the American national body, arguing that in the face of the violent encounters the novel details, Carlos's faith in the American Dream is less a willed naiveté than a "postcolonial humanism" that questions the promise of American liberalism by linking the workers' struggle in the United States to the causes of poverty of the peasantry in the Philippines and the fight against fascism in Spain. This is a humanism that, for Roe, seeks to encompass "the history of all subjugated men and women," thereby rejecting the limitations of national consciousness and providing a model of "universal humanism."[21]

Such commentaries attempt to resolve the text's most central contradiction by reading it as either Bulosan's capitulation to the patriotic postwar political climate in which the text was first published, or as a rhetorical strategy by which Carlos, through his own naïve faith in the American Dream, demonstrates for the reader the hypocrisy of the promises embedded there. I think, however, there is much to be gained by suspending the impulse to resolve this contradiction between the ideal "America" in which Carlos has faith, and the material conditions of exploitation and legal exclusion that the novel depicts so vividly. In fact, what is at stake is an epistemological impasse whose irresolvability provides a critical key to discerning the novel's critique of the imperial occupation of the Philippines, a critique that, superficially, seems conspicuously absent from the text.

I would suggest that the productive ambiguity that underpins such contradictions isolates Carlos's movement between knowing and not knowing as episodes that foreground the politics of knowledge as central to Bulosan's critical perspective on the imperial conquest of the Philippines. What is at stake in Carlos's seemingly incredulous refusal to "know" the hypocrisy of the idyllic America he has learned through books is not his own status as a naïve (and therefore untrustworthy) narrator, but rather a profound commentary on the politics of knowledge production as that endeavor was used to justify the colonization of the Philippines within the progressive discourse of the early twentieth century. Through such textual contradictions, Bulosan engages with the logic of President McKinley's project of benevolent assimilation to mark the imposition of the U.S.

educational system as part of a violent regime of colonial dominance. In these moments, we see the novel's latent critique of U.S. imperialism within the fluctuations of Carlos's own investments in knowledge production as the privileged site of access to the American Dream, fluctuations that are inextricably linked to the politics of knowledge production and the educational history that justified the U.S. occupation of the islands. It is thus not Carlos's refusal to know and resolve this contradiction, but rather his difficulty in negotiating his own different ways of knowing, that make the novel a productive, challenging text, a "repository of counter-memory and counter-history" that seeks to contain and illuminate the repressed history of U.S. imperialism.[22]

America begins in the Philippines, with the protagonist, Allos (later called Carlos upon his migration to the United States), helping his father in the fields when he notices a stranger approaching them from a long distance. Recognizing the man from a photo in the family home, Allos alerts his father that his oldest brother is returning, to which his father responds incredulously, remarking that Leon "is still fighting in Europe. Maybe he is dead now" (4). As Leon approaches and his homecoming is complete, Allos moves quickly from the moment of first recognition to reflect on their separation, the "strange war in Europe," and the "radical social change" taking hold of the Philippines, in which the "young generation" was "inspired by false American ideals and modes of living" (5). Sensing that the islands were being "torn from their roots" in the midst of such social change, Allos is positioned at this juncture as an uncomprehending spectator, the scene a collage of images that linger in his mind, awaiting for their elucidation the development of Carlos's own skill as an interpreter. In this way, the novel opens by foregrounding Carlos's exceptionality in his family: he is first witness, then scribe, who will know and write the family story. The novel's opening line establishes that he was, after all, "the first to see [Leon] coming," the first to recognize the return of the eldest son and, subsequently, the irrevocable changes beginning to transform the country and the impending loss of their village way of life. At the same time, however, such changes are events that Allos can not yet comprehend, and as such, their telling invests part 1 of the novel with a sense of precariousness and foreboding about the outcome of such changes.

This opening strategy of narrative incomprehension on Allos's part establishes a dialectical tension between knowing and unknowing that structures the entire novel's progression, as the story that Carlos tells is one of his gradual enlightenment toward the knowledge through which he is able to find the meaning in the struggles of his life. This tension is marked explicitly at several stages in the text, when Carlos leaves the present tense of the narrative scene to return to his place as narrator, looking back to the past to read the meaning of his life experiences. In this way, much of the narrative builds toward the future, anticipating the time when he will have gained the necessary perspective to fully understand the moment at hand. Such a dialectical movement is clear in an early passage after the family's crop is taken by a "strange man" who claims the land for a landlord in Manila. Having already sold their small property to support the education of one son, Macario, the family is left destitute, and uncomprehending about the legal process that would deprive them of the fruits of their hard labor. Of this scene, Carlos remarks:

> This family tragedy marked the beginning of my conscious life, when my responses to outward influences grew so acute that I almost wrecked my whole future. I became sensitive in the presence of poverty and degradation, so sensitive that my unexpressed feelings tempered my psychological relation to the world. It was long afterward in a land far away, long after these conflicts were conquered and forged as a weapon against another chaos that threatened to plunge me into despair and rootlessness, that the full significance of our tragedy burst into a flaming reality. (29)

Here Carlos marks the episode of injustice as one that inaugurates his "conscious life," thus highlighting class conflict as central to the knowledge he will acquire. Tellingly, however, he emphasizes his own inability to make sense of this scene, anticipating a future moment when the "full significance" of the events can be comprehended.

Such incomprehension dominates the telling of these early episodes in the Philippines, especially in relation to his family, where his place as observer is early secured. He describes the knowledge of his parents as noble and straightforward, but fundamentally unequal to the task of assimilating their life circumstances to the new economic and social relations that surround them. Noting his mother's skillful trading in the market, he reflects that "like my father, she could not read or write, but her practical sense was sharper than most who had learned to read. Her common sense had kept our family going for many desperate years" (36). Likewise, Allos works alongside his father with great respect for him, noting his father's wise and perseverant manner in the face of adversity; as he writes so admiringly: "illiterate as he was, my father had an instinct for the truth. It was this that had kept him going in a country rapidly changing to new conditions and ideals" (23). Despite such wisdom, however, his parents are unable to prevent the family from descending deeper and deeper into poverty, thus forcing each brother to leave home to make his way elsewhere. Despite Carlos's admiration for their wisdom, the knowledge of his parents is ultimately a powerless one, rendered anachronistic in the face of the changes that Carlos, retrospectively, can appreciate. Tellingly, at this point the narrative skips forward, to "years afterward," when, convalescing in a hospital in the United States, Carlos remembers these scenes and is driven to speak and write them in the hope of making concrete their meaning; he avers, "my rememberance gave me a strange courage and vision of a better life," vowing, finally, "Yes, I will be a writer and make all of you live again in my words" (57).

Early in the novel, we witness Bulosan's own investment in the politics of knowledge and, more specifically, in Carlos's power to interpret the circumstances of his life. Poised to reflect on the meaning of his parents' struggle as well as his own, Carlos is a transitional narrator, translating across two generations, two historical moments, and two worldviews. In this sense, the novel builds in teleological fashion, marking the conflicts of Carlos's early years as the latent seeds that, once he is in the United States, will flower into a new, expansive consciousness. At the same time, the novel links his experience of the United States with a particular kind of knowledge acquisition, one that is heavily invested in the perpetuation of U.S. cultural hegemony through the ideological primacy of the literary. As the son of parents who neither read nor write, Carlos invests remarkable power in the literary as the mode through which he reads his experience in the world. Preparing for his passage to the United States, he begins to work in a library under the supervision of a white American, Mary Strandon, who expresses great interest in inculcating him with the stories of American literature. Describing this primary attachment to books, Carlos proclaims that his growing knowledge of the library's holdings find him "beginning to understand what was going on around [him]," so that "the darkness that had covered [his] present life was lifting." Thus, "emerging into sunlight," Carlos finds in the library that "a whole new world was opened to [him]" (70–71). The fulfillment of such opportunity is confirmed at the end of this passage, when Carlos again skips ahead to the future to tell of his attempt, fifteen years later, to find Strandon in Iowa. Learning that she had died long before, he donates a copy of his first book to the local library, marking, in no uncertain terms, his own place in the "new world" she had introduced to him.

Literary production is a highly gendered and racialized endeavor, one that, for Carlos, both results from the U.S. colonial occupation of the archipelago and obscures the material effects of that occupation. As yet, however, Carlos describes his relation to the literary as an individual one, as yet unconnected to a systematic or structural critique of racism and class oppression that, in their institutionalized forms, construct the very conditions of necessity for his presence in the United States. This is, at times, a glaring omission, as when Carlos, while still in the Philippines doing domestic work for an American woman in Baguio, tells a fellow houseboy that he plans to save for passage to America and is told, "You don't need money, you could work on the boat. But English is the best weapon" (69).[23] Such advice launches Carlos's instruction in English and concretizes his immersion in the grand mythologies of American democracy, signaled shortly thereafter by his enchantment with the story of Abraham Lincoln, with whom he quickly identifies.

Stories thus become crucial points of identification for Carlos, who learns that Abe "walked miles and miles to borrow a book so that he would know more about his country" and internalizes this tale as it speaks to his own experience: "deep down in me something was touched, was springing out, demanding to be born, to be given a name. I was fascinated by the story of this boy who was born in a log cabin and became a president of the United States" (69). As the Abe Lincoln story makes sufficiently clear, English was a primary weapon of the U.S. occupation of the Philippines, and was crucial both to its exploitative mission in the islands and to its massive recruitment of Filipino men as labor for industry and agriculture in Hawaii, Alaska, and along the west coast of the mainland United States.[24] Carlos's identification with the foundational stories of U.S. nationalism thus takes on multiple meanings within Bulosan's text, as it seems to offer a sort of intellectual illumination for Carlos even as it marks another level of his subjection to U.S. imperialism; as Bulosan makes abundantly clear, to be a colonial subject is to be subjected to the cultural as well as economic demands of the U.S. nation-state.

The necessity of formal education and of fluency in English taps into a key ambivalence in the text, one that points to a broader contradiction between the democratic principles of inclusion and uplift that underpinned the philosophies of democratic education used to justify the U.S. invasion and occupation of the Philippines, and the lived reality of exclusion, disenfranchisement, and forced, or "necessitious" mobility.[25] This is an ambivalence demonstrated not by Carlos, who seems to accept the logic of democratic education as a key to his self-realization, but by Bulosan, in his careful juxtapositioning and cross-referencing of scenes. Inasmuch as education functioned as a central promise offered by U.S. officials looking to legitimate the occupation of the Philippines, its importance in *America* allows us to explore the contradictions inherent in the project of "benevolent assimilation," and to consider education as the critical nexus for Bulosan's implicit critique of U.S. imperialism.[26]

This dual nature of English education—the tandem workings of pacification and "uplift," and the school's status as a colonial apparatus—is not lost on Bulosan, who again and again opens up the question of what is lost and what is gained in the colonial subject's interpellation by the institutions of formal schooling. The importance of education and the rewards it promises are, in fact, the subject of much longing in the text, particularly in part 1, where the privilege of going to school is desired by Carlos and his siblings. Only Macario, "who was [the] pride and the star of all [the family's] hope" (12), is able to attend high school, and the family's many sacrifices to keep him there, "so that he could come back to Binalonan to teach school and, perhaps, to help support [his] large family" (10), force them to sell their land and sink further into poverty. From the text's opening pages, education is at best a fraught privilege, holding out the promise of security for the family while forcing its eventual disintegration.

This contradiction is offered in starker terms in the pages that follow. Refusing to acquiesce to the logic of benevolent U.S. rule, Carlos insists upon the ameliorative potential of popular education as an improvement for the Philippines:

Popular education was spreading throughout the archipelago and this opened up new opportunities. It was a new and democratic system brought by the American government into the Philippines, and a nation hitherto illiterate and backward was beginning to awaken. In Spanish times education was something that belonged exclusively to the rulers and to some fortunate natives affluent enough to go to Europe. But the poor people, the peasants, were denied even the most elementary schooling. When the free education that the United States had introduced spread throughout the islands, every family who had a son pooled its resources and sent him to school. (14)

The passage begins as a discourse espousing the progressive, democratic potential of colonial education, adopting the language of U.S. colonial policy in deeming the Philippines a "backward" nation poised to reap great benefits from the benevolent presence of the United States and its cultural institutions. The final line, however, destabilizes this claim by pointing to the sacrifices demanded even of "free" education, and these hidden costs, both economic and familial, emerge as the most devastating threat to the family's survival. As Carlos laments: "My father and mother, who could not read or write, were willing to sacrifice anything and everything to put my brother Macario through high school.... We had deprived ourselves of any form of leisure and simple luxury so that my brother could finish high school. But even then he kept asking for more money.... The thought that he would really stop terrified us" (14).

Education is thus at the center of an exploitative patriarchal, colonial arrangement masquerading as a democratic intervention. Despite the sacrifices it entails, however, it continues to hold a powerful promise for Carlos, encapsulating the contradictory status of America as that ideological entity that promises what it structurally cannot deliver. It is the subject of an almost magical attachment, as evidenced when, after a long period of work in the fields and in the market, Carlos is told by his mother, "You can go to school now, son." He remembers: "the prospect of going to school made the whole night enchanted. My bleeding hands were forgotten. The long and weary road to Binalonan was as nothing. Yes, even the hard work with my father in the village was also forgotten" (41). This remarkable passage foregrounds the dangerous dynamic in which one kind of knowing— formal education—is predicated upon a kind of forgetting—the labor and sacrifice that will enable his attendance. Such forgetting is essential to the mystifying function of the democratic rhetoric of which education is a crucial part. "Forgetting," at least for a time, the hard labor he has performed with his father, as well as the family's sacrifices that must inevitably occur to assure his attendance at school, Carlos effectively jettisons the knowledge of his peasant life, and the privileged perspective it might afford him to decipher the contradictory claims of the U.S. occupation and its story of colonial benevolence, the story of colonialism as a scene of national tutelage.

Here Bulosan points us to a critical void, the mark of precious knowledge lost under the enchantment of a promise made—and ultimately unfulfilled—by the U.S. colonial regime. Such moments, however, point to a more crucial omission, a larger episode of forgetting, which is marked by an absence in the text of any discussion of the Philippine-American War and conflicts engendered by the U.S. occupation. These matters are not separable from the question of education, to be sure, as the narrative of public education as uplift, as we have seen, was crucial to the occupation's popular support in the United States, despite the horrific casualties sustained by the Filipino population.[27] And in this respect, Carlos's dream of formal education in the colonial schools and his professed faith in the possibility of an America without racial prejudice or class exploitation seem all the more difficult to reconcile.

Such an absence, however, might be precisely the point. That is, such moments of strategic forgetting on Carlos's part mirror the more urgent, national forgetting of the devastating imperial war between the U.S. military and Filipino resistance, producing a curious and clever disjuncture, a chance to see Bulosan's implicit critique within the very professing of Carlos's belief. In such moments, Bulosan achieves an essential distance from Carlos, investing the novel with layers of reflection and commentary made implicit through the significant disjunctures in the narrative form. Through the continual deferral of Carlos's education and the sacrifice behind Macario's schooling, Bulosan undercuts the rhetoric of free education, pointing to the hypocrisy implicit in the kinds of stories and histories reproduced as part of such an education. Facing the void left by Macario's absence and the dissolution of the family's resources as the cost of Macario's education, Carlos's longing can read only as a sharp critique of the failure of the occupying government's "benevolent" rule.

Such a critique is reinforced through Bulosan's retrospective positioning of Carlos's successes and failures, offering a broader critique of U.S. cultural hegemony. Upon discovering his facility in English, Carlos immerses himself in his project of literary education, asking: "Who were the men that contributed something positive to society? Show me the books about them! I would read them all! I would educate myself to be like them!" (181). In a sense, Carlos seeks the literary as the venue for his own transformation, one in which the capacity to tell the world of the injustices he has faced is also to take on a new role, "to be like" other men whose stories have already been told. Such a proclamation emphasizes the importance of the life story as a form of example and instruction even as it reinvests in the individualist logic of self-uplift, resonating with Carlos's continued fascination and identification with the stories of Robinson Crusoe, Moses, Abraham Lincoln, and Richard Wright. Likewise, it prefigures Carlos's later "discovery" of, and immersion in, the canon of American literature as that form of self-instruction that, quite literally, saves him during the two years that he is hospitalized. Accordingly, this passage is one of our first signposts marking the important place that literary education plays in the text, as an inspired mode of self-transformation and a realization of the latent potential of humanity, on both an individual and collective scale.

Tempering this realization, however, is a narrative style that refuses the transformative effects of Carlos's epiphany just as soon as it hints at them. This is not the first time that Carlos is inspired by the potential of literature to give meaning and form to his experience. The novel is replete with such moments, in which the literary serves as Carlos's passage to the opportunities he identifies with the promise of America. In one earlier passage, young Allos is inspired by the desire to learn English by reading the story of Abraham Lincoln, "a poor boy who became president of the United States" (69). Later, he makes the "sudden discovery of America" through the writings of Walt Whitman, whose "passionate dream of an America of equality for all races" becomes a fantasy that "enchants" Carlos, becoming "burned [in his] consciousness" as he himself begins to write (251–52). These moments make explicit the connection between writing and nation-building, situating Carlos in seemingly collaborative relation to the ideals that such writing presents. Taking as models those writers he encounters, Carlos looks to literature as the means of his own self-realization; as he realizes, much later in the novel, that "the time had come, . . . for [him] to utilize [his] experiences in written form. [He] had something to live for now" (306). It is this regard for literature that reanimates his drive, time and again, to contribute to those ideals, promises of recognition and equality that remain formally and legally out of his grasp. In this sense, the literary becomes the venue for Carlos's participation in the idyllic American national body.

At the same time, the lesson of such textual moments is contradictory, even duplicitous; while Carlos seems ever inspired by the ideals articulated in the canonical texts of American literature, these moments serve as well to illustrate the gap between his own experience and the utopian promise such texts offer. Carlos comes to perceive literature not simply as the source of a most idyllic "America," but also as a vehicle for social justice, through his efforts to catalogue his experiences of injustice, racism, and imperialist conquest. This power of the literary is reflected in moments of desperation, when Carlos, "full of loneliness and love" for what he has left behind, turns to writing as a way to insert himself into the fabric of the American national body. As he reflects upon a friend's urging that he again write and try to be published: "It will be the last pull. . . . I have tried it several times. If I fail again, it will be horrible. I could become the most vicious Filipino criminal in America." Significantly, his companion inspires him with the urgency of the project as a means to validate the sacrifices of the community more broadly: "That is why you must not fail this time. . . . You've got to succeed for all our sakes" (309).

It is telling, then, that Carlos's first act, after his self-proclaimed rebirth through writing, is to wander the streets of San Luis Obispo searching for the house in which a Filipino friend, Max Smith, shot and killed his wife's white lover. That event is one of many violent acts Carlos witnesses, the sum of which converge to concretize Carlos's role as witness, and eventual scribe, to the multiple violences perpetrated against and by the disenfranchised Filipino community.[28] This act, like many others, is described as one that Carlos cannot fully comprehend at the time of its enactment; rather, it is one of the stories that Carlos internalizes and carries with him in his travels; "the farther I went away, the more the thought of the crime possessed me" (167). Revisiting the scene of the crime, Carlos thus embarks not upon a strategic quest for formal knowledge (i.e., the stories already committed to paper) but an impulsive drive toward his own past, a revisiting of his own story and the stories of others he has encountered along the way. Such a move is important because it immediately counters Carlos's emphasis on formal knowledge by locating his own lived history as an important source of his own education. As such, it introduces a tension in the text between formal and informal sites of education, between the textual and the experiential as valorized archives of knowledge.

Carlos's quest to revisit his own past, to revisit the scene of the crime that continues to haunt him seems a logical step in a text that consistently stages his growth and education as a process in which he moves forward toward new experiences and challenges in order to reconsider the past with new insight before moving ahead again. It seems, in fact, like a return that will allow him to begin to understand and relate his own story, adding it to the others he has collected. Interestingly, however, Bulosan describes this drive as "an impulse" that compels Carlos to search for the house despite the "difficult time" he has remembering it and the pain he has in facing the memory that has become "too vivid in my imagination" (181). This depiction subtly undermines Carlos's own narrative authority by depicting the next step in this growth as one driven as much by chance as by will. Precisely by marking his quest as an impulse rather than a well-considered decision, Bulosan gives his reader cause to doubt Carlos's resolve to re-create himself. Rather, his transformation seems to comprise unlikely coincidences, repetitions, and crossed paths. Witness the example that immediately follows Carlos's resolution. "At last" finding Max Smith's wife's house, he is greeted by a white woman who, seemingly inexplicably, immediately invites him in and serves him a glass of wine. Meanwhile, Carlos looks around the room appraisingly, noting apprehensively to himself, "This was a new experience" (181). Noticing a bedroom door, he surmises, "that must be the place where Max shot the white man" and begins to edge cautiously toward the exit. Now, curiously, Carlos's desire to begin a new life has led him into yet another strange and unexplained encounter in which he has neither the understanding nor the security to know how, exactly, to manage the situation. In fact, the situation takes a dramatic turn for the good—Carlos is no sooner seated when he discovers that the white woman and her Filipino husband share his sympathy toward Filipino laborers and, more miraculously, two old friends, José and Gazamen, appear in the house and explain that they are all involved in labor organizing. The point here is that this meeting, which effectively launches Carlos on the route to critical self-consciousness and awareness of the antiracist, working-class struggle, is the result not of conscious planning or decisive action, but of unlikely coincidence. Despite Carlos's knowing resolution to be the agent behind his own education, it is this chance meeting that offers him his first important lesson: "here was the answer to my confusion. Pascual [the Filipino husband] was a socialist" (182).

By insisting upon the importance of coincidence in this narrative sequence, I want to point to the importance of such unlikely turns and chance encounters in the text, as markers of a profound incompatibility between the two visions of America that circulate there. In such moments, the novel undermines Carlos's own status as the typical bildungsroman hero by showing the faulty premise upon which lies his faith in the American dream, marking his own faith in education as complicitous, in fact, with the logic of colonial rule. Thus Carlos can declare himself a "new man," on the cusp of a new destiny, and yet time and again the text challenges his authority by guiding his experiences, both positive and negative, in large part through fortuitous coincidences, chance meetings, or simple luck. Such moments exist in tension with Carlos's drive toward self education, pointing to the ways in which he will continue to be guided by what he does not, or cannot, know. In this gap between his insight and the reader's, however, lingers a second important revelation: that the question of knowledge acquisition—what Carlos can know—is fundamental to the novel's otherwise obscured critique of U.S. imperialism. It is precisely because the text vacillates between a valorization of the institutionalized, formal education used to justify the imperialist occupation of the Philippines on the one hand, and the challenges Carlos faces living within the racist logic of that occupation on the other, that the reader is forced to confront the contradiction between these two paradigms and acknowledge the hollowness of liberal humanist justifications behind the occupation of the Philippines. It is precisely because Carlos seems to believe so strongly in the redemptive power of formal education that its continual deferral works to delegitimate the colonial occupation even as, on a literal level, Carlos fails to articulate a consistent critique of that occupation.

In this sense, the novel's temporal framework, often confusing, seems quite strategic here.[29] At times, the text appears to work on a teleological scale, where events in the present are comprehended much later in the future, and Carlos progresses toward greater and greater comprehension of his life and its relation to the world around him. The temporal gap between experience and comprehension is registered from the early chapters of the text, as Carlos frequently looks toward the future as that period where he will have the necessary tools to interpret his experiences. This is a narrative style that informs much of the text's description of Carlos's coming to consciousness; Carlos's narrative repeatedly insists on his own latent potential whose realization is continually deferred. As he says when witness to an early moment of brutality, "My bravery was still nameless, still waiting to express itself" (109). Similarly, events unfold, one after the other, whose meaning becomes clear to him only much later. He says several times that he had not yet learned to "see things historically," pointing to the distinction between experience and comprehension. Experience is thus the base of knowledge; however, for true understanding, Bulosan seems to suggest, a broader perspective and a more systematic analysis is necessary.

This understanding of self-education emerges in several important scenes: soon after his arrival in the United States, already witness to numerous injustices perpetrated against Filipino workers, and poor workers more generally, Carlos meets a friend who tries to politicize Carlos by interpreting for him the connections between such injustices. To this, Carlos cannot respond, except to gesture toward the future: "Perhaps in another year I will be able to understand what you are saying" (118).

Similarly, meeting Estevan, a young Filipino writer, Carlos remembers: "I carried [his short story] with me for years reading it again a decade after, when I was intellectually equipped to understand the significance of Estevan's tragic death and the merit of the story. Thus it was that I began to rediscover my native land, and the cultural roots there that had nourished me, and I felt a great urge to identify myself with the social awakening of my people" (139). For Carlos, moving forward is a process of continually revisiting and reevaluating the experiences of his past. This culminates in a final scene when he tells an organizing group of workers about Moses, remembering Macario explaining the story to him, and saying "Now, here among common laborers, I understood the full significance of Moses's flight from the enemy of his people" (312). As such, his learning process is described as a sort of dialectical arrangement in which he revisits the past in order to reemerge in the present with a more critical awareness, another lesson learned.

Against this teleological momentum toward greater and greater knowledge, however, the reader is simultaneously presented with the weight of so many lessons not yet learned, and so many exchanges never explained. That is, what Carlos cannot know, and what the narrative can never resolve for us, is as important as what he does discover, because such limitations, both of his own narrative position and in the overall coherence of the text, point to the irresolvable contradictions that face Bulosan as author. There is a closing scene in the text that illustrates this textual ambivalence perfectly. Reunited with his friend José, Carlos describes his efforts teaching workers about unionism and proclaims: "I was sure now that we were at last beginning to play our own role in the turbulent drama of history. I did not understand it then, did not realize that this was the one and only common thread that bound us together, white and black and brown, in America. I felt a great surge of happiness inside me!" (313). What we see here is the understated tension between knowledge and its failure; Carlos begins by insisting upon his certainty of his entry into a larger historical framework, suggesting that he has learned to interpret his own experiences within the broader scope of history, in terms of the structural dynamics of expansion and exploitation that orient his very presence in the United States. And yet, he then offers that this is, in fact, the very thing that he has yet to understand; in retrospect, he sees that he did not fully comprehend the dynamic of this struggle. Such narrative turns continually position Carlos at arm's length from the realization he believes he has made. By framing this episode as something that he later realizes he "did not understand then," Bulosan pushes the reader to question Carlos's progress toward the enlightenment that the narrative seems to promise. The moment of comprehension is consistently withheld from the reader's gaze, and as such, the sense of resolution and comprehension which Carlos, as narrator, works to impose upon the scenes of his earlier life, is rendered suspect.

Finally, Bulosan leaves the reader to learn from those moments that Carlos cannot fully comprehend. Such is the didactic function of text, and a central critical intervention on Bulosan's part. Such a deferral, I would argue, calls into question Carlos's own insistence upon his progressive enlightenment, pointing instead to the sum of his experiences as an archive of oppressions and violences that stands in fundamental opposition to the ideals of America in which Carlos invests so much hope. Here, we see such repetitions of incomprehension as a rhetorical strategy, an insightful troubling of the promises of racial equality that the novel superficially seems to support. Left unresolved, those contradictions point to the fundamental contradiction of U.S. imperialism, between the exploitative and racist logic behind extraterritorial expansion and the humanist language of democracy and rule of law. Carlos's episodes of overwhelming confusion point to the hypocrisy at the heart of the U.S. "civilizing mission" in the Philippines and contradict the narrative of gradual advancement that proved to be so persuasive a justification for the U.S. military and economic control of the archipelago. Through Carlos's own belief in the fundamental promises of the American civilization, we as readers are granted our own education in the violence of such a gesture.

In this vein, the closing passage offers an apt vision of the text's unresolved tensions in relation to the America Carlos wants to find:

> Then I heard bells ringing from the hills—like the bells that had tolled in the church tower when I had left Binalonan. . . . It came to me that no man—no one at all—could destroy my faith in America again. It was something that had grown out of my defeats and successes, something shaped by my struggles for a place in this vast land. . . . It was something that grew out of the sacrifices and loneliness of my friends, of my brothers in America and my family in the Philippines—something that grew out of our desire to know America, and to become a part of her great tradition, and to contribute something toward her final fulfillment. I knew that no man could destroy my faith in America that had sprung from all our hopes and aspirations, *ever*. (327)

One reading of this passage would cite it as the "conversion" ending typical of the bildungsroman form. Indeed, many critics have read Bulosan's text this way, pointing to the "mental gymnastics" involved in any vindication of American democracy and reading the nationalist resolution as a compromise made for the purposes of publication and marketing the text during a highly nationalist period.[30] However, I would argue that this closure already hints at its own failure. Taken back to Binalonan by the sound of the bells ringing, Carlos leaves unspoken the subtext of his belief in America, the backdrop to those "defeats and successes"—the history of U.S. imperialism. It is a history that reasserts itself, however, one that structures this epiphany and lingers as the interpretive framework for the knowledge Carlos acquires. While Carlos asserts, in the final sentence, that "no man could destroy my faith in America," it appears that this *faith* cannot stand up to the knowledge Bulosan imparts to his readers (327). Carlos thus strays from knowledge to faith as the source of his conviction. As such, Bulosan ends his text by pointing to the glaring contradictions that Carlos cannot resolve, leaving this task for his readers.

In the end, Bulosan's text refuses to comply with the linear, individualist narrative structure of autobiography. Instead, the text encompasses a multiplicity of circumstances and experiences in suspended tension together. Refusing, too, the progressive narrative form of the bildungsroman, Bulosan offers chance occurrences and unlikely coincidence as structure for the narrative movement; these work as symptoms of the incommensurability between the forms of knowing—formal and experiential—that Carlos embodies. It is thus the unresolved contradiction between American exceptionalism and American imperialism that become unresolved formal ambiguities in the text. Leaving such ambiguities unresolved, Bulosan refuses the "resolution" of the nation-state's exploitative, exclusionary practices through the legal disenfranchisement of racialized immigrants, here giving voice and presence to the lived experience of those Americans and exposing the lie that is the American dream.

Conclusion

"An Empire of Letters": Literary Tradition, National Sovereignty, and Neocolonialism

> But for now, we still have a republic and not yet an empire of letters, and no one is obliged to read silly books. There are plenty of wise ones which some of us have not read.
>
> —W. D. Howells, "The New Historical Romances,"
>
> December 1900

In the December 1900 issue of *North American Review*, William Dean Howells offered a scathing critique of the "new historical romances," as fiction that would "in a measure and for a while debauch the minds and through their minds the morals of their readers."[1] Warning that the American sentimental and spectacular texts risked effecting a collective lowering of the intellectual and literary spirit of the nation, Howells clarified his critique, saying:

> I do not think it by any means a despicable thing to have hit the fancy of our enormous commonplace average. Some of the best and truest books have done this.... But what is despicable, what is lamentable is to have hit the popular fancy and not have done anything to change it, but everything to fix it; to flatter it with false dreams of splendor in the past, when life was mainly as simple and sad-colored as it is now; to corrupt it to an ignominious discontent with patience and humility, and every-day duty, and peace.[2]

Howells's charge is that such books glorify a past that holds little glory, and make false heroes in the present through fantasies of conflict rather than the more palatable virtues of responsibility and equanimity. In so doing, he confers to such texts an enormous power, to enrich the character of their readers or to degrade it. He laments, in other words, the failure of such books to put to good use their own transformative power. After expressing his reasoned distaste for the form, however, Howells concludes on a curious note by adding, "we still have a republic and not yet an empire of letters, and no one is obliged to read silly books. There are plenty of wise ones which some of us have not read."[3]

Attentive readers may remember that Howells was a vocal critic of the late nineteenth-century imperialists, and he wrote often and decisively against the U.S. occupation of the Philippines and the brutalities that resulted from its rule. He outlined this position quite clearly in the *New York Evening Post*: "I think our wrong consists in forcing sovereignty over a people who are unwilling to accept the change. I know our position is well enough supported by international law, but, to my mind, that is not a sufficient justification for us. . . . Stop the fighting, I say. My position is that it is 'never too late to do right.'"[4] His position as the vice president of the Anti-Imperialist League further solidified his reputation as a foremost critic of the Spanish-American War, the Philippine-American War, and the U.S. occupation of the Philippines. Thus his passing reference to the shame of empire is not an altogether surprising one. But in this otherwise light moment of Howells's distinction between empires and republics of letters, we are presented with an indication of the *political* power of the literary. Howells is upending the notion that literature necessarily effects its change for good; rather than exercising its ameliorative potential, the historical romance, he charges, mobilizes the power of the literary toward undesirable ends. But my sense is that the distinction matters more than this, that for Howells, and for us, it resonates beyond the escapist attractions of the historical romances. If the literary, for Howells and, as we have seen, for many of his contemporaries, is a potentially transformative agent, then the nation's status as an empire or as a republic of letters matters, because the power of letters represents the conditions of possibility for a range of other transformations, positive or negative, political, cultural, and moral. Taking Howells's admonition as a warning about the political power of the literary, how might readers understand the enduring legacy of the American ideological mobilization of English and of American literature as arms of empire? Was this, in other words, a republic or an empire of letters?

While the emphasis of the book has been on the formation of *American* literary study and its field history, I take Howells's insistence on the

freedom to read as a directive to consider the legacy of the project of benevolent assimilation in terms of literary production in the Philippines
and outside of it. That is to say, I would like to conclude by noting briefly
some of the long-term effects of that program of U.S. cultural imperialism and its relation to the political question of national sovereignty. In the
end, this investigation points to new sites of struggle, in Iraq and Afghanistan, where U.S. military operations have reanimated the use of American
literature as "textbooks for democracy" in zones of conflict.

Legacies of Literary Imperialism

Critics and scholars of twentieth-century Philippine literature have written at length about the legacy of the program of Benevolent Assimilation
on Philippine cultural production; most have agreed that the conditions
of American influence extended long beyond the occupation of the islands, with myriad cultural and political consequences. Citing the sinister
effects of the pervasiveness of English in the Philippines, the historian and
critic Renato Constantino has urged contemporary writers to take seri-
ously the "literary underdevelopment" that has been the result of both
"colonial education and upbringing" and "the pervasiveness of the media
of dominant nations."[5] "A pernicious effect of the imposition of English,"
writes Constantino, "has been the shameful notion that serious thought
and artistic effort must be articulated in English for the so-called intel-
ligentsia and that the masses deserve only pap, escapist stuff and shoddy
work." As a result, the "liberation of consciousness" he argues, is "as important as . . . economic and political liberation."[6]

In his admonition about the effects of a literary monopoly that impov-
erishes its readers, Constantino's words echo Howells's fear about the failure of literary democracy and its effects on the reading public. However,
the history of cultural production to which Constantino refers is not the
simple erosion of taste, as in Howells's case, but the systematic challenge
to nationalist literary production as part of a strategy for consolidating
U.S. hegemony. As E. San Juan Jr., Jonathan Chua, Shirley Geok-Lin Lim,
and others have argued, one of the most notable results of the American
educational system in the Philippines has been the position of privilege
accorded to Philippine literatures in English, at the expense of indigenous
literary traditions.[7] Jonathan Chua has noted that the first two decades of
the twentieth century, what Resil Mojares has called the "Golden Age of

literature in Philippine languages," witnessed the growth of politically oriented literary societies, whose raison d'être was to validate the moral and intellectual strengths of Philippine literature.[8] Noting the "extrinsic tendency of Philippine literary criticism," Chua asserts that the politicized nature of early twentieth-century vernacular literatures stemmed from the desire to counteract the influence of American colonial policies, with decided efforts to preserve local tradition and culture, and to contain the "influx of American values, deemed loose or immoral and destructive of local mores."[9] San Juan Jr. goes further, arguing that the nineteenth-century tradition of vernacular expression was intimately tied to the history of revolution and resistance in the Philippines; with the revolution of 1896 and the radical reformist works of the propagandists, this native resistant tradition incorporated elements of European revolutionary thought that presented a radical alternative to the collaborationist politics of those intellectuals educated through the American education system.

In contrast, by the 1930s, after a full generation of writers and intellectuals had been educated through the American system and many more had traveled to the United States, the dominant tide of Philippine literary criticism turned decisively away from the view of literature as a site of political struggle and cultural contestation, and toward a hierarchy of value as it accrued to the principles of literary experimentation and formal mastery.[10] "Whereas the vernacular writers in Tagalog and other native languages continued their exploration of alternatives initiated by the 1896 propagandists (Rizal, Jaena, del Pilar) in dialogue with Fournier, Bakunin, Zola, Spencer, and Marx," San Juan Jr. writes, "the practitioners of English nourished themselves to a large extent with Washington Irving, Whittier, and Longfellow's *Evangeline*."[11] The result, San Juan Jr. asserts, was a systematic "alienation of the Filipino artist from the Filipino masses" and the degradation of the political principles that subtended the work of artists in the vernaculars. The point is not that these revolutionary traditions were extinguished altogether, but that the continued assertion of U.S. hegemony was enacted, well beyond the official end of its sovereignty on the islands, in part under the aegis of value-neutral literary production in English. Consider, as one example, the Writers' Club established at the University of the Philippines; its fidelity to the priority of English and to establishing the high value accorded to Anglo-Saxon cultural traditions was expressed directly in its founding pledge to promote Philippine writing in English and to recruit its members as "faithful followers of Shakespeare."[12]

The characterization of vernacular literatures in the literary-critical circles that emerged in the early part of the century reveals the hierarchy of literary value at work in those sites as well. Reflecting on the accomplishments of Philippine literature in English, writers dismissed Tagalog literature for not "keeping pace with the progress of the times."[13] One author deemed its writers "literary quacks"; others emphasized the inferiority of Tagalog literature to literature in English.[14] A. V. H. Hartendorp, editor of the *Philippine Magazine,* asserted, moreover, that "Filipino literature in English is way ahead of literature in the vernacular insofar as artistic values are concerned" and attributed this valuation to an impression that "the English-reading public in the Philippines demands a higher standard of writing and editing than is demanded by those who read in the vernacular. Vernacular periodicals," Hartendorp insisted, "have gone after mass circulation and have made no effort to anything but the most unformed tastes."[15]

These characterizations matter, not least because they suggest a certain longevity to the dynamics of cultural persuasion in the form of arrangements of literary value. While the work of Carlos Bulosan represents one vibrant vein of literary production informed by the traditions of mass organization and revolutionary solidarity, Bulosan's is not the only cultural legacy of Philippine literature in English.[16] Rather, the notable popularity and influence of poet and critic Jose Garcia Villa demonstrates that this revolutionary perspective exists in tension with the formalist, seemingly apolitical literary tradition for which there has been extensive institutional and material support.[17] One of the most well-known and highly praised of that generation of Filipino writers, Villa was, according to San Juan Jr., the scholar who "almost singlehandedly founded modern writing in English in the Philippines in the 1920s."[18] As a modernist poet, essayist, and critic, Villa found ready praise from both American modernists in the United States and Filipino writers and scholars in the Philippines; his formalist innovations, including the "comma poem," remain significant contributions. At the same time, Villa's popularity and his enduring influence have been suspect; the formalist ethos he championed, and the valorization of art for art's sake, "may be said to encapsulate the triumph of 'Manifest Destiny,' with its peculiar ensemble of essentialism, a romantic rejection of historical reification, and the myth of the autonomous ego in liberal thought."[19] Chua, too, posits that Villa's popularity was timed perfectly to "reproduce colonialist discourse on the level of cultural practice" and that his formalist aesthetics, influenced by European and American modernists, "were tantamount to a tacit affirmation of the superiority of the colonizer."[20] Such affirmations, Chua argues, did not end with the waning of Villa's influence, but have continued inasmuch as authors he championed (among them Paz Latorena, N. V. M. Gonzales, Manuel Arguilla, and Nick Joaquin) have since become "revered names in Philippine literature."[21]

As we have seen, the efficacy of the program of American education in the Philippines relied upon the persuasiveness of literature as an apparatus of colonial rule that appeared to be politically neutral, merely a gesture of benevolent address. As it was in the U.S. colonial occupation, so it continues in the neocolonial relationship between the Philippines and the United States. What should be clear, then, is that these systems of value have effects well beyond the realm of literature, and they register specific material and political consequences that exceed questions of cultural taste. As many researchers have shown, the material legacy of U.S. colonialism in the Philippines endures. The heavy agricultural-export economy installed under U.S. rule has hindered efforts for national autonomy, and the current policies enforced by the World Bank and IMF continue to exact a high cost for "development" in the Philippines, thus perpetuating the neocolonial dependency that has made the country more hospitable to the military and economic interests of the United States.[22] The islands have been a crucial site for the demonstration of U.S. military force in Asia as well; the period of economic prosperity in the Philippines under President Ferdinand Marcos in the 1960s was largely dependent upon the U.S. war in Vietnam, and U.S. military and economic support continued after Marcos declared martial law in 1972.[23] By the late 1980s, the Philippines suffered from high inflation, high foreign debt, and the instability of markets for agricultural exports; at the same time, under the name of the fight against communism, the United States fought vociferously against the politics of land reform in the Philippines and continued to support the consolidation of resources in the hands of its wealthy pro-American allies. In such ways, Philippine domestic policy continues to be affected by U.S. foreign policy. The closing of U.S. military bases in no way ended the "special relationship" of neocolonial, militaristic exploitation between the Philippines and the U.S.[24]

The neocolonial logic that underpins the rhetoric of that "special relationship" is inextricably linked to the questions of cultural production at stake in this debate about literary value, regardless of how far apart these topics might seem. To use Constantino's words, the "liberation of consciousness" is inextricably linked to "economic and political liberation."

In this sense, the literary remains a site of struggle in the consolidation of political power and the articulation of national autonomy.[25] To the extent that neocolonialist policies continue the relentless exploitation of the Philippines, the colonial presence of the United States is not a matter left to the past. An interrogation into the politics of cultural persuasion and literary value that form the roots of that "special relationship" remains essential for efforts to conceive of more democratic and ethical futures.

Literary State-Building in Iraq

In the fall of 2004, the Library of America designed a new program to connect the state-building projects in Iraq and Afghanistan with the cultural power of the classics of American literature. The Library of America's subdivision LOA Worldwide announced that it would be sending one-hundred-volume sets of the Library of America to libraries and universities in Iraq and Afghanistan, funded through a private foundation and individual sponsors.[26] In the article announcing the program, the editors remind potential contributors that "previous governments made little or no investment in libraries for many years, and both countries have been wracked by war and economic and social turmoil for decades." Interestingly, the article makes no explicit reference to the U.S. military operations in Iraq or Afghanistan, other than to note that the program was designed with the consultation of the U.S. State Department's Bureau of Educational and Cultural Affairs. In this respect, Alberto M. Fernandez, the director for public diplomacy in the Office of Iraq Affairs, offers optimistically, "These books are very beneficial because they introduce (or in some cases reintroduce) the human and universal values that make America so attractive to the rest of the world—freedom, creativity, humanity, a restless and enquiring spirit." Fernandez adds, somewhat euphemistically, "this is a side of us that is sometimes lost, especially these days."

The article's plea for individual sponsorship of the volumes is thus pitched as a humanitarian effort to save Iraqis and Afghans from the destruction befallen their countries from unnamed sources; importantly, the words "war," "invasion," "sanctions," and "occupation" are conspicuously absent from the prose. In this picture, it is the misconduct of irresponsible or corrupt citizens themselves who, first by failing to invest in libraries and universities, and then by looting buildings, destroying classrooms, and destabilizing the intellectual culture of Iraq and Afghanistan, rendered

necessary this generous intervention. Rather than focus on political turmoil, opportunism, or greed, the reader is encouraged to contemplate the
enduring cultural values through which "Iraqis and Afghans have a deep
appreciation for books," and to be reassured that despite "years of conflict," the "demand for education is high."[27] Finally, the books are granted
a diplomatic function, that "readers . . . can gain a better understanding of
the United States and its culture." The book, in this manner, becomes the
ambassador of American goodwill, serving as both gesture of generosity
and archive of cultural values, meanings, and national identities.

The Library of America program has not received wide publicity, though by 2006 it had placed LOA sets in eighteen libraries in Iraq
and seven in Afghanistan.[28] It should be noted, however, that the effort
is in keeping with the pedagogical-as-humanitarian philosophy through
which the United States and its "coalition" forces have attempted to recast
the military aggression in Iraq into a democratic state-building effort. The
point was emphasized in a radio address in October 2003, when President
George W. Bush focused his remarks on the topic of education by outlining the strategic link between school programs and nation-building in
Iraq. Using language strikingly similar to that of McKinley's proclamation
of benevolent assimilation to outline the United States as a progressive,
liberating force, Bush isolated the importance of education as an essential
part of "efforts to build a stable and secure Iraq" and assured listeners that
"we are working to rebuild Iraq's schools, to get the teachers back to work
and to make sure Iraqi children have the supplies they need."[29] Important
to the effort was the construction of a stark contrast between the decadent rule of Saddam Hussein and the benevolent generosity of the United
States and the coalition forces: "During the decades of Saddam Hussein's
oppression and misrule, all Iraqis suffered, including children. While Saddam built palaces and monuments to himself, Iraqi schools crumbled.
While Saddam supported a massive war machine, Iraqi schoolchildren
went without books, and sometimes teachers went unpaid." By contrast,
Bush portrayed the United States as a marvel of efficiency in providing
the necessary infrastructure just months after the invasion: "Today, all 22
universities and 43 technical institutes and colleges are open, as are nearly
all primary and secondary schools in the country." Even better, listeners
were assured, the progress has exceeded all expectations: "Earlier this year
we said we would rehabilitate 1,000 schools by the time school started.
This month, just days before the first day of class, our coalition and our
Iraqi partners had refurbished over 1,500 schools."

Importantly, the speech lacked most specific details about the educational rebuilding project; reliable data on the actual rebuilding of schools, student enrollment and attendance, and the distribution of textbooks are difficult to come by, not in the least because the U.S. Agency for International Development (USAID) directed its subcontracting agency, Creative Associates International, Inc. (CAII), not to speak to the news media about the progress of its work; USAID also rejected a Freedom of Information Act request for the documents that resulted from external and internal audits of the rebuilding program.[30] What we do know is that since the military invasion of Iraq in 2003, more than $100 billion has been spent on education projects, largely funding private corporations through no-bid contracts who operate with little to no governmental oversight. However, a senior education advisor with the provisional authority in Iraq, Williamson M. Evers, declared a "mixed verdict" on the quality of the work, stating that while CAII had done well in preparing for the start of the school year, "all the other things in the contract that had to do with the longer-term development of the Education Ministry—and what is called capacity building—were not done well."[31] Others concurred with Evers's evaluation of the "poor, sloppy" work; one former employee of CAII reported that USAID had charged the firm with training 44,000 teachers, and the firm's concern to meet the appointed number outweighed any gauge of the effectiveness of the training or the teaching: "it doesn't matter who comes, where they come from . . . just count so that we have 44,000."[32]

Beyond the important question of war profiteering, one of the most crucial matters regarding the educational "reconstruction" of Iraq is that of curriculum design. In his radio address, Bush asserted that "Saddam used schools for his own purposes: to indoctrinate the youth of Iraq and to teach hatred"; by contrast, the work of the U.S. forces would help Iraq "rejoin the world" through a "modern" curriculum, presumably free from the subjective influence of politics: "we're working with UNESCO to print 5 million revised and modern textbooks free of Ba'athist propaganda, and to distribute them to Iraqi students." But this, in fact, was a point of considerable ideological tension as well as practical difficulty. Several news reports in October and November 2003 confirmed that there had been conflicts redesigning the textbooks for Iraq. The *Guardian* reported that 563 texts were "heavily edited and revised" in the summer of 2003, with "every image of Saddam and the Ba'ath party" removed.[33] In addition, the *Economist* disclosed that "the team revamping the curriculum has deleted anything deemed controversial, including any mention of the war between

Iraq and Iran in the 1980s, the Gulf War of 1991, all references to Jews and Israel, Shias, Sunnis and Kurds, and anything critical of America."[34]

The absurdity of touting a fully "modern" and "revised" textbook where, as a U.S. Defense Department employee put it, "entire swaths of the 20th century have been deleted," is outweighed only by the pronounced hubris with which U.S. officials reveal their own censorship in this process.[35] Though the textbook redesigning was reputed to be in the hands of Iraqis themselves, U.S. influence in this process was somewhat obscured from view but no less determined. As Gregg Sullivan of the Near Eastern Affairs Bureau of the State Department put it, "we will strongly recommend concepts of tolerance, and be against anything that is anti-semitic or anti-west-content that would sow the seeds for future intoler-ance." Clarifying the role of U.S. officials, he continued, "We hope it's only an advisory role, but if something develops that's disadvantageous to the Iraqi people, we'd weigh in on a stronger level."[36] Clearly, the language of paternalism is familiar here. One wonders by what expertise Sullivan can know what is "disadvantageous to the Iraqi people" and by what le-gitimate means the United States might make its own influence felt "on a stronger level." But it is not even left to the State Department to make such distinctions from the outside, as Fuad Hussein, the expatriate Iraqi in charge of the curriculum redesign effort, declares himself to be already on board with the program: "We considered anything anti-American to be propaganda."[37]

One also wonders, however, what the end result of such an education will be. Clearly, if any criticism of America is deemed "propaganda," then this constitutes a distinct attempt to foreclose the possibility of sustained, engaged critique of the United States and its role in the Middle East. In fact, given the history that this book has traced, this position is hardly surprising. What is more unexpected is the openness with which U.S. of-ficials have revealed these interests, thus giving the lie to the notion of de-mocracy promotion and democratic education as Bush and other officials promoted the system. Thus we see in Iraq a familiar utility of education in the service of empire. Functioning as a way of rationalizing the invasion by recourse to the avowed benevolent intentions of the occupation and its policies, the school system has also worked to establish the ideological conditions necessary for the continued U.S. presence by rewriting text-books, designing curriculum, and training teachers according to a prin-ciple of corporate education. Even according to neoconservative policy advocates, the centrality of education has been the result in no small part of its efficacy both as a form of social control and as a persuasive public relations device. Contrary to the charges of most of its critics, the issue is not simply one of war profiteering, though the work of CAII certainly indicates that such profit-mongering is at work. Rather, this is a paradigm of social engineering, an effort to "rebuild" Iraqi society that is every bit as militarized and instrumental to U.S. foreign policy as the process of Indian removal and assimilation, the "pacification" of the Philippine insurrection, and other such actions. The question is what kind of social order this produces, and what opportunities remain for contesting it. At stake, too, is the contemporary meaning of the field of American letters in light of its continued use as a pacifying measure and an index of cultural sophistication.

Such developments make all the more striking the academic revolution envisioned by the U.S. senior advisor to Iraq's Ministry of Education, Dr. John Agresto, who has promoted an education in the humanities as a "liberation of the mind" that would complement the political liberation of Iraq. As Agresto asserts: "I would worry about a country that was liberated politically but not intellectually. . . . For a country to produce leaders it has to be a country where the humanities can grow, where literature of the world is prized, where people can think clearly and write persuasively." He continues: "I'm not sure what good it is to free a country without freeing their mind."[38] Consider, too, the latest manifestation of the literature-for-democracy paradigm: as recently as June 2008, Slate.com contributor Christopher Hitchens called for a "book drive for Iraq" and urged Americans to "make a contribution, however small, to the effort to build democracy in Iraq" by donating books to "lay the foundation of a liberal and cosmopolitan education for the next generation of educated Iraqis."[39] In the face of such assertions about the instrumentality of the humanities in this new phase of U.S. imperialism, the question remains as to how scholars and critics in these fields will now understand the use-value of the work that they do, and become participants in the struggle over the meanings of our disciplines and the larger causes they serve.

Shalmali Guttal has argued that "reconstruction" must be understood as a euphemism for "sophisticated colonialism," part of the increasingly familiar strategy of what Naomi Klein has identified as the "predatory form of capitalism that uses desperation and fear created by catastrophe to engage in radical social and economic engineering."[40] In the wake of the powerful emergence of this "disaster capitalism" in the past decade, it behooves us to pay special care to the forms this social engineering is taking in Iraq and, on a smaller scale, in Afghanistan. What does it mean that the practice of English education is again being deployed in these newly occupied territories? How do we engage in the struggle for ethical political futures with the knowledge that humanism's intellectual project is presented, in the context of Iraq's "reconstruction," to be a liberation?

This book has endeavored to address the stakes of the discipline of American literary study by reading its origins in the struggle to assert and to maintain U.S. political dominance in the Philippines. More broadly, I have outlined how the impulse for imperial power became instrumental to the consolidation of the field as it was taught in the Philippines, where American literature was invested with a particular qualities of moral suasion and persuasive force deemed necessary as a counterpart to violent military action used to "subdue" the native resistance to U.S. rule and to rescript the project of imperial dominance as a program of benevolent tutelage. As E. San Juan Jr. has asked, "what is tutelage but a euphemism for the self-reproducing apparatus of colonial discourse, conforming to the requirements of capital accumulation?"[41] It is precisely through the discourse of tutelage that we witness the disciplinary structure of American literature take shape as a complement to the military domination and material exploitation of the islands, serving as the keystone in a curriculum designed to emphasize the linguistic, cultural, and political advancement of Anglo-Europeans and to win the consent of Filipinos to the benevolent authority of the colonial government. That the project failed to win Filipinos' consent, and that they continue to resist the cultural and political hegemony of the United States in no way diminishes the import of American literature's origins as an instrument of colonial rule.

Literary formations have political histories whose traces remain. At a time when scholars across the humanities are reacting with alarm to the very real threats to our fields' institutional health –university budget cuts, decreasing amounts of available outside funding, the scaling back of scholarly presses, and the pervasive culture of anti-intellectualism that challenges the very raison d'être of humanistic inquiry—it is worth reconsidering the complex histories that have produced these fields as we know them today. The irony of the fact that many bemoan the death of the humanities in the United States at a time when its intellectual traditions are being used in the hopes of facilitating U.S. economic and military exploitation in other regions should not be lost. This new imperialism uses the rhetoric of liberal studies not simply as a cover for its military interventions but as a training regimen for the next generation of pro-American political class. This should give us pause to consider the consequences of the instrumentalization of these fields, even as we undertake to resist the undoing of our institutional relevance. Such examples demonstrate that the work that literary scholars (and other humanists) perform is necessarily political. Whether Longfellow in the Philippines or the Library of America in Iraq and Afghanistan, the politics of English are vitally a part of our past programs of expansion and struggles for domination. My hope is that by illuminating the specificities of one aspect of this history, this book will contribute to the imaginings of alternative, more hopeful futures.

Notes

NOTES TO THE INTRODUCTION

1. Speech by Albert Beveridge before the U.S. Senate, Jan. 9, 1900, 56th Cong., 1st sess., *Congressional Record* 33, pt. 1 (1899–1900): 704–11.

2. This statement is attributed to a speech President McKinley made on November 21, 1899, as reported in General James Rushling, "Interview with President William McKinley," *Christian Advocate*, New York, January 22, 1903, in *The Philippines Reader: A History of Colonialism, Neocolonialism, Dictatorship, and Resistance*, ed. Daniel B. Schirmer and Stephen Rosskamm Shalom (Quezon City: KEN: 1987), 22–23.

3. Importantly, the Philippines were also home to the University of Santo Tomas, established in 1611 (twenty-five years before Harvard), and the large class of European-educated *ilustrados*. For more on the history of missionary work in Asia, see Jane Hunter, *The Gospel of Gentility: American Women Missionaries in Turn-of-the-Century China* (New Haven: Yale University Press, 1984); and Patricia Ruth Hill, *The World Their Household: The American Woman's Foreign Mission Movement and Cultural Transformation, 1870–1920* (Ann Arbor: University of Michigan Press, 1985).

4. Andrew Carnegie, "Distant Possessions—The Parting of the Ways," *North American Review* 167 (August 1898): 239.

5. William Dean Howells, quoted in William M. Gibson, "Mark Twain and Howells: Anti-Imperialists," *New England Quarterly* 20, no. 4 (December 1947): 437.

6. Col. E. Rice, 26th Infantry, U.S. Volunteers, reported in Elihu Root, *Education in the Philippines: Letter from the Secretary of War* (Washington, D.C.: U.S. Government Printing Office, 1901), 48, National Archives and Records Administration (hereafter NARA), Record Group (hereafter RG) 350, File 470, #15.

7. *Report of the First Philippine Commission to the Secretary of War* (Washington, D.C.: U.S. Government Printing Office, 1900), 17.

8. Phelps Whitmarsh, "Conditions in Manila," *Outlook* 63 (1899): 921, quoted in John Morgan Gates, *Schoolbooks and Krags: The United States Army in the Philippines, 1898–1902* (Westport, Conn.: Greenwood Press, 1973), 87.

9. Katherine Cook, "Public Education in the Philippine Islands," in *U.S. Bureau of Education Bulletins, 1935* (Washington, D.C.: U.S. Government Printing Office, 1935), 5.

10. Emma Sarepta Yule, *An Introduction to the Study of Colonial History for Use in Secondary Schools* (Manila: Bureau of Printing, 1912): 209, NARA, RG 350, File 2618, #68.

11. *Education in the Philippines,* May 15, 1902, anonymous pamphlet included in the NARA, RG 350, File 2618, #12; "Public Schools in Manila," *Washington Evening Star,* August 25, 1899, NARA, RG 350, File 470, #2.

12. E. San Juan Jr., *The Philippine Temptation: Dialectics of Philippines–U.S. Literary Relations* (Philadelphia: Temple University Press, 1996), 24.

13. I specify this period because, as other critics have charted, the idea of what constitutes the canon has gone through several important changes. Certainly the texts that I explore here, such as Stowe's *Uncle Tom's Cabin* and Longfellow's *Evangeline,* were notably absent from ideas about the canon that developed after World War I; likewise, the list of American authors that would become canonized by F. O. Matthiessen: Emerson, Thoreau, Melville, Whitman, and Hawthorne, are conspicuously absent from the reading lists developed in the Philippines (see *American Renaissance: Art and Expression in the Age of Emerson and Whitman* [New York: Oxford University Press, 1941]).

14. David Barrows, *Annual Report of the General Superintendent of Education, September 1904* (Manila: Bureau of Public Printing, 1904), 36.

15. Gauri Viswanathan, *Masks of Conquest: Literary Study and British Rule in India* (New York: Columbia University Press, 1989), 3. For more on the international politics of literature and imperial power, see Pascale Casanova, *The World Republic of Letters,* trans. M. B. DeBevoise (Cambridge: Harvard University Press, 2007).

16. Gerald Graff, *Professing Literature: An Institutional History* (Chicago: University of Chicago Press, 1987); Kermit Vanderbilt, *American Literature and the Academy: The Roots, Growth, and Maturity of a Profession* (Philadelphia: University of Pennsylvania Press, 1986); Arthur N. Applebee, *Tradition and Reform in the Teaching of English: A History* (Urbana: National Council of Teachers of English, 1974); Michael Warner, *The Letters of the Republic: Publication and the Public Sphere in Eighteenth-Century America* (Cambridge: Harvard University Press, 1990); Gerald Graff and Michael Warner, *The Origins of Literary Studies in America: A Documentary Anthology* (New York: Routledge, 1989).

17. Amy Kaplan and Donald Pease, *Cultures of U.S. Imperialism* (Durham: Duke University Press, 1993); Donald Pease and Robyn Wiegman, *The Futures of American Studies* (Durham: Duke University Press, 2002); John Carlos Rowe, *Literary Culture and U.S. Imperialism* (New York: Oxford University Press, 2000); José David Saldívar, *Border Matters: Remapping American Cultural Studies* (Berkeley and Los Angeles: University of California Press, 1997); and Lisa Lowe, *Immigrant Acts: On Asian American Cultural Politics* (Durham: Duke University Press, 1996), to name a very few.

18. According to the *Historical Statistics of the United States,* as of 1899, 42 percent of public day school students were enrolled in English courses, compared with 50.6 percent in Latin. By 1909, the numbers are reversed, with 49 percent for Latin and 57 percent for English. Statistics are published online at *Historical Statistics of the United States,* http://hsus. cambridge.org.proxy.library.cornell.edu/HSUSWeb/HSUSEntryServlet (accessed April 26, 2008).

19. Bureau of Education of the Philippine Islands, *Suggested Course of Study* (Manila: Bureau of Printing, 1902), NARA, RG 350, File 2618, #10.

20. *Selected Short Poems by Representative American Authors,* annotated by George W. St. Clair. (Manila: Bureau of Printers, 1911), 7–8.

21. See especially Paul A. Kramer, *The Blood of Government: Race, Empire, the United States, and the Philippines* (Chapel Hill: University of North Carolina Press, 2006); Stuart Creighton Miller, "Benevolent Assimilation": The American Conquest of the Philippines, *1899–1903* (New Haven: Yale University Press, 1982); Leon Wolff, *Little Brown Brother: How the United States Purchased and Pacified the Philippine Islands at the Century's Turn* (1960; repr., New York: History Book Club, 2006); Julian Go and Anne L. Foster, eds. *The American Colonial State in the Philippines: Global Perspectives* (Durham: Duke University Press, 2003); Renato Constantino, *The Philippines: A Past Revisited* (Manila: Tala, 1975); and Vicente Rafael, *White Love and Other Events in Filipino History* (Durham: Duke University Press, 2000).

22. Inquiries into the gender politics of the Spanish-Cuban-American War include Gail Bederman, *Manliness and Civilization: A Cultural History of Gender and Race in the United States, 1880–1917* (Chicago: University of Chicago Press, 1996); and Kristin L. Hoganson, *Fighting for American Manhood: How Gender Politics Provoked the Spanish-American and Philippine-American Wars* (New Haven: Yale University Press, 1998).

23. Extract from the report of Major General Arthur MacArthur, excerpted in Elihu Root, *Education in the Philippines: Letter from the Secretary of War* (Washington, D.C.: U.S. Government Printing Office, 1901), 48, NARA, RG 350, File 470, #15.

24. Louis Althusser, "Ideology and Ideological State Apparatuses," in *Lenin and Philosophy and Other Essays* (New York: Monthly Review Press, 1971), 181–82.

25. Ibid.

26. Senate Committee on the Philippines, *Affairs in the Philippine Islands,* 57th Cong., 1st sess., 1902., S. Doc. 331, pt. 1, 65–68.

27. Legislation against Chinese immigrants began with the Miners' License Tax Law in 1850, and the California State Supreme Court decision, in 1854, to deny Chinese residents the right to testify against white men in courts of law. The depression of the 1870s further fueled anti-Asian sentiment, particularly in areas with significant unemployment, where Asian immigrants, underpaid and exploited, were scapegoated for the lack of available jobs. The Chinese Exclusion Act of 1882 barred Chinese skilled and unskilled laborers from immigrating for ten years; it was the first major legislative act restricting immigration. It further defined Chinese residents in the United States as ineligible for citizenship, and required certification for Chinese residents to reenter the country upon leaving (see Lowe, *Immigrant Acts;* and Harry Kitano and Roger Daniels, *Asian Americans: Emerging Minorities* [New York: Prentice Hall, 1988]).

28. Michael Salman, *The Embarrassment of Slavery: Controversies over Bondage and Nationalism in the American Colonial Philippines* (Berkeley and Los Angeles: University of California Press, 2001), 26–27.

29. Quoted in Ronald T. Takaki, *Iron Cages: Race and Culture in Nineteenth-Century America* (New York: Knopf, 1979), 258.

30. Ibid., 258–59.

31. Albert J. Beveridge, "The Development of a Colonial Policy for the United States,"

Annals of the American Academy of Political and Social Science 30, no. 1 (July 1907): "opportunity," 11; "American markets," 13.

32. William McKinley, "Remarks to Methodist Delegation," in *The Philippines Reader: A History of Colonialism, Neocolonialism, Dictatorship, and Resistance*, ed. Daniel B. Schirmer and Stephen Rosskamm Shalom (Quezon City: KEN, 1987), 22.

33. David P. Barrows, "Education and Social Progress in the Philippines," *Annals of the American Academy of Political and Social Science* 30, no. 1 (July 1907): 69.

34. Dean C. Worcester, *The Philippines, Past and Present*, 2 vols. (New York: Macmillan, 1914), 501.

35. For a more detailed account of the regulation of hygiene and the colonial ideologies of sexuality, gender, and reproduction, see Laura Briggs, *Reproducing Empire: Sex, Science, and U.S. Imperialism in Puerto Rico* (Berkeley and Los Angeles: University of California Press, 2002); and Catherine Ceniza Choy, *Empire of Care: Nursing and Migration in Filipino American History* (Durham: Duke University Press, 2003).

36. United States Insular Commission, *Report of the United States Insular Commission to the Secretary of War upon Investigations Made into the Civil Affairs of the Island of Porto Rico, with Recommendations,* United States War Department, Division of Customs and Insular Affairs, June 9, 1899 (Washington D.C.: U.S. Government Printing Office, 1899), 53.

37. General John Eaton, "Education in Puerto Rico" (1900), in *Annual Reports of the Department of the Interior for the Fiscal Year Ended June 30, 1900, Report of the Commissioner of Education*, vol. 1, 56th Cong., H. Doc. 5 (Washington, D.C.: U.S. Government Printing Office, 1901), 251.

38. Henry K. Carroll, *Report on the Island of Porto Rico; Its Population, Civil Government, and Commerce, Industries, Productions, Roads, Tariff, and Currency, With Recommendations* (1899; repr., New York: Arno Press, 1975), 59.

39. Victor Selden Clark, *Teachers' Manual for the Public Schools of Puerto Rico* (New York: Silver, Burdett, 1900), 70.

40. United States Insular Commission, *Report of the United States Insular Commission to the Secretary of War upon Investigations Made into the Civil Affairs of the Island of Porto Rico, with Recommendations*, 21.

41. For a study of the curricular design of Puerto Rican schools under U.S. control, see José-Manuel Navarro, *Creating Tropical Yankees: Social Science Textbooks and U.S. Ideological Control in Puerto Rico, 1898–1908* (New York: Routledge, 2002); Aida Negrón de Montilla, *Americanization in Puerto Rico and the Public School System, 1900–1930* (Río Piedras, Puerto Rico: Editorial Edil, 1971); Sonia Nieto, "Puerto Rican Students in U.S. Schools: A Brief History," in *Puerto Rican Students in U.S. Schools*, ed. Sonia Nieto, 5–38 (Mahwah, N.J.: Erlbaum, 2000); and Juan José Osuna, *A History of Education in Puerto Rico* (New York: Arno Press, 1975).

42. Fred W. Atkinson, "Present Educational Movements in the Philippines," 417–18, Scrapbook 5, Bernard Moses Papers, Bancroft Library, University of California, Berkeley.

43. Navarro, *Creating Tropical Yankees* 125.

44. Samuel McCune Lindsay, *Report of the Commissioner of Education for Porto Rico* (1903), quoted in Navarro, *Creating Tropical Yankees*, 125.

45. For a reading of the feminist politics of nationalism, colonialism, and the history of U.S.–Hawaiian relations, see Haunani-Kay Trask, *From a Native Daughter: Colonialism and Sovereignty in Hawai'i* (Monroe, Me.: Common Courage Press, 1993). For a detailed reading of the history of education in Puerto Rico and its political stakes, see José Solís, *Public School Reform in Puerto Rico: Sustaining Colonial Models of Development* (Westport, Conn.: Greenwood Press, 1994), esp. 47–74. On the subject of the economic and political takeover of Hawai'i by representatives of U.S. business interests, see Gary Y. Okihiro's masterful *Pineapple Culture: A History of the Tropical and Temperate Zones* (Berkeley and Los Angeles: University of California Press, 2009).

46. Katherine M. Cook, *Public Education in Hawaii,* Bulletin, 1935, no. 10 (Washington, D.C.: U.S. Government Printing Office, 1935), 38.

47. Ibid., 45.

48. Peter Schmidt, *Sitting in Darkness: New South Fiction, Education, and the Rise of Jim Crow Colonialism, 1865–1920* (Jackson: University of Mississippi Press, 2008), 14, 110.

49. Yen Le Espiritu, *Filipino American Lives* (Philadelphia: Temple University Press, 1995), 9.

50. Julian Go, "The Chains of Empire," in *The American Colonial State in the Philippines: Global Perspectives,* ed. Julian Go and Anne L. Foster, 182–216 (Durham: Duke University Press, 2003).

51. Constantino, "Identity and Consciousness: The Philippine Experience," quoted in Espiritu, *Filipino American Lives,* 3.

52. Jefferson famously rallied for elementary education for all white residents of Virginia, but asserted that secondary education should be available only to those who could afford it. Others he referred to as "rubbish" who should instead learn the skills of the trades or of homemaking from their parents (see Thomas Jefferson, *Notes on the State of Virginia,* ed. Frank Shuffelton [New York: Penguin, 1999]; and James Bryant Conant, *Thomas Jefferson and American Public Education* [Berkeley and Los Angeles: University of California Press, 1962]).

53. Benjamin Franklin, *Idea of the English School, sketch'd out for the consideration of the trustees of the Philadelphia Academy* (Philadelphia: Printed by B. Franklin, 1751), 3.

54. Ibid., 8.

55. Frederick Douglass, *Narrative of the Life of Frederick Douglass, an American Slave, Written by Himself* (1845; repr., New York: Anchor Books, 1973), 36.

56. As I explain later in the introduction, in referencing the "public sphere" I do not mean to posit an idealized sphere of democratic access to and of "the public" but rather to consider how the idea of such publics are constituted through institutional forms, within historically specific contexts, and at the exclusion of other public forms.

57. For a detailed account of the educational opportunities and debates of the eighteenth century, see Lawrence A. Cremin, *American Education: The National Experience, 1783–1876* (New York: Harper and Row, 1980).

58. Lawrence A. Cremin, *The Transformation of the School: Progressivism in American Education, 1876–1957* (New York: Knopf, 1961), 8–9.

59. Horace Mann, *Annual Report on Education* (1848), quoted in Mike Starr, *Labor Looks at Education* (Cambridge: Harvard University Press, 1947).

60. Richard Brodhead notes that the first truancy officer was hired in Boston in 1850, under Mann's influence as secretary of the Massachusetts State Board of Education (see Horace Mann, *The Common School Controversy* [Boston: Dutton and Wentworth, 1844]; and Richard Brodhead, "Sparing the Rod: Discipline and Fiction in Antebellum America," *Representations* 21 [Winter 1988]: 74).

61. Brodhead, "Sparing the Rod," 75.

62. Cremin, *American Education*, 51.

63. Antonio Gramsci, *Selections from the Prison Notebooks*, trans. Quintin Hoare and Geoffrey Nowell Smith (New York: International, 1971), 57–58.

64. By 1860, most states had established some primary public school systems, though until the latter part of the century, public education was neither compulsory nor guaranteed. In 1852, Massachusetts was the first state to pass legislation establishing compulsory attendance, and the nation's first tax-supported public school system started in Illinois as late as 1855. Only 57 percent of eligible children were enrolled in school in 1870; few offered public secondary education like New York, Massachusetts, and Pennsylvania, and even fewer had public universities. Moreover, the development of public schooling varied widely by region, as many of the southern states established no popular schooling until after the Civil War (see Lawrence A. Cremin, *Traditions of American Education* [New York: Basic Books, 1976], 69; Cremin, *Transformation of the School*, 13; and R. Freeman Butts and Lawrence Cremin, *History of Education in American Culture* [New York: Holt, Rinehart and Winston, 1953], 357, 408). It took until the mid-1920s for the enrollment rate for both primary and secondary schools to reach 90 percent (Robert Franciosi, *The Rise and Fall of American Public Schools: The Political Economy of Public Education in the Twentieth Century* [Westport, Conn.: Praeger, 2004], 99–100).

65. Christopher Newfield, *Ivy and Industry: Business and the Making of the American University, 1880–1980* (Durham: Duke University Press, 2003), 45.

66. Ibid., 48.

67. Ibid., 46.

68. This is, to some degree, the success story repeated in many histories of education in the United States. See especially Cremin, *American Education*; Cremin, *The Transformation of the School*; and Butts and Cremin, *A History of Education in American Culture*.

69. Ward Churchill has estimated the number of casualties of the Indian boarding schools alone at as high as 50 percent of the children who attended them, the result of insufficient food, harsh living conditions, inadequate health care, and hard labor (see *Kill the Indian, Save the Man: The Genocidal Impact of American Indian Residential Schools* [San Francisco: City Lights Books, 2004], 29–50).

70. "Height of foolishness" is the characterization offered by William Roscoe Davis, a leading freedman of Hampton, Virginia; he is quoted in Robert Engs, *Freedom's First Generation: Black Hampton, Virginia, 1861–1890* (1979; repr., New York: Fordham University, 2004), 118. "Moral way" quoted in Engs, *Freedom's First Generation*, 119.

71. Laura Wexler, *Tender Violence: Domestic Visions in an Age of U. S. Imperialism* (Chapel Hill: University of North Carolina Press, 2000), 149.

72. For more on the history of Native American education, see Churchill, *Kill the Indian, Save the Man*; Jon Reyhner and Jeanne Eder, *American Indian Education: A History* (Norman: University of Oklahoma Press, 2004); and Frederick E. Hoxie, *A Final Promise: The Campaign to Assimilate the Indians, 1880–1920* (Lincoln: University of Nebraska Press, 1984).

73. As Jon Reyhner and Jeanne Eder note, "the difficulty of convincing parents to send their children to schools can be seen in the 1857 Pawnee treaty that stipulated that parents who refused to send their children to school regularly would have money deducted from their annuities" (*American Indian Education*, 47).

74. Jürgen Habermas, "The Public Sphere," *New German Critique* 3 (1974): 49.

75. Nancy Fraser, "Rethinking the Public Sphere: A Contribution to the Critique of Actually Existing Democracy," in *Habermas and the Public Sphere*, ed. Craig Calhoun (Cambridge: MIT Press, 1992).

76. George Eley, "Nations, Publics, and Political Cultures: Placing Habermas in the Nineteenth Century," in *Habermas and the Public Sphere*, ed. Craig Calhoun (Cambridge: MIT Press, 1992).

77. Anna Brickhouse, *Transamerican Literary Relations and the Nineteenth-Century Public Sphere* (Cambridge: Cambridge University Press, 2004), 27–28, 30.

78. Gramsci, *Selections from the Prison Notebooks*, 247.

79. See, for example, the collections *Tales of the American Teachers in the Philippines*, ed. Geronima T. Pecson and Maria Racelis (Manila: Carmelo and Bauermann, 1959); and Mary Racelis and Judy Celine Ick, eds., *Bearers of Benevolence: The Thomasites and Public Education in the Philippines* (Pasig City: Anvil Press, 2001).

80. See Vicente Rafael, "White Love: Census and Melodrama in the U. S. Colonization of the Philippines," in *White Love and Other Events in Filipino History* (Durham: Duke University Press, 2000), 19–51; and John D. Blanco, *Frontier Constitutions: Christianity and Colonial Empire in the Nineteenth-Century Philippines* (Berkeley and Los Angeles: University of California Press, 2009), 7.

81. Priya Joshi, *In Another Country: Colonialism, Culture, and the English Novel in India* (New York: Columbia University Press, 2002).

82. Lisa Lowe, "The Intimacies of Four Continents," in *Haunted by Empire*, ed. Ann L. Stoler (Durham: Duke University Press, 2006), 206.

83. C. J. Wan-ling Wee, *Culture, Empire, and the Question of Being Modern* (Lanham, Md.: Lexington Books, 2003).

84. This was the appellation given to Filipinos and other colonized peoples in Mark Twain's scathingly satirical critique of the U. S. and European colonial projects, "To the Person Sitting in Darkness" (*North American Review*, February 1901).

NOTES TO CHAPTER 1

1. R. W. B. Lewis, "1898–1907: The Founders' Story," in *A Century of Arts and Letters: The History of the National Institute of Arts & Letters*, ed. John Updike (New York: Columbia University Press, 1998), 1.

2. Address by Institute President Charles Dudley Warner, made before the meeting of the National Institute of Arts and Letters in New York City, January 30, 1900, quoted in Lewis, "The Founders' Story," 4.

3. Charles A. Fenton, "The Founding of the National Institute of Arts and Letters in 1898," *New England Quarterly* 32, no. 4 (December 1959): 437.

4. John Bigelow, chairman, "Report of the Executive Committee," circular letter to the members of the Academy, February 5, 1908, quoted in Louis Auchincloss, "1908–1917: Idealism and Patriotism," in *A Century of Arts and Letters: The History of the National Institute of Arts & Letters*, ed. John Updike (New York: Columbia University Press, 1998), 28.

5. Quoted in Lewis, "The Founders' Story," 20.

6. William Dean Howells, "Opening Address of the President," *Proceedings of the American Academy of Arts and Letters and of the National Institute of Arts and Letters* 1, no. 1 (June 10, 1910): 6.

7. Fenton, "The Founding of the National Institute of Arts and Letters in 1898."

8. This is a history illuminated in detail by Raymond Williams in *Marxism and Literature* (New York: Oxford University Press, 1977), 47–52.

9. Richard Brodhead, *Cultures of Letters: Scenes of Reading and Writing in Nineteenth-Century America* (Chicago: University of Chicago Press, 1993), 157.

10. Pierre Bourdieu elaborates on the notion of "symbolic capital" in *Outline of a Theory of Practice* (Cambridge: Cambridge University Press, 1977).

11. For a more detailed discussion of the value of the literary at the end of the nineteenth century, see David R. Shumway, *Creating American Civilization: A Genealogy of American Literature as an Academic Discipline* (Minneapolis: University of Minnesota Press, 1994), esp. 26–40.

12. Fenton, "The Founding of the National Institute of Arts and Letters in 1898," 435.

13. McKinley quoted in Paul A. Kramer, *The Blood of Government: Race, Empire, The United States and the Philippines* (Chapel Hill: University of North Carolina Press, 2006), 98.

14. Ibid.

15. William McKinley, "Instructions to the Taft Commission, April 7, 1900," in Maximo M. Kalaw, *The Development of Philippine Politics, 1872–1920* (Manila: Oriental Book Company, 1926), 459.

16. "Cultural capital" is John Guillory's phrase, derived from the work of Pierre Bourdieu, meant to resituate the canon debate with a more pointed focus on class, and to index the political stakes in the "production, exchange, distribution, and consumption" of forms of capital that are "specifically symbolic or cultural," of which literacy and canonical representation are a part. Canon-formation, according to Guillory, is "best understood as a problem in the constitution and distribution of cultural capital, or more specifically, a problem of access

to the means of literary production and consumption" that is regulated through the school as an institution which aids in "the *reproduction* of the social order, with all of its various inequalities" (see John Guillory, *Cultural Capital: The Problem of Literary Canon-Formation* [Chicago: University of Chicago Press, 1993], viii–ix).

17. Longer inquiries into the history of literature in the academy can be found in Gerald Graff, *Professing Literature: An Institutional History* (Chicago: University of Chicago Press, 1987); Kermit Vanderbilt, *American Literature and the Academy: The Roots, Growth, and Maturity of a Profession* (Philadelphia: University of Pennsylvania Press, 1986); Arthur N. Applebee, *Tradition and Reform in the Teaching of English: A History* (Urbana, Ill.: National Council of Teachers of English, 1974); and William Riley Parker, "Where Do English Departments Come From?" *College English* 28, no. 5 (February 1967). On the standardization of American literary texts, see Joseph Csicsila, *Canons by Consensus: Critical Trends and American Literature Anthologies* (Tuscaloosa: University of Alabama, 2004); Jane Tompkins, *Sensational Designs: The Cultural Work of American Fiction, 1790–1860* (New York: Oxford University Press, 1985); Paul Lauter, *Canons and Contexts* (New York: Oxford University Press, 1991); and Wendell V. Harris, "Canonicity," *PMLA* 106, no. 1 (January 1991). On literature in the high-school curriculum, see Joseph Mersand, "The Teaching of Literature in American High Schools, 1865–1900," in *Perspectives on English: Essays to Honor W. Wilbur Hatfield,* ed. Robert C. Pooley (New York: Appleton-Century-Crofts, 1960); and Ruth Windhover, "Literature in the Nineteenth Century," *English Journal: An Historical Primer on the Teaching of English* 68, no. 4 (April 1979). For an insightful reading of the cultural and political stakes of canon-formation, curriculum design, and literacy training, see Guillory, *Cultural Capital.*

18. Shumway, *Creating American Civilization,* 30.

19. See Horace Scudder, "The Place of Literature in Common School Education," in *Literature in School* (Boston: Houghton Mifflin, 1888).

20. Nina Baym, "Early Histories of American Literature: A Chapter in the Institutionalization of New England," *American Literary History* 1 (1989): 463.

21. Applebee, *Tradition and Reform,* 33.

22. Parker, "Where Do English Departments Come From?" 339–51.

23. Applebee, *Tradition and Reform,* 27–28.

24. Applebee traces the origins of English to three traditions: "An ethical tradition which placed its emphasis on moral and cultural development, a classical tradition of intellectual discipline and close textual study, and a nonacademic tradition more concerned with 'enjoyment' and 'appreciation'" (ibid., 1).

25. For more on the early primers and their function in the instruction of English, see Paul Leicester Ford, *The New England Primer* (New York: Teachers College, Columbia University, 1962).

26. The *Speller* was the first of Webster's three-volume compendium titled *The Grammatical Institute;* the second part, a grammar, and the third, a reader, followed in consecutive years. The *Speller* was notable, however, as a sign of the importance of language as constitutive of the national identity of the new Republic. For Webster, this meant standardizing

American English as distinct from the English of the nation's former colonial master, Great Britain.

27. Noah Webster, *Dissertation on the English Language* (Boston: Isaiah Thomas and Company, 1789), quoted in Noah Webster, "Declaration of Linguistic Independence," in *Language Loyalties: A Source Book on the Official English Controversy,* ed. James Crawford (Chicago: University of Chicago Press, 1992), 34.

28. Webster, "Declaration" in Crawford, *Language Loyalties,* 34.

29. Ibid.; "American," in Dennis Baron, "Federal English," in Crawford, *Language Loyalties,* 38.

30. Marc Shell, "Babel in America; or, The Politics of Language Diversity in the United States," *Critical Inquiry* 20 (Autumn 1993): 104.

31. Ibid., 105–6; Shirley Brice Heath, "Why No Official Tongue?" in Crawford, *Language Loyalties,* 20–31.

32. Eric Cheyfitz has detailed how the acquisition of English was an integral part of the attempted assimilation of Native peoples in North America, as well as their disenfranchisement and displacement, inasmuch as its very structure embodied a particular relationship to property that was incommensurate with most Native worldviews. This relation was outlined clearly by Jimmie Durham, a Cherokee, as he comments on the effects of the General Allotment Act of 1887: "The mere concept of parcels of owned land is an insult to Cherokees. . . . Talking about it is impossible; in our own language the possessive pronouns can only be used for things that you can physically give to another person, such as, 'my woodcarving,' 'my basket'" (quoted in Cheyfitz, *The Poetics of Imperialism Translation and Colonization from* The Tempest *to* Tarzan [New York: Oxford University Press, 1991], 8).

33. What is more, the early days of the Republic saw eager discussion about what language, if any, would be the national one. English-German bilingualism was considered, as well as the singular adoption of either German (already spoken by many colonists) or French (as a final blow to the pride of the British). Also considered was the revivification of an ancient language, such as Greek or Hebrew, "the language of that other 'chosen people'" (Shell, "Babel in America," 105, 108).

34. Vicente Rafael has written exquisitely about the relation between the privileging of American English and the historical formations of U.S. empire, in his essay "Translation, American English and the National Insecurities of Empire," *Social Text 101* 27, no. 4 (Winter 2009): 1–23.

35. For a more involved and detailed discussion of the secular makings of Webster's *Grammatical Institute* and the McGuffey readers, see Applebee, *Tradition and Reform,* 4.

36. The original McGuffey readers were a series of six books published by William Holmes McGuffey, though numerous editions proliferated and new versions continued to be published after his death.

37. John Pierpont, preface to the first edition of *The American First Class Book* (1820), quoted in George R. Carpenter, Franklin T. Baker, and Fred N. Scott, *The Teaching of English in the Elementary and the Secondary School* (New York: Longmans, Green, 1905), 43.

38. Some notable exceptions were attempted courses in English literature at Dartmouth

in 1822, Amherst in 1827, and Middlebury in 1848–49 (see Parker, "Where Do English Departments Come From?" 343).

39. This emphasis on grammar, with its regular and prescriptive study of rules and its rigid exercises of the parsing and diagramming of sentences, drew heavily from the standardized methods used in the study of classical languages. The College of New Jersey, which would later become Princeton, set an acquaintance with English grammar as a prerequisite for admission in 1819; this was the first example in which "competence in any aspect of the vernacular had been requited for entrance to any college in America" (Applebee, *Tradition and Reform*, 8). On university English, see Parker, "Where Do English Departments Come From?" 342; and Applebee, *Tradition and Reform*, 8–10.

40. This constituted a substantive divide between ways of using the literary and of conceiving of it as an object of study. Rhetoricians represented an older cadre aligned with the tradition of appreciation—one that held that the literary had moral and spiritual value which, upon contact, would edify and ennoble the reader or listener. The best example of this was Cornell professor Hiram Corson, who posited a theory of "interpretive reading" in which the literary work's true import would be gained not through scholarship but proper oral delivery. Corson argued that the poem reached the "non-intellectual, non-discursive" part of man, expressing his "essential absolute being," and devoted his classes to oral performance, "thundering Shakespeare to his classes" in the style of an evangelical preacher on a mission to save souls through literature. A less spectacular example would be found in future U. S. president Woodrow Wilson's oft-cited essay "Mere Literature," published in *Atlantic Monthly* in 1893. Then a professor of political economy at Princeton, Wilson argued against specialized research and linguistic methodology, instead glorifying the literary as an "expression of spirit" that "has a quality to move you . . . if you have any blood in you," and that "has also a power to instruct you which is as effective as it is subtle (Hiram Corson, *The Voice and Spiritual Education* [1896], quoted in Gerald Graff, *Professing Literature: An Institutional History* [Chicago: University of Chicago Press, 1987], 48).

41. Similarly, Wordsworth claimed for the poet the place as "the rock of defence for human nature," an artist who "binds together by passion and knowledge the vast empire of human society." Shelley quoted in Applebee, *Tradition and Reform*, 23. Wordsworth quoted from the Preface to *Lyrical Ballads*, quoted in Raymond Williams, *Culture and Society, 1780–1950* (1958; repr., New York: Columbia University Press, 1983), 41.

42. Matthew Arnold, *Culture and Anarchy* (New York: Oxford University Press, 2006), 37.

43. See Jim McWilliams and Cicero Bruce, "Matthew Arnold's Visit to St. Louis," *Nineteenth-Century Literature* 50, no. 2 (September 1995): 225–31; and Chilson Hathaway Leonard, "Arnold in America: A Study of Matthew Arnold's Literary Relations with America and of His Visits to This Country in 1883 and 1886" (Ph.D. diss., Yale University, 1932).

44. See Edna Hays, *College Entrance Requirements in English: Their Effects on the High Schools* (New York: Teachers College, Columbia University, 1936), 31; Carpenter, Baker, and Scott, *The Teaching of English in the Elementary and the Secondary School*, 134; and Arthur N. Applebee, *Tradition and Reform*, 31. This method quickly became standard when, one year later, the Commission of New England Colleges on Admission Examinations approved it.

Such changes quickly spread beyond New England to other regions and institutions, such as the University of Illinois, which based its entrance examination of 1896 on knowledge of the content of pre-assigned "classics," including Shakespeare's *A Midsummer Night's Dream,* Irving's *Tales of a Traveler,* and Longfellow's *Evangeline"* (see John E. Stout, *The Development of High School Curricula in the North Central States from 1860–1918* [Chicago: University of Chicago Press, 1921]; and Mersand, "The Teaching of Literature in American High Schools, 1865–1900").

45. See Francis H. Stoddard, "Conference on Uniform Entrance Requirements in English," *Educational Review* (1905): 375–83.

46. Peter Novick, *That Noble Dream: The "Objectivity Question" and the American Historical Profession* (New York: Cambridge University Press, 1998), 48.

47. Laurence Veysey, "The Plural Organized Worlds of the Humanities," in *The Organization of Knowledge in Modern America, 1860–1920,* ed. Alexandra Oleson and John Voss (Baltimore: Johns Hopkins University Press, 1979), 71. For more on the development of the field of history, see Ian Tyrrell, "Making Nations/Making States: American Historians in the Context of Empire," *Journal of American History* 86 (1999): 1015–44; and Thomas Bender, "Introduction: Historians, the Nation and the Plentitude of Narratives," in *Rethinking American History in a Global Age* (Berkeley and Los Angeles: University of California Press, 2002), esp. 1–12; 19–21.

48. Michael A. Elliott, *The Culture Concept: Writing and Difference in the Age of Realism* (Minneapolis: University of Minnesota Press, 2002), 4. Two of the field's main journals, *American Anthropologist* and *Journal of American Folk-Lore,* appeared for the first time in 1888. See also Dorothy Ross, *The Origins of American Social Science* (New York: Cambridge University Press, 1991).

49. Fascinating in this regard is Nina Baym's study of the "canonizing" of *The Scarlet Letter* and *Moby-Dick,* which became classics of American literature through two very different routes (see "Hawthorne's *Scarlet Letter*: Producing and Maintaining an American Literary Classic," *Journal of Aesthetic Education* 30, no. 2 [Summer 1996]: 61–75).

50. *Report of the First Philippine Commission* (Washington, D.C.: U. S. Government Printing Office, 1900), 1:17.

51. Ibid., 1:34.

52. Ibid.

53. Capt. Albert Todd, quoted in Elihu Root, *Education in the Philippines: Letter from the Secretary of War* (Washington, D.C.: U. S. Government Printing Office, 1901), 48, NARA, RG 350, File 470, #15.

54. Records of soldiers' activity indicate that soldiers began teaching in Corregidor in August 1898, and opened seven schools in September of that year (see Leonardo Estioko, *History of Education: A Filipino Perspective* [Manila: Society of Divine Word, 1994], 186; Dalmacio Martin, *A Century of Education in the Philippines: 1861–1961* [Manila: Philippine Historical Association, 1980], 117; and Isabel Pefianco Martin, "Longfellow's Legacy: Education and the Shaping of Philippine Writing," *World Englishes* 23, no. 1 [2004]: 129–39).

55. Capt. Albert Todd, Sixth Artillery, quoted in Frederick W. Nash, "Education in the Philippines," *Educational Review* 22, no. 3 (October 1901): 218.

56. Katherine Cook, "Public Education in the Philippine Islands," in *U. S. Bureau of Education Bulletins, 1935* (Washington, D.C.: U. S. Government Printing Office, 1935).

57. Quoted in Fred W. Atkinson, "Present Educational Movements in the Philippines," 15, Scrapbook 5, Bernard Moses Papers, Bancroft Library, University of California, Berkeley.

58. Moses was a professor of history and political science from the University of California; Fred W. Atkinson had been a high-school principal from Springfield, Massachusetts; David P. Barrows was an anthropologist from California whose research on the Native Americans of Southern California first landed him the job as head of the Bureau of Non-Christian Tribes in the Philippines before becoming the superintendent of schools in Manila and then the general superintendent of public instruction for the Philippines. After their work in the Philippines, both Moses and Barrows returned to the United States to work at the University of California, Berkeley.

59. The original draft of the bill, as well as the suggested revisions of Superintendent Fred Atkinson, can be found in Atkinson, "Present Educational Movements," 24–45.

60. McKinley, quoted in Kalaw, *The Development of Philippine Politics,* 457.

61. May, *Social Engineering,* 83.

62. Extract from the Report of Major General Arthur MacArthur, printed in Elihu Root, *Education in the Philippines: Letter from the Secretary of War* (Washington, D.C.: U. S. Government Printing Office, 1901), 48, NARA, RG 350, File 470, #15.

63. "Extract of Reports Rendered by Brig. Gen. S. B. M. Young, excerpted in Elihu Root, *Education in the Philippines: Letter from the Secretary of War* (Washington, D.C.: U. S. Government Printing Office, 1901), 48, NARA, RG 350, File 470, #15.

64. It will be of interest, perhaps, that Dean C. Worcester was the grandson of the abolitionist Samuel Worcester, who argued on behalf of the Cherokee in the landmark case *Worcester v. Georgia* in 1832. The status of Native Americans as "domestic dependent wards of the nation" that resulted from the decision in that case bear a striking resemblance to the status Dean Worcester seemed to envision for Filipinos, against whose independence he argued vociferously (see Michael Salman, *The Embarrassment of Slavery,* 34).

65. "The Philippine Report," *Harper's Weekly* 43, no. 2239 (1899): 1154.

66. "The Native Peoples of the Philippines," in *Report of the First Philippine Commission,* 1:11.

67. Ibid., 1:15.

68. "Preliminary Report: Capacity for Self-Government" (November 2, 1899), in *Report of the First Philippine Commission,* 1:182.

69. "Spanish Language Rights in California: Constitutional Debates," excerpted from *Debates and Proceedings of the Constitutional Convention of the State of California, 1878–1879* (Sacramento, 1880–81), 2:801–2, in Crawford, *Language Loyalties,* 51–57.

70. Examples of these would be the Philippine Education series, in which were published *The First Year Book, The Second Year Book,* etc. (New York and Manila: World Book, 1907); the Philippine English series, which featured grade-specific readers starting in 1904 (Boston: Ginn, 1904); and Mary Fee, *Constructive Lessons in English* (Manila: Bureau of Printing, 1910).

71. Though lessons on hygiene and manners formed part of every course of study, there were specific guidelines given to teachers on this point as well (see, for example, *Outline of Teaching of Manners and Right Conduct* [1905], in NARA, RG 350, File 2618, #44). On the larger implications of this, see Warwick Anderson, *Colonial Pathologies: American Tropical Medicine, Race, and Hygiene in the Philippines* (Durham: Duke University Press, 2006).

72. Sidney C. Newsom and Levona Payne Newsom, *Primer,* Philippine English series (Boston: Ginn, 1904), 3.

73. Newsom and Newsom, Philippine English series; Mary Fee, *The First Year Book* (New York and Manila: World Book, 1907); Mary Fee, "Learning English: A Plea for New Methods," *Teachers' Assembly Herald,* May 11, 1911, 113–15.

74. Emma Sarepta Yule, *An Introduction to the Study of Colonial History* (Manila: Bureau of Printing, 1912), 207–8. See also Prescott F. Jernegan, *The Philippine Citizen: A Text-book of Civics, Describing the Nature of Government, the Philippine Government, and the Rights and Duties of Citizens of the Philippines* (Manila: Philippine Education Publishers, 1907); *Course of Study in Character Education and Citizenship* (Manila: Bureau of Printing, 1938).

75. Arthur Stanley Riggs, *The Filipino Drama, 1905* (Manila: Ministry of Human Settlements, Intramuros Administration, 1981), 1, 6, 20, quoted in Kramer, *The Blood of Government,* 197.

76. "Philippine English," *Philippine Teacher* 2, no. 9 (February 1906): 1.

77. Everett E. Thompson, "Exhibit C: Civil Service in Oriental Possessions," in *4th Annual Report of the Philippine Civil Service Board: Report of the Philippine Commission to the Secretary of War for 1904,* 259–68 (Washington, D.C.: U.S. Government Printing Office, 1905), quoted in Kramer, *The Blood of Government,* 204.

78. Bernard Moses, "American Control of the Philippines," handwritten and printed manuscript, 1913: 104, Carton 1, Bernard Moses Papers.

79. *Report of the First Philippine Commission,* 1:38.

80. Ibid., 1:32.

81. Atkinson, "Present Educational Movements," 122, 251.

82. David P. Barrows, "Education and Social Progress in the Philippines," *Annals of the American Academy of Political and Social Science* 30 (July 1907): 74.

83. Russell C. Langdon, first lieutenant, Third Artillery, Bulacan, excerpted in Elihu Root, *Education in the Philippines: Letter from the Secretary of War* (Washington, D.C.: U.S. Government Printing Office, 1901), 48, NARA, RG 350, File 470, #15.

84. Ruter W. Springer, chaplain, U.S. Army, Angeles, P.I., excerpted in Elihu Root, *Education in the Philippines: Letter from the Secretary of War* (Washington, D.C.: U.S. Government Printing Office, 1901), 48, NARA, RG 350, File 470, #15.

85. Pardo de Tavera to Arthur MacArthur, May 14, 1901, NARA, RG 350, File 364, #23.

86. Franz Boas was key to the institutionalization of anthropology but also to the popularization of a particular classification of culture and race that was integral to the management of difference both within and outside of the expanding borders of the United States at the end of the nineteenth century. As both a museum anthropologist and, later, a professor of anthropology at Columbia University, Boas's career included essential venues for the popular

digestion of his notions of culture (including his work for the Chicago World's Fair in 1893), as well as situating him at the center of professional, academic anthropology (see Michael Elliott, *The Culture Concept: Writing and Difference in the Age of Realism*, esp. 1–34). Similarly, Neil Smith has compellingly argued that Isaiah Bowman served as such a figure for the field of geography. Part of the first generation of university-trained geographers, Bowman was influential as an academic and a politician, working as president of Johns Hopkins University and of the American Geographical Society as well as serving in Franklin D. Roosevelt's State Department. From such positions, Bowman was able to work both toward the professionalization of geography as a discipline and to popularize/develop the tools of political geography that were crucial to the exploitation of world resources for U.S. capital and the maintenance of American hegemony after World War II. Smith argues, in fact, that Bowman's notion of "trusteeship" was meant to disturb the advancement of British colonialism in favor of self-determination, effectively replacing the colonial notion of territorial control in favor of a form of globalization that privileged the opening up access to both resources and markets across the globe (see Neil Smith, *American Empire: Roosevelt's Geographer and the Prelude to Globalization* [Berkeley and Los Angeles: University of California Press, 2003]).

87. Henry Luce, "The American Century," in *The Ambiguous Legacy*. ed. Michael J. Hogan (Cambridge: Cambridge University Press. 1999), 11–29. Originally published in *Life* magazine, February 7, 1941.

88. Thomas Babington Macaulay, *Speeches by Lord Macaulay, with the Minute on Indian Education*, ed. G. M. Young (London: Oxford University Press, 1935); Gauri Viswanathan, *Masks of Conquest: Literary Study and British Rule in India* (New York: Oxford University Press, 1989).

89. Viswanathan, *Masks of Conquest*, 37.

90. U.S. Senate, *Affairs in the Philippine Islands. Hearings before the Committee on the Philippines of the United States Senate*. 57th Cong., 1st sess., 1902, S. Doc. 331, 699.

91. Ibid., 702.

92. Barrows to Bailey, January 9, 1901, Folder: "Jan.–Nov. 1901," Box 1, David P. Barrows Papers, Bancroft Library, University of California, Berkeley; Atkinson, "Present Educational Movement," 369.

93. Bernard Moses, "The Education of the Stranger," *San Francisco Bulletin*, August 28, 1903, Carton 1, Bernard Moses Papers.

94. Bernard Moses, "Use of the English Language in Schools," handwritten manuscript, n.d., 9, Carton 2, Bernard Moses Papers.

95. Atkinson, "Present Educational Movement," 417–18.

96. U.S. Senate, *Affairs in the Philippine Islands*, 697.

97. Ibid., 702, 699.

98. Moses, "Education of the Stranger," 4–5.

99. Moses, "American Control of the Philippines," 105.

100. Bernard Moses, "The Philippine Assembly," handwritten manuscript, n. d., 2–3, Carton 1, Bernard Moses Papers.

101. Moses, "American Control of the Philippines," 105. Moses justified this distinction

on the basis of literature: "This difference in policy is justified by the different conditions of the two countries. In the first place, the native languages of India are languages of cultivation. There exists in each of those most widely used an extensive literature adequate for the principal intellectual needs of a civilized people. This literature, embracing poetry, books of religion, and laws, cannot be set aside without destroying an important force among the people that makes for civilization. The Filipinos have no such literature in any of their various dialects; and, therefore, to teach them the English language and open to them the views of the world that may be gained through the use of that tongue is not to subject them to any intellectual loss, but, on the other hand, to furnish them a most powerful stimulus to intellectual progress. . . .The civilization of India is a native product, tempered and modified by English influence. In so far as the inhabitants of the Philippine Islands are civilized, their civilization is an European product spread over a barbaric past. . . . The only language of cultivation available to the Filipinos is a European language" (Moses, "Use of the English Language in Schools," 5–7).

102. Atkinson, "Present Educational Movement," 62, 273–307.

103. Bernard Moses, "In the Wilds of the Philippines," 7, Carton 1, Bernard Moses Papers.

104. *Annual Report of the Commissioner of Indian Affairs to the Secretary of the Interior* (Washington, D.C.: U.S. Government Printing Office, 1878), xxv–xxvi, 174. "Destitute," from William Swinton, *A Condensed School History of the United States* (New York: Ivison, Blakeman and Taylor, 1875), 21, quoted in John Reyhner, "Policies toward American Indian Languages: A Historical Sketch," in Crawford, *Language Loyalties*, 42.

105. Francis Paul Prucha, ed., *Americanizing the American Indians* (Cambridge: Harvard University Press, 1973), 199.

106. J. D. C. Atkins, *Annual Report of the Commissioner of Indian Affairs* (Washington, D.C.: U.S. Government Printing Office, 1887), quoted in Crawford, *Language Loyalties*, 51.

107. Lonna M. Malmsheimer, "'Imitation White Man': Images of Transformation at the Carlisle Indian School," *Studies in Visual Communication* 2 (Fall 1985): 69.

108. Reyhner, "Policies toward American Indian Languages," 41–47.

109. Leti Volpp, "American Mestizo: Filipinos and Antimiscegenation Laws in California," *U.S. Davis Law Review* 33 (Summer 2000): 829.

110. Jacob Gould Schurman, *Philippine Affairs: A Retrospect and Outlook* (New York: Charles Scribner's Sons, 1902), 41–42.

111. U.S. Senate, 56th Cong., 1st sess., Jan. 9, 1900, 710.

NOTES TO CHAPTER 2

Epigraph: Printed in General James F. Smith, "An Address Delivered at the Zorrilla Theatre, Manila, December 30, 1905," *Philippine Teacher: A Periodical for Philippine Progress* 2, no. 7 (December 1905): 4 (my italics).

1. Harriet Beecher Stowe, *Uncle Tom's Cabin*, ed. Elizabeth Ammons (New York: Norton, 1994), 217. Hereafter cited parenthetically.

2. Declaring an end date of the Philippine-American War is difficult, particularly because

U. S. officials proclaimed its finale not once, but three times, each while the resistance continued. Current official documents date the close of the war to 1902, though hostilities continued until 1913.

3. Twain's work in this regard is compiled in Jim Zwick, *Mark Twain's Weapons of Satire: Anti-Imperialist Writings on the Philippine-American War* (Syracuse: Syracuse University Press, 1992). For an unabashedly pro-imperialist view, see Albert J. Beveridge, *The Meaning of the Times and Other Speeches* (Indianapolis: Bobbs-Merrill, 1908).

4. For more thorough discussion of the insular cases which decided the legal status of the United States' insular possessions, see Christina Duffy Burnett and Burke Marshall, eds., *Foreign in a Domestic Sense: Puerto Rico, American Expansion, and the Constitution* (Durham: Duke University Press, 2001); and Amy Kaplan, *The Anarchy of Empire in the Making of U. S. Culture* (Cambridge: Harvard University Press, 2002), 1–12.

5. *Uncle Tom's Cabin* was the best-selling novel of the century, surpassed in book sales only by the Bible.

6. On the centrality of Little Eva's death to nineteenth-century mourning and spiritualism, see Bridget Bennett, "Spirited Away: The Death of Little Eva and the Farewell Performances of 'Katie King,'" *Journal of American Studies* 40, no. 1 (2006): 1–16.

7. George Sand, "Review of *Uncle Tom's Cabin,*" *La Presse*, December 17, 1852, included in Stowe, *Uncle Tom's Cabin*, 462.

8. Ibid.

9. Ann Douglas, *The Feminization of American Culture* (New York: Knopf, 1977), 3–4.

10. Jane Tompkins, "Sentimental Power: *Uncle Tom's Cabin* and the Politics of Literary History," *Glyph* 2 (1978), included in Stowe, *Uncle Tom's Cabin*, 507.

11. Ibid., 507.

12. Ibid., 512–13.

13. Hortense J. Spillers, "Changing the Letter: The Yokes, the Jokes of Discourse, or, Mrs. Stowe, Mr. Reed," in *Slavery and the Literary Imagination*, ed. Deborah McDowell and Arnold Rampersad (Baltimore: Johns Hopkins University Press, 1989), 43.

14. Rayford W. Logan, *The Betrayal of the Negro: From Rutherford B. Hayes to Woodrow Wilson*, rev. ed. (1965; repr., New York: Da Capo Press, 1997).

15. This statistic is reported in Vron Ware, *Beyond the Pale: White Women, Racism, and History* (London: Verso, 1992), 171.

16. Richard Slotkin, *Gunfighter Nation: The Myth of the Frontier in Twentieth-Century America* (New York: Macmillan, 1992), 114.

17. Andrew Wadsworth, in a letter to aunt Jennie Wadsworth, March 8, 1899, Folder 173, Hussey-Wadsworth Papers, Clements Library, University of Michigan; Earl Pearsall Diary, Folder: "Pearsal, Earl, 1898–W-1521, 1st Neb. Vol. Inf., Diary for 1899," Box 97, Nebraska Infantry, 1st Regiment, SAWS, February 24, 1899, quoted in Paul A. Kramer, *The Blood of Government: Race, Empire, the United States, and the Philippines* (Chapel Hill: University of North Carolina Press, 2006), 125.

18. Kramer, *The Blood of Government*, 130–45.

19. For a more thorough discussion of Asian immigration and U. S. exclusion acts, see

Lisa Lowe, *Immigrant Acts: On Asian American Cultural Politics* (Durham: Duke University Press, 1996); and Leti Volpp, "American Mestizo: Filipinos and Antimiscegenation Laws in California," *U. S. Davis Law Review* 33 (Summer 2000): 795–835.

20. Nellie Foster, Inter-Racial Council of San Diego, to Mr. L. E. Lampton, County Clerk of Los Angeles, Nov. 7, 1930, quoted in Volpp, "American Mestizo," 813–14.

21. Hugh Tinker, *A New System of Slavery: The Export of Indian Labour Overseas, 1830–1920* (London: Oxford University Press, 1974), 69–70, quoted in Moon-Ho Jung, "Outlawing 'Coolies': Race, Nation, and Empire in the Age of Emancipation," *American Quarterly* (November 2005): 680.

22. Moon-Ho Jung, "Outlawing 'Coolies.'"

23. David Starr Jordan, *The Question of the Philippines: An Address Delivered before the Graduate Club of Leland Stanford Junior University, February 14, 1899* (Palo Alto, Calif.: J. J. Valentine, 1899), 20, 54, quoted in Michael Salman, *The Embarrassment of Slavery: Controversies over Bondage and Nationalism in the American Colonial Philippines* (Berkeley and Los Angeles: University of California Press, 2001), 32.

24. Its presence haunts the text, however. When St. Clare warns of a coming "San Domingo hour," prophesying that the "divine law in our times" is "that the masses are to rise, and the under class become the upper one" (234), his casual mention belies the actual threat that the Haitian revolution posed to the stability of the American slave system.

25. See Carolyn Vellenga Berman, "Creole Family Politics in *Uncle Tom's Cabin* and *Incidents in the Life of a Slave Girl*," *NOVEL: A Forum on Fiction* 33, no. 3 (Summer 2000): 328–52; and Robin Blackburn, *The Overthrow of Colonial Slavery, 1776–1848* (New York: Verso, 1988).

26. See Blackburn, 275–80, and Paul F. Lachance, "The Foreign French," in *Creole New Orleans: Race and Americanization*, ed. Arnold R. Hirsch and Joseph Logsdon (Baton Rouge: Louisiana State University Press, 1992), 101–30.

27. This relation is discussed in more detail in Gillian Brown, *Domestic Individualism: Imagining Self in Nineteenth-Century America* (Berkeley and Los Angeles: University of California Press, 1990).

28. Laura Wexler, *Tender Violence: Domestic Visions in an Age of U. S. Imperialism* (Chapel Hill: University of North Carolina Press, 2000), 101–2.

29. Samuel Chapman Armstrong, quoted in Robert F. Engs, *Freedom's First Generation: Black Hampton, Virginia, 1861–1890* (1979; repr., New York: Fordham University, 2004), 114.

30. I am referring to Frances Benjamin Johnston's photographs of Hampton Institute, taken in December 1899. These are collected in Lincoln Kirstein, ed., *The Hampton Album* (New York: Museum of Modern Art, 1966), 12–15. Wexler offers a stunning reading of these in *Tender Violence*, 127–76.

31. Samuel Chapman Armstrong, *Proceedings of the Department of Superintendence, Circulars of Information*, No. 3 (Washington, D.C.: Bureau of Education, 1883), 139, quoted in Jacqueline Fear-Segal, "Nineteenth-Century Indian Education: Universalism Versus Evolutionism," *Journal of American Studies* 33, no. 2 (1999): 323.

32. Francis Greenwood Peabody, *Education for Life: The Story of Hampton Institute* (New York: Doubleday, Page, 1918), 118–19.

33. "Conviction," from Armstrong, *Report of the Principal of Hampton* 1888, quoted in Fear-Segal, 331; "domestic arts" from Hollis Burke Frisell, untitled article, *Southern Workman* 14 (June 1885): 85, quoted in Wexler, *Tender Violence*, 130.

34. *Annual Reports for Academic and Fiscal Year Ending June, 1880* (Hampton, 1880), 5–6, quoted in Engs, *Freedom's First Generation*, 116.

35. For example, Stowe's donation of one thousand dollars from the royalties of *Uncle Tom's Cabin* enabled the opening of the Colored Girls School in Washington, D.C., which offered primary school and classes in domestic arts (see Robert McHenry, ed., *Famous American Women: A Biographical Dictionary from the Colonial Times to the Present* [Boston: Dover, 1983], 284).

36. Harriet Beecher Stowe to her brother Charles Beecher, quoted in Mary B. Graff's biographical introduction to Stowe's memoir, *Palmetto Leaves* (1873; repr., Gainesville: University of Florida Press, 1968), x.

37. Joan D. Hedrick, *Harriet Beecher Stowe: A Life* (New York: Oxford University Press, 1994), 341.

38. Stowe, *Palmetto-Leaves*, 317.

39. Charles W. Dabney and George T. Winston, quoted in James D. Anderson, *The Education of Blacks in the South, 1860–1935* (Chapel Hill: University of North Carolina Press, 1988), 85. Michael Dennis asserts that "progressive" southern educators were in fact crucial in advocating for an industrial education system that effectively maintained racial control in the post-Emancipation South (see Dennis, "Schooling along the Color Line: Progressives and the Education of Blacks in the New South," *Journal of Negro Education* 67, no. 2 [1998]: 142–56).

40. Richard Henry Pratt, quoted in Lonna M. Malmsheimer, "'Imitation White Man': Images of Transformation at the Carlisle Indian School," *Studies in Visual Communication* 2 (Fall 1985): 55.

41. See Ward Churchill, *Kill the Indian, Save the Man: The Genocidal Impact of American Indian Residential Schools* (San Francisco: City Lights Books, 2004); Frederick E. Hoxie, *A Final Promise: The Campaign to Assimilate the Indians, 1880–1920* (Lincoln: University of Nebraska, 1984); and Jon Allan Reyhner and Jeanne Eder, *American Indian Education: A History* (Norman: University of Oklahoma Press, 2004).

42. Helen Sekaquaptewa, quoted in Churchill, *Kill the Indian, Save the Man*, 25.

43. William H. Taft to Fred Atkinson, memorandum, May 5, 1900, NARA, RG 350, File 470, #5.

44. Fred Atkinson, "Present Educational Movement in the Philippines," typescript, Bernard Moses Papers, Bancroft Library, University of California, Berkeley, Scrapbook 5, p. 414.

45. William Roscoe Davis, quoted in Engs, *Freedom's First Generation*, 118.

46. Fred Atkinson to Booker T. Washington, April 8, 1900, Booker T. Washington Papers, container 166, Manuscripts Division, Library of Congress, quoted in May, *Social Engineering*, 89–92.

47. Horace Taft to William Howard Taft, February 19, 1901, series 1, box 32, William Howard Taft Papers, Manuscripts Division, Library of Congress, Washington, D.C., quoted in May, *Social Engineering*, 92.

48. "Tender violence" is Samuel Armstrong's phrase, used in reference to the discipline needed when working with African American students; it is quoted in Laura Wexler's eloquent and insightful book by the same name. I repeat it here because it so precisely and sinisterly foreshadows the violent repression enacted under the name of benevolence in the Philippines (see Wexler, *Tender Violence*, 108).

49. "Industrial Work," *Philippine Teacher* 2, no. 2 (July 1905): 22.

50. Salman, *The Embarrassment of Slavery*, 32.

51. Armstrong quoted in Peabody, *Education for Life*, 118.

52. The Lake Mohonk Conference of Friends of the Indians and Other Dependent Peoples was founded in 1883 as a venue for officials, missionaries, and reformers to discuss the progress of current Indian policy. Thoroughly imbued with an ethos of Christian paternalism, it expanded its mission and amended its name, in 1898, to address the incorporation of new "dependent" peoples. On the Lake Mohonk conferences, see Larry E. Burgess, "The Lake Mohonk Conferences on the Indian, 1883–1916" (Ph.D. diss., Claremont Graduate School, 1972). For comparisons between Native Americans and Filipinos in official and reformist policy, see Walter L. Williams, "United States Indian Policy and the Debate over Philippine Annexation: Implications for the Origins of American Imperialism," *Journal of American History* 66, no. 4 (March 1980): 810–31.

53. "The Teaching Process," *Philippine Teacher* 2, no. 2 (July 1905): 24.

54. Gauri Viswanathan, *Masks of Conquest: Literary Study and British Rule in India* (1989; repr., New Delhi: Oxford University Press, 2003), 19.

55. Matthew Arnold, *Culture and Anarchy: An Essay in Political and Social Criticism* (1869; repr., Oxford: Oxford University Press, 2006), 37.

56. Horace E. Scudder, "The Place of Literature in Common School Education," in *Literature in School* (Boston: Houghton Mifflin, 1888), 7.

57. Ibid., 7.

58. Ibid., 28.

59. Ibid., 31.

60. Horace E. Scudder, "American Classics in School," in *Literature in School* (Boston: Houghton Mifflin, 1888), 46–47.

61. Ibid., 49.

62. Ibid., 50.

63. Ibid., 51.

64. Bernard Moses, *First Annual Report of the Secretary of Public Instruction to the Philippine Commission, for the Year Ending October 15, 1902* (Manila: Bureau of Public Printing, 1902), 23–24.

65. Arthur N. Applebee, *Tradition and Reform in the Teaching of English: A History* (Urbana, Ill.: National Council of Teachers of English, 1974), 37.

66. *Selected Short Poems by Representative American Authors*, annotated by George W. St. Clair (Manila: Bureau of Printers, 1911), 7–8.

67. Estelle Reel, *Course of Study for Indian Schools of the United States* (Washington, D.C.: U. S. Government Printing Office, 1901), 210.

68. See, by way of comparison, the curriculum for primary education for public schools in Massachusetts, where Atkinson had last worked (John T. Prince, "A Preliminary Report upon a Course of Studies for Elementary Schools," in *Sixtieth Annual Report: 1895–96* [Massachusetts Board of Education, 1896], 441).

69. Fred W. Atkinson, "Present Educational Movements in the Philippines," 274, Scrapbook 5, Bernard Moses Papers.

70. James Baldwin, *School Reading by Grades* (New York: American Book Company, 1897). Charles Eliot Norton, ed., *Fairy Stories and Classic Tales of Adventure*, third book of *the* Heart of Oak Books (Boston: Heath, 1901), ix.

71. Atkinson, "Present Educational Movements," 274

72. Sidney C. Newsom and Levona Payne Newsom, *Third Reader*, Philippine English series (Boston: Ginn, 1904), 5–6.

73. Board of Educational Survey, *A Survey of the Educational System of the Philippine Islands* (Manila: Bureau of Printing, 1925), 374.

74. James Baldwin, *School Reading by Grades*, 3.

75. Reynaldo Ileto, "The Philippine Revolution of 1896 and U.S. Colonial Education," in *Knowing America's Colony: A Hundred Years from the Philippine War* (Manoa: University of Hawaii, 1999), 1–17. The comparisons to feudalism are clear throughout the correspondence of the colonial administrators, as when Atkinson declared that "Custom and long years of servitude have rendered [the hombre] contented with serfdom" (Atkinson, "Present Educational Movements," 135).

76. Sidney C. Newsom and Levona Payne Newsom, *Primer*, Philippine English series (Boston: Ginn, 1904), 3–4.

77. Atkinson, "Present Educational Movements," 94.

78. *Selected Short Poems by Representative American Authors*, annotated by George W. St. Clair (Manila: Bureau of Printing, 1911), 5.

79. Board of Educational Survey, *A Survey of the Educational System of the Philippine Islands*, 378.

80. David Barrows, *Annual Report of the General Superintendent of Education, September 1904* (Manila: Bureau of Public Printing, 1904), 36.

81. Rizal's *Noli Me Tangere* was published as *Eagle Flight* by McClure, Phillips, and Co. in 1900. For more on the strategy behind Rizal's mobilization as an ally to American colonial interests, see Renato Constantino, *Insight and Foresight* (Quezon City: Foundation for Nationalist Studies, 1977), 27–32; and Sharon Delmendo, *The Star-Entangled Banner: One Hundred Years of America in the Philippines* (New Brunswick, N.J.: Rutgers University Press, 2004), esp. 22–29.

82. Renato Constantino, *Insight and Foresight* (Quezon City: Foundation for Nationalist Studies, 1977), 28.

83. William Cameron Forbes, *The Philippine Islands*, vol. 2 (Boston: Houghton Mifflin, 1928), 495.

84. San Juan Jr., *The Philippine Temptation*, 29–30. Importantly, it was William Dean Howells who first reviewed Rizal's work and brought it to the attention of U.S. audiences by

reviewing it in his "Editor's Easy Chair" column for *Harper's Monthly Magazine* 102 (December 1900), 805–6.

85. Bureau of Education, *Libraries for Philippine Public Schools* (Manila: Bureau of Printing, 1912), 22–40.

86. Bureau of Education, *Approved Library Lists* (Manila: Bureau of Printing, 1928), x–xi.

87. For a full account of the American reception to Matthew Arnold's two speaking tours in the 1880s, see C. Leonard, "Arnold in America: A Study of Matthew Arnold's Literary Relations with American and of his Visits to this Country in 1883 and 1886" (Ph.D. diss., Yale University, 1932).

88. Dean C. Worcester, "Knotty Problems of the Philippines," *Century Magazine* 56, no. 6 (October 1898): 874.

89. Richard Brodhead, "Sparing the Rod: Discipline and Fiction in Antebellum America," *Representations* 21 (Winter 1988): 70.

90. Ibid., 90.

91. Ibid.

92. Ibid., 87.

93. Albert J. Beveridge, "The Development of a Colonial Policy for the United States," *Annals of the American Academy of Political and Social Science* 30, no. 1 (July 1907): 3.

94. For more on the increasing restriction between the literary and the popular at the end of the nineteenth century, see Raymond Williams, *Marxism and Literature* (New York: Oxford University Press, 1977), 45–54; Janice A. Radway, *A Feeling for Books: The Book-of-the-Month Club, Literary Taste, and Middle-Class Desire* (Chapel Hill: University of North Carolina Press, 1997), 138–42. Interestingly, Stowe's novel served multiple purposes as a text of popular reform; as Mary Chapman notes, *Uncle Tom's Cabin* was translated into Chinese as *A Chronicle of the Black Slaves' Appeals to Heaven,* and served to mobilize Chinese women in the interests of political reform (see Chapman, "A 'Revolution in Ink': Sui Sin Far and Chinese Reform Discourse," *American Quarterly* [2008]: 975–1001).

95. Ruter W. Springer, chaplain, U.S. Army, Angeles, P.I., excerpted in Elihu Root, *Education in the Philippines: Letter from the Secretary of War* (Washington, D.C.: U.S. Government Printing Office, 1901), 48, NARA, RG 350, File 470, #15.

96. As noted earlier, *Evangeline* was required reading for all Filipino high-school students by at least 1904; as late as 1925, it was still the object of prolonged study, as a survey of the Philippine educational system laments: "Practically an entire semester of the freshman year is given to an intensive study of Evangeline, a selection that can be read by an ordinary reader in two or three hours. Obviously this poem is read intensively. It is analyzed, taken to pieces, put back together, looked at from every angle, and considered in all of its relations" (Board of Educational Survey, *A Survey of the Educational System of the Philippine Islands,* 378).

97. *Littell's Living Age,* quoted in Kenneth Walter Cameron, *Longfellow among His Contemporaries* (Hartford: Transcendental Press, 1978), 23.

98. William Charvat, *The Profession of Authorship in America, 1800–1870,* ed. Matthew J. Bruccoli (Columbus: Ohio State University Press, 1968).

99. The history of Longfellow's reception indicates that many school administrators

found his epic poem to be overly didactic for classroom use in the United States (see Frank-lyn B. Snyder and Edward D. Snyder, "Henry Wadsworth Longfellow," in *A Book of American Literature* [New York: Macmillan, 1953], 583–84).

100. Arthur Applebee notes that in the list of the ten most-taught texts in a 1907 survey, three were by Shakespeare, and the only American text was James Russell Lowell's *The Vision of Launfal* (Applebee, *Tradition and Reform*, 49–50). Ruth Windhover reports that Washington Irving, William Cullen Bryant, and Longfellow were the three writers most often included in literature readers (see "Literature in the Nineteenth Century," *English Journal: An Historical Primer on the Teaching of English* 68, no. 4 [April 1979]: 31).

101. *Evangeline* is first included in David Barrows's *Annual Report of the General Superintendent of Public Instruction, September 1904* (Manila: Bureau of Public Printing, 1904). In the 1925 curricular survey commissioned by the Philippine legislature, the authors lament that "practically an entire semester of the freshman year is given to an intensive study of *Evangeline*, a selection that can be read by an ordinary reader in two or three hours" (see Board of Educational Survey, *Survey of the Educational System of the Islands*, 378).

102. Lewis B. Semple, introduction to *Evangeline*, by Henry Wadsworth Longfellow (Gretna: Pelican, 2003), xviii.

103. Henry Wadsworth Longfellow, *Evangeline* (Gretna: Pelican, 2003). Hereafter cited parenthetically.

104. Kirsten Silva Gruesz, "El Gran Poeta Longfellow and a Psalm of Exile," *American Literary History* 10, no. 3 (Autumn 1998): 406.

105. Coventry Patmore's "The Angel in the House," written in praise of what he perceived to be the submissive virtues of his wife, Emily, was originally published in 1854.

106. Gruesz's discussion on this point is instructive, particularly given the emphasis on *Evangeline*'s Catholicism in readings of the poem in Latin America (see Gruesz, "El Gran Poeta Longfellow").

107. I. P. Soliongco, "Pan American Literature and Filipino Society," in *Rediscovery: Essays on Philippine Life and Culture*, ed. Cynthia Lumbera and Teresita Maceda (Manila: National Bookstore, 1983), 210.

108. Semple, introduction to *Evangeline*, xxvii.

109. Worcester, "Knotty Problems of the Philippines," 877.

NOTES TO CHAPTER 3

1. This number, which includes 368 men and 141 women, is taken from the data recorded in the ship's log. Many historical accounts give the number as 540, which more likely reflects the total number of passengers on board, including not just the teachers, but 14 children, 4 American nurses, and accompanying spouses (see Ronald P. Gleason, ed., *The Log of the "Thomas," July 23– August 21, 1901*. 1901).

2. Adeline Knapp, "A Notable Educational Experiment," in Gleason, *The Log of the "Thomas,"* 12.

3. There were three declared "ends" to the Philippine-American War in the early years

of the conflict, though fighting continued in parts of the islands for over a decade. General Arthur MacArthur had pronounced the war over in November 1899, declaring all further attacks to be "banditry" or murder. Hostilities continued well beyond 1901, however, such that President Theodore Roosevelt was obliged to make a similar proclamation on July 4, 1902 (see Paul A. Kramer, *The Blood of Government: Race, Empire, the United States and the Philippines* [Chapel Hill: University of North Carolina Press, 2006], 130–54).

4. Quoted in Adjutant General of the Army, *Correspondence Relating to the War with Spain.* (Washington, D.C.: U. S. Government Printing Office, 1902), 2:1352–53.

5. The "water cure" was a practice in which water was forced down the throat of a captive Filipino, until the captive individual confessed or drowned (*Soldiers' Letters: Being Materials for the History of a War of Criminal Aggression* [Boston: Anti-Imperialist League, 1899]).

6. Adeline Knapp, "A Notable Educational Experiment," in Gleason, *The Log of the "Thomas,"* 12.

7. Ann Laura Stoler, "Tense and Tender Ties: The Politics of Comparison in North American History and (Post) Colonial Studies," *Journal of American History* 88, no. 3 (December 2001): 830.

8. Laura Wexler, *Tender Violence: Domestic Visions in an Age of U. S. Imperialism* (Chapel Hill: University of North Carolina Press, 2000), 9.

9. Among these, particularly relevant studies include Gillian Brown, *Domestic Individualism: Imagining Self in Nineteenth-Century America* (Berkeley and Los Angeles: University of California Press, 1990); Shirley Samuels, ed., *The Culture of Sentiment: Race, Gender, and Sentimentality in Nineteenth-Century America* (New York: Oxford University Press, 1992); Lora Romero, *Home Fronts: Domesticity and Its Critics in the Antebellum United States* (Durham: Duke University Press, 1997); Ann Laura Stoler, *Carnal Knowledge and Imperial Power* (Berkeley and Los Angeles: University of California Press, 2002); and Laura Wexler, *Tender Violence: Domestic Visions in an Age of U. S. Imperialism* (Chapel Hill: University of North Carolina Press, 2000).

10. Rosemary Marangoly George, *The Politics of Home: Postcolonial Relocations and Twentieth-Century Fiction* (Cambridge: Cambridge University Press, 1996), 36. For other feminist critiques of imperialism and its relation to contemporary feminism, see Kumkum Sangari and Sudesh Vaid, eds., *Recasting Women: Essays in Indian Colonial History* (New Brunswick, N.J.: Rutgers University Press, 1990); Chandra Talpade Mohanty, *Feminism without Borders: Decolonizing Theory, Practicing Solidarity* (Durham: Duke University Press, 2003); Chela Sandoval, *Methodology of the Oppressed* (Minneapolis: University of Minnesota Press, 2000).

11. Amy Kaplan, *The Anarchy of Empire in the Making of U. S. Culture* (Cambridge: Harvard University Press, 2002), 25–26.

12. Vicente Rafael, *White Love and Other Events in Filipino History* (Durham: Duke University Press, 2000), 54–56.

13. Kimberly Alidio, "'When I Get Home I Want to Forget': Memory and Amnesia in the Occupied Philippines, 1901–1904," *Social Text* 59 (Summer 1999): 110.

14. Depictions of the Philippines as the new frontier of American settlement were quite

explicit. For contemporary examples, see Albert J. Beveridge, *The Meaning of the Times and Other Speeches* (Indianapolis: Bobbs-Merrill, 1908); William Howard Taft, "The Philippines," *National Geographic Magazine* 16, no. 8 (1905): 361–75; and Caroline S. Shunk, *An Army Woman Writing in the Philippines* (Kansas City, Mo.: Franklin Hudson, 1914). For current scholarship on this point, see Richard Drinnon, *Facing West: The Metaphysics of Indian-Hating and Empire-Building* (Norman: University of Oklahoma Press, 1980); and Sidney Lens, *The Forging of the American Empire* (1971; repr., Chicago: Haymarket Press, 2003).

15. Michael Elliott, *The Culture Concept: Writing and Difference in the Age of Realism* (Minneapolis: University of Minnesota Press, 2002), 9.

16. C. H. Maxon, "The Voyage of The 'Thomas,'" in Gleason, *The Log of the "Thomas,"* "tender young Tagalogs," 24; N. C. Abbott, "The Cost of the Expedition," ibid., "orphans," "adopted," "Uncle Sam," 23.

17. Ibid., 11–12.

18. Glenn May reports that, according to Capt. Albert Todd, the director of the Department of Public Instruction under General Otis, "the primary goal of the army's teaching program was not to educate Filipinos but rather to pacify them by convincing them of U. S. good will" (Glenn May, *Social Engineering in the Philippines: The Aims, Execution, and Impact of American Colonial Policy, 1900–1913* (Westport, Conn: Greenwood Press, 1980), 79, 85.

19. Katherine Cook, "Public Education in the Philippine Islands," in *U. S. Bureau of Education Bulletins, 1935* (Washington, D.C.: U. S. Government Printing Office, 1935), 5.

20. Helen Herron Taft, *Recollections of Full Years* (New York: Dodd, Mead, 1914), 124–25.

21. U. S. House, *Papers Relating to the Foreign Relations*, 12.

22. Cited in Adjutant General of the Army, *Correspondence Relating to the War with Spain* (Washington, D.C.: U. S. Government Printing Office, 1902), 2:1352–53.

23. J. F. Bell, "Telegraphic Circulars Issued by Brig. Gen. J. F. Bell to Station Commanders in the Provinces of Tayabas, Batangas, and Laguna," in Senate Committee on the Philippines, *Affairs of the Philippine Islands*, 1607, quoted in Kramer, *Blood of Government*, 154.

24. Bell, *Telegraphic Circular No. 3* (December 9, 1901), 1608, quoted in Kramer, *Blood of Government*, 154.

25. Jane Hunter, *The Gospel of Gentility: American Women Missionaries in Turn-of-the-Century China* (New Haven: Yale University Press, 1984), 5; Karen Sánchez-Eppler, *Dependent States: The Child's Part in Nineteenth-Century American Culture* (Chicago: University of Chicago Press, 2005), 187. See also Patricia Ruth Hill, *The World Their Household: The American Woman's Foreign Mission Movement and Cultural Transformation, 1870–1920* (Ann Arbor: University of Michigan Press, 1985).

26. Louise Michele Newman, *White Woman's Rights: The Racial Origins of Feminism in the United States* (New York: Oxford University Press, 1999), 52.

27. Bureau of Education of the Philippine Islands, *A Statement of Organization and Aims Published for General Information, December 1907* (Manila: Bureau of Printing, 1907).

28. Alidio, "When I Get Home," 109.

29. Harry N. Cole to Helen M. N. Cole, October 20, 1901, Harry N. Cole Papers, Michigan

Historical Collections, Bentley Historical Library, University of Michigan, quoted in Alidio, "When I Get Home," 108.

30. Ibid.

31. Mary Cole to J. E. Scott, January 26, 1902, Harry N. Cole Papers, quoted in Alidio, "When I Get Home," 109.

32. Quoted in Kramer, *Blood of Government*, 145.

33. Mary Cole to J. E. Scott, 20 January 1902, quoted in Alidio, "When I Get Home," 112.

34. Ibid., 109.

35. For more on the Samar campaign, see John Morgan Gates, *Schoolbooks and Krags: The United States Army in the Philippines* (Westport, Conn.: Greenwood, 1973); Joseph L. Schott, *The Ordeal at Samar* (Indianapolis: Bobbs-Merrill, 1964), 286–87; and Moorfield Storey and Marcial P. Lichauco, *The Conquest of the Philippines by the United States, 1898–1925* (New York: G. P. Putnam's Sons, 1926), 138–39.

36. Mary Fee, *A Woman's Impressions of the Philippines* (1910; repr., Chicago: McClurg, 1912), cited parenthetically; William Freer, *The Philippine Experiences of an American Teacher: A Narrative of Work and Travel in the Philippine Islands* (New York: Charles Scribner's Sons, 1906), cited parenthetically.

37. Rafael, *White Love*, 55.

38. Fee's own text describes this paradox, but she was not alone in this experience. While men were paid more than women for their teaching service, salaries in the Philippines were typically higher than those in public schools in the United States, this despite the fact that teachers' salaries were paid in devalued Mexican currency. The Coles, for example, were in a similar predicament. Harry Cole was a chemistry professor at the University of Michigan; his wife, Mary, worked as a public school elementary teacher. They enlisted in the civil service in the Philippines for financial reasons, as their salaries in their employments in the United States did not allow them to buy a house (see Alidio, "When I Get Home," 107).

39. See, for example, Helen Taft, *Recollections of Full Years; Unofficial Letters of an Official's Wife*; Caroline S. Shunk, *An Army Woman in the Philippines* (Kansas City, Mo.: Franklin Hudson, 1914); and Campbell Dauncy, *An Englishwoman in the Philippines* (New York: Dutton, 1906).

40. Kamala Visweswaran, "'Wild West' Anthropology and the Disciplining of Gender," in *Gender and American Social Science: The Formative Years*, ed. Helene Silverberg (Princeton: Princeton University Press, 1998), 87.

41. As the recruitment brochure explained, "In many cases, however, a man and wife are assigned together in a town, the man carrying on the work of supervision and the woman the instruction of the advanced classes in the central municipal school" (Bureau of Education of the Philippine Islands, *A Statement of Organization and Aims Published for General Information, December 1907* [Manila: Bureau of Printing, 1907]).

42. For more on the relations between domestic advice and female complaint as a route to white American women's entry into the political sphere, see Lauren Berlant, "Uncle Sam Needs a Wife: Citizenship and Denegation," in *Materializing Democracy: Towards a*

Revitalized Cultural Politics, ed. Russ Castronovo and Dana D. Nelson (Durham: Duke University Press, 2002), 144–74.

43. Ibid., 155.

44. Louise Newman, *White Women's Rights: The Racial Origins of Feminism in the United States* (New York: Oxford University Press, 1999), 34.

45. Atkinson, quoted in Daniel B. Schirmer, "The Conception and Gestation of a Neocolony," in *The Philippines Reader: A History of Colonialism, Neocolonialism, Dictatorship, and Resistance*, ed. Schirmer and Stephen Rosskamm Shalom (Quezon City: KEN 1987), 43–44.

46. Mary A. Livermore, quoted in Kristin Hoganson, "'As Badly Off as the Filipinos': U.S. Women's Suffragists and the Imperial Issue at the Turn of the Twentieth Century," *Journal of Women's History* 13, no. 2 (Summer 2001): 9. See also Allison Lee Sneider, "Reconstruction, Expansion, and Empire: The U.S. Woman Suffrage Movement and the Re-Making of National Political Community, 1870–1900" (Ph.D. diss., University of California, Los Angeles, 1999), 169–209.

47. Stanton, diary entry from 30 September 1899, quoted in Hoganson, "As Badly Off as the Filipinos," 13.

48. Gayatri Chakravorty Spivak, "Can the Subaltern Speak?" in *Marxism and the Interpretation of Culture*, ed. Cary Nelson and Lawrence Grossberg (Urbana: University of Illinois, 1988), 271–316.

49. Representative James R. Mann, *Congressional Record* 31, pt. 5, April 28, 1898, p. 4362, quoted in Kristin Hoganson, "'Honor Comes First': The Imperatives of Manhood in the Congressional Debate over War," in *Whose America? The War of 1898 and the Battles to Define the Nation*, ed. Virginia M. Bouvier (Westport, Conn.: Praeger, 2001), 126.

50. Senator Richard R. Kenney, *Congressional Record* 31, pt. 4, April 5, 1898, p. 3547, quoted in Hoganson, "Honor Comes First," 124.

51. This would be to extend Richard Slotkin's notion of the American fantasy of the frontier as the site of "regeneration through violence" (see Slotkin, *Regeneration through Violence: The Myth of the American Frontier* [Middletown, Conn.: Wesleyan University Press, 1973]).

52. For a thorough account of the overlap between the Indian Wars, the War of 1898, and the Philippine-American War, see Drinnon, *Facing West*, 255–354.

53. Gail Bederman, *Manliness and Civilization: A Cultural History of Gender and Race in the United States, 1880–1917* (Chicago: University of Chicago Press, 1996); Kristin L. Hoganson, *Fighting for American Manhood: How Gender Politics Provoked the Spanish-American and Philippine-American Wars* (New Haven: Yale University Press, 1998).

54. Quoted in Bederman, *Manliness and Civilization*, 170.

55. Ibid., 192–93.

56. Ibid., 193–94.

57. As I discuss in more detail below, the spectre of same-sex desire haunts constructions of masculinity of the Spanish-American War, thus pointing to the central role of sexual regulation in nation-building and empire.

58. Quoted in Ann Laura Stoler, *Carnal Knowledge and Imperial Power: Race and the Intimate in Colonial Rule* (Berkeley and Los Angeles: University of California Press, 2002), 1.

59. Quoted in Paul A. Kramer, "The Darkness that Enters the Home: The Politics of Prostitution during the Philippine American War," in *Haunted by Empire*, ed. Ann Laura Stoler (Durham: Duke University Press, 2006), 370.

60. Ibid., 397.

61. Brig. Gen. R. P. Hughes to Major George Andrews, January 25, 1901, NARA, RG 350, File 357, #5.

62. J. W. Clark to Senator W. B. Allison, January 8, 1901, NARA, RG 350, File 363, # 2.

63. Ellsworth Huntington, *Civilization and Climate* (New Haven: Yale University Press, 1915), 8, 42, 44.

64. Quoted in Warwick Anderson, *Colonial Pathologies: American Tropical Medicine, Race, and Hygiene in the Philippines* (Durham: Duke University Press, 2006), 138–39.

65. Bernard Moses, "In the Wilds of the Philippines," May 4, 1904, Folder: "In the Wilds of the Philippines," Carton 1, Bernard Moses Papers; William Cameron Forbes, *The Philippine Islands*, vol. 1 (Boston: Houghton Mifflin, 1928), 442.

66. David P. Barrows to S. T. Black, president, State Normal School, San Diego, Calif., May 4, 1903, Folder: "Jan-Dec. 1903," Carton 1, David P. Barrows Papers, Bancroft Library, University of California, Berkeley.

67. Barrows, "Review of the Year 1906," 51, and "Review of the Year 1908," 105, Cartons 2 and 3, David P. Barrows Papers.

68. "Gov. Forbes Ill," *New York Times*, June 22, 1912.

69. Anderson, *Colonial Pathologies*, 134.

70. Warwick Anderson notes that despite the feminized nature of the neurasthenia diagnosis, there are few accounts of tropical neurasthenia among white women (ibid.,140).

71. Rafael, *White Love*, 21.

72. See Renato Rosaldo, "Imperialist Nostalgia," *Representations* 26 (Spring 1989): 108.

73. G. Frank Lydson, "Sexual Perversion, Satyriasis and Nymphomania," *Medical and Surgical Reporter* 61 (1889): 254, quoted in George Chauncey, *Gay New York: Gender, Urban Culture, and the Making of the Gay Male World, 1890–1940* (New York: Basic Books, 1994), 12.

74. Chauncey, *Gay New York*, 36–37.

75. Mrinalini Sinha has written about the management of this paradox in the British colonial system in India, in which the figure of the "effeminate *babu*" emerges in the second half of the nineteenth century as a foil to the "manly Englishman" in ways that were intricately tied to the changing conditions of the British rule in India and of the regulation of sexual practices and identities in Britain (see Sinha, *Colonial Masculinity: The 'Manly Englishman' and the 'Effeminate Bengali' in the Late Nineteenth Century* [New York: Manchester University Press, 1995]).

NOTES TO CHAPTER 4

1. R. H. Pratt to Adjutant General, U.S.A., December 5, 1902, NARA, RG 350, File 363, #25.

2. Ibid.

3. See NARA, RG 350, File 363, for letters on Filipino students in the United States.

4. R. H. Pratt to Adjutant General, U.S.A., December 5, 1902, NARA, RG 350, File 363, #25.

5. Quoted in Adjutant General of the Army, *Correspondence Relating to the War with Spain*, 2 vols. (Washington, D.C.: U.S. Government Printing Office, 1902), 2:1352–53.

6. R. H. Pratt to Adjutant General, U.S.A., December 5, 1902, NARA, RG 350, File 363, #25.

7. R. H. Pratt to Major-General H. C. Corbin, Adjutant General, U.S.A., December 30, 1902, Washington, D.C., NARA, RG 350, File 363, #28.

8. Quoted in Frederick E. Hoxie, *A Final Promise: The Campaign to Assimilate the Indians, 1880–1920* (1984; repr., Lincoln: University of Nebraska Press, 2001), 192.

9. On the *pensionado* program, see Steffi San Buenaventura, "Filipino Immigration to the United States," in *The Asian American Encyclopedia* (New York: Marshall Cavendish, 1995), 2:443–46; and Paul Kramer, *The Blood of Government: Race, Empire, the United States, and the Philippines* (Chapel Hill: University of North Carolina Press, 2006), 203–4.

10. Yen Le Espiritu, *Home Bound: Filipino Lives Across Cultures, Communities, and Countries* (Berkeley and Los Angeles: University of California, 2003), 27; San Buenaventura, "Filipino Immigration to the United States," 443–46.

11. Lisa Lowe, *Immigrant Acts: On Asian American Cultural Politics* (Durham: Duke University Press, 1996), 188 n. 36.

12. Ibid., 6–22.

13. I take these statistics from Espiritu, *Home Bound*, 27; San Buenaventura, "Filipino Immigration," 444; and E. San Juan Jr., *The Philippine Temptation*, 132.

14. Espiritu, *Home Bound*, 47.

15. Among the important collections of Philippine literature in English, see Luis H. Francia, *Brown River, White Ocean: An Anthology of Twentieth-Century Philippine Literature in English* (New Brunswick, N.J.: Rutgers University Press, 1993); Luis H. Francia and Eric Gamalinda, eds., *Flippin': Filipinos on America* (New Brunswick, N.J.: Rutgers University Press, 1996); Leonard Casper, *New Writing from the Philippines: A Critique and Anthology* (Syracuse: Syracuse University Press, 1966); and Arturo G. Roseburg, ed., *Pathways to Philippine Literature in English: Anthology with Biographical and Critical Introduction* (Quezon City: Alemar-Phoenix 1966). For critical work on the history and politics of Philippine literature in English, see E. San Juan Jr., *The Philippine Temptation: Dialectics of Philippines–U.S. Literary Relations* (Philadelphia: Temple University Press, 1996); Resil B. Mojares, *Panitikan: An Essay on the American Colonial and Contemporary Traditions in Philippine Literature* (Manila: Sentrong Pangkultura ng Pilipinas, 1994); Antonio G. Manuud, ed., *Brown Heritage: Essays on Philippine Cultural Tradition and Literature* (Quezon City: Ateneo de Manila University Press, 1967); and Shirley Geok-Lin Lim, *Nationalism and Literature: English-Language Writing from the Philippines and Singapore* (Quezon City: New Day, 1993).

16. In particular, E. San Juan Jr. reads Bulosan as a "fictional representative of about 30,000 Filipinos resident in California" and "an organic intellectual of the masses" (*The Philippine Temptation*, 137, 133).

17. Carlos Bulosan, *America Is in the Heart*, (1946; repr., Seattle: University of Washington, 1973), 188. Hereafter cited parenthetically. Following the bulk of criticism on *America Is in the Heart*, I distinguish between Carlos Bulosan, the author, and "Carlos," the text's narrator and protagonist, by using the first name to refer to the character, the last to refer to the author. As I discuss later in the chapter, this distinction is a tenuous one, as the text's generic location between fiction and autobiography continues to be the subject of significant critical debate. Nevertheless, I hope this provisional distinction will allow for greater analytical clarity.

18. This is the conclusion reached in several studies of *America Is in the Heart*, each of which reads Carlos's continued admiration for an unrealized idyllic America as demonstrative of Bulosan's own affiliation with that ideal. See especially Kenneth Mostern, "Why Is America in the Heart?" *Critical Mass: A Journal of Asian American Cultural Criticism* 2, no. 2 (1995): 35–65; and Jae H. Roe, "Revisiting the Sign of 'America': The Postcolonial Humanism of *America Is in the Heart*," *English Language and Literature* 49, no. 9 (2003): 905–20.

19. On this point, Marilyn Alquizola argues for a reading of the narrative that emphasizes the ironic distance between Bulosan the author and Carlos the narrator, calling Carlos a "collective protagonist" who exhibits a "naïve optimism" mobilized to provoke the suspicion of his readers as well as their sympathy. In this sense, Alquizola's reading has much in common with my own, though to my mind, what the text renders clear in Carlos's seeming naïveté is less consistent a disavowal than Alquizola suggests, and instead a series of contradictions that Bulosan himself must also fail to resolve (Alquizola, "The Fictive Narrator of *America Is in the Heart*," in *Frontiers of Asian American Studies,* ed. Gail Nomura, Russell Endo, Stephen H. Sumida, and Russell C. Leong [Pullman: Washington State University Press, 1989], 211–17).

20. E. San Juan Jr., "Searching for the Heart of 'America,'" in *Teaching American Ethnic Literatures: Nineteen Essays,* ed. John Maitino and David R. Peck (Albuquerque: University of New Mexico Press, 1996), 216.

21. Roe, "Revisiting the Sign of America," 906.

22. Lowe, *Immigrant Acts,* 127.

23. This is the subject of an insightful essay by Oscar V. Campomanes and Todd S. Gernes, who argue for the interconnectedness of literary awakening and social consciousness in Bulosan's work more generally. With regard to *America Is in the Heart*, Campomanes and Gernes note that "striking out and communicating are the conflicting impulses behind the act of writing," impulses that Bulosan resolves through his access to written expression, discovering that "writing is both a form of violent rebellion and liberating communication" (see "Carlos Bulosan and the Act of Writing," *Philippine Studies* 40, no. 1 [1992], 78).

24. See Ronald Takaki, *Strangers from a Different Shore: A History of Asian Americans* (New York: Penguin Books, 1989); Michael Omi and Howard Winant, *Racial Formation in the United States* (New York: Routledge, 1994); and Gary Okihiro, *Margins and Mainstreams: Asians in American History and Culture* (Seattle: University of Washington Press, 1994).

25. "Necessitous mobility" is Sau-ling Wong's term for the text's unmappable quality, by which she refers not only to Carlos's ceaseless movement from town to town, but also to

the forced or involuntary quality of this mobility, demanded by poverty and the threat (or actuality) of violence. Such mobility, for Wong, counters the fascination in American letters with mobility's promise of liberation and its status as a privileged sign of freedom. As she argues, "*America Is in the Heart* (the title bearing a single place name) betokens a promise to undo the hurt of Necessitous mobility, to subsume the unruly Many of specific injustices into the liberating One of the heartfelt, shared creed. The place names crowding the pages . . . threaten to undermine this reassurance by contrasting with its insubstantiality: if America is in the heart, doesn't it mean that it is nowhere, that its rallying aspirations have not been realized in any of these actual places" (134). In this sense, it is Carlos's proclaimed belief in the American Dream and its promise of social mobility that is undercut by the compelled mobility of the novel's protagonist (*Reading Asian American Literature: From Necessity to Extravagance* [Princeton: Princeton University Press, 1993]).

26. Importantly, while the U.S. presence in the Philippines is mentioned in part 1 of the text, it is never cited as a colonial occupation, thus making U.S. imperialism curiously absent from Bulosan's otherwise explicitly critical gaze. E. San Juan Jr. usefully argues for the narrative importance of U.S. colonialism as a textual absence, noting that it receives almost no direct mention in *America* while serving as the unarticulated motor behind the events of the text; thus, the U.S. occupation is that which "the bulk of this narrative wants to forget but cannot." That is to say, Bulosan cannot directly name the history of U.S. imperialism, which exists as a backdrop for the text's deroulement, one that, surprisingly, never makes its way to the foreground as the precise object of Carlos's critical gaze ("Searching for the Heart of 'America,'" in *Teaching American Ethnic Literatures: Nineteen Essays*, ed. John Maitino and David R. Peck [Albuquerque: University of New Mexico Press, 1996], 266).

27. The distinction between civilian and resistance fighters is one that the U.S. military officials determinedly refused to make, authorizing the torture or slaughter of any Filipino not "proved" to be supportive of the U.S. authority in the archipelago. By no means do I wish to be understood to be arguing for a strict delineation between the two, since it is precisely the modes of resistance carried out by the Philippine population en masse, particularly in the face of the technological advantage held by the U.S. military, that marks the overwhelming popular resistance to the colonial rule.

28. San Juan Jr. argues that *America Is in the Heart* is not an autobiography as such because Carlos is not the hero; rather, he views Carlos as "mediating device" representing the Filipino worker more generally, thus depicting "the objective force of the peasant-working class" (San Juan Jr., *Carlos Bulosan and the Imagination of the Class Struggle* [Quezon City: University of the Philippines Press, 1972], 94).

29. Critics have been quick to note that the text is formally quite complicated, if not incoherent, due to the overflow of place-names, the unchartable passage of time, and the quick moves between past and present. Similarly, events in the text are rendered difficult to interpret, as they remain unaccompanied by sufficient elaboration to place them chronologically, thereby denying its readers an easily deciphered developmental narrative upon which the bildungsroman would seem to depend (see Alquizola, "The Fictive Narrator of *America Is in the Heart*"; Roe, "Revisiting the Sign of 'America'"; and Wong, *Reading Asian American Literature*).

30. See, particularly, Elaine Kim, *Asian American Literature: An Introduction to the Writings and Their Social Context* (Philadelphia: Temple University Press, 1982); and Wong, *Reading Asian American Literature.*

NOTES TO THE CONCLUSION

1. W. D. Howells, "The New Historical Romances," *North American Review* 171, no. 6 (December 1900): 941.

2. Ibid., 943.

3. Ibid., 948.

4. William Dean Howells, "The Philippine Problem: How to Secure the Peace," *New York Evening Post,* October 17, 1899.

5. Renato Constantino, *Insight and Foresight* (Quezon City: Foundation for Nationalist Studies, 1977), 101.

6. Ibid., 98.

7. Among these, see E. San Juan Jr., *The Philippine Temptation: Dialectics of Philippines–U. S. Literary Relations* (Philadelphia: Temple University Press, 1996), esp. chaps. 1, 2, and 6; Shirley Geok-Lin Lim, *Nationalism and Literature: English-Language Writing from the Philippines and Singapore* (Quezon City: New Day, 1993); Mina Roces, "Filipino Identity in Fiction, 1945–1972," *Modern Asian Studies* 28, no. 2 (1994): 279–315; Jonathan Chua, introduction to *The Critical Villa: Essays in Literary Criticism* (Quezon City: Ateneo de Manila University Press, 2002), 1–31. While the field of Philippine literature in English is said to have been inaugurated with the publication of Paz Márquez-Benítez's short story "Dead Stars" in the *Philippine Herald* in 1925, the proliferation of collections of writing in English in the 1930s marks this as a significant period of literary production in English, made all the more striking by fact of the official end of American rule in the islands and the reclassification of Filipinos as "aliens" in 1934. Thus, in highly visible terms, U. S. cultural hegemony in the form of English made a discernable emergence at the very period that its official political sovereignty was coming to an end.

8. Chua notes that the founding of the Aklatang Bayan in 1910 set forth the objectives of "fight[ing] vices, evil habits and beliefs, whether these be found in politics, religion, or even day to day life" and the Ilaw at Panitik in 1912, whose name advocated the advancement of literature as a path toward 'Freedom and Redemption'" (Chua, *The Critical Villa,* 9). See also Resil B. Mojares, *Panitikan: An Essay on the American Colonial and Contemporary Traditions in Philippine Literature* (Manila: Sentrong Pangkultura Ng Pilipinas, 1994), 32.

9. Chua, *The Critical Villa,* 9.

10. Chris Friday reports that between 1920 and 1925, about two thousand Filipinos attended high school or college in the United States; in 1928, that number jumped by one thousand that year alone (*Organizing Asian American Labor: The Pacific Coast Canned-Salmon Industry, 1870–1942* [Philadelphia: Temple University Press, 1994]), 135, quoted in Yen Le Espiritu, *Filipino American Lives* (Philadelphia: Temple University Press, 1995), 4.

11. E. San Juan Jr., *The Philippine Temptation: Dialectics of Philippines–U. S. Literary Relations* (Philadelphia: Temple University Press, 1996), 33–34.

12. Founded in 1908, the University of the Philippines was overwhelmingly dominated by American officials and scholars, who formed the majority both on the Board of Regents and among the faculty. The first university president, an American educator named Dr. Murray Bartlett, avowed in his inaugural address that "the surest and quickest way of bringing about the Filipinization of the government is through the university"; officially dedicating the university to the tutelary functioning of the American colonial state, Bartlett added that its role would be to function as "a training school for the development of character" and as "the expert advisor of the State." Even after the presidency passed to the control of Filipino scholars, the ideological sway of the institution remained steadily aligned with the American political power; its College of Education continued to produce Filipino teachers well-versed in the curriculum designed by the American superintendents of education, and many of its scholars were initially educated through the pensionado program, which brought Filipino students of "good moral character" to study in advanced institutions in the United States as a way of more closely molding future leaders "of recognized merit" for the islands. Numerous scholars have traced the history of the University of the Philippines and recorded its close links to the project of American dominance in the Pacific. Reynaldo Ileto, in particular, has traced how the scholarship of its faculty, themselves educated through the American educational system, rehearsed the same racialized notions of "progress" that characterized the American colonial system (see Harry L. Case and Robert A. Bunnell, *The University of the Philippines: External Assistance and Development* [East Lansing: Michigan State University, 1970], 10; William Cameron Forbes, *The Philippine Islands* [Boston: Houghton Mifflin, 1928], 1:457; Oscar M. Alfonso and Leslie E. Bauzon, eds., *The University of the Philippines: The First 75 Years* [Quezon City: University of the Philippines Press, 1985]; Belinda Aquino, ed., *The University Experience: Essays on the 82nd Anniversary of the University of the Philippines* [Quezon City: University of the Philippines Press, 1991]; Helen E. Lopez, *At the Helm of the U.P.: Presidential Accents* [Quezon City: University of the Philippines Press, 1999]; and Reynaldo Ileto, "The Philippine Revolution of 1896 and U.S. Colonial Education," in *Knowing America's Colony: A Hundred Years from the Philippine War* (Manoa: University of Hawaii, 1999), 8.

13. Alvaro L. Martinez, "The Vernacular Short Story," *Philippine Magazine*, October 1930, 298–99, quoted in Chua, introduction to *The Critical Villa*, 11.

14. Genario Virtusio, "Vernacular Literature and Literary Quacks," *Philippines Herald*, August 7, 1935, 7, quoted in Chua, introduction to *The Critical Villa*, 11.

15. A. V. H. Hartendorp, "The Importance of Philippine Literature in English," *Philippine Magazine*, January 1937, 18–19. Isabel Pefianco Martin makes the important point that such characterizations continued to be connected to racialized assumptions about Filipinos, such that "what was considered as a weakness of Philippine writing was also perceived as a weakness of the Filipino race. These observations from Filipino critics and educators, as well as from influential American educators, only perpetuated the dichotomies between Occidental and Oriental languages, realistic and romantic literatures, high literature and low literature,

good taste and poor taste, maturity and adolescence, intelligence and ignorance" ("Longfellow's Legacy: Education and the Shaping of Philippine Writing," *World Englishes* 23, no. 1 [2004]: 138).

16. Notably, the traditions of Filipino American literature do play out just such a critical perspective, making visible the contradictions of U. S. colonial rule and speaking out the legacy of that period. One particularly interesting example is Faye Caronan, "Making History from U. S. Colonial Amnesia: Filipino American and U. S. Puerto Rican Poetic Genealogies" (Ph.D. diss., University of California, San Diego, 2007), which studies the vectors of this critique through performance poetry by Filipino Americans in Los Angeles and Puerto Ricans in New York.

17. Villa's career as a foremost poet, critic, and essayist in English dramatizes some of the contradictions that attend the dynamics between English and vernacular literatures. As a modernist poet, story writer, and critic, Villa found ready praise from both American and Filipino writers and scholars. Edward O'Brian wrote the introduction to Villa's 1933 story collection *Footnote to Youth,* and included Villa's work in his collection of *Best American Stories of 1932.* Villa's poetry earned high praise from central figures in U. S. modernism like e.e. cummings, Marianne Moore, and Conrad Aiken, particularly after Villa's move to Greenwich Village in the 1940s. More than anything else, Villa is remembered as a formal innovator, whose invention of reverse consonance and the "comma poem" placed him in the thick of stylistic experimentation and artistic exploration. In the Philippines, Villa published annual lists of the best Filipino short stories and poems, a "Roll of Honor," from 1927 until the start of World War II, and Chua reports that such lists were anticipated "with bated breath" (20).

18. San Juan Jr., *The Philippine Temptation,* 171.

19. Ibid., 34.

20. Chua, *The Critical Villa,* 13.

21. Ibid., 20.

22. Amy Blitz, *The Contested State: American Foreign Policy and Regime Change in the Philippines* (New York: Rowman and Littlefield, 2000); William H. Blanchard, *Neocolonialism American Style, 1960–2000* (Westport, Conn.: Greenwood Press, 1996); Daniel B. Schirmer and Stephen Rosskamm Shalom, eds., *The Philippines Reader: A History of Colonialism, Neocolonialism, Dictatorship, and Resistance* (Boston: South End Press, 1987).

23. John M. Liu and Lucie Cheng, "Pacific Rim Development and the Duality of Post-1965 Immigration to the United States," in *The New Asian Immigration in Los Angeles and Global Restructuring,* ed. Paul Ong, Edna Bonacich, and Lucie Chang (Philadelphia: Temple University Press, 1994), 77; Alejandro Lichauco, *Hunger, Corruption, and Betrayal: A Primer on U. S. Neocolonialism and the Philippines Crisis* (Manila: Citizens' Committee on the National Crisis, 2005).

24. On the importance of Clark air base and Subic naval base, see Donald Kirk, *Looted: The Philippines after the Bases* (New York: St. Martin's Press, 1998); and Blitz, *The Contested State,* 197–200.

25. More recently, Filipino writers have spoken out about the limitations of English-language fiction as an arena of expression and political motivation for Filipino writers. Nick

Joaquin asserted that Philippine literature "has to assert its roots outside American culture; now it has to assert its continuity with the rest of our history"; F. Sionil Jose insisted upon the importance of revolutionary tradition to Philippine literature by saying that "in the Philippine context, the writer has no choice but be a revolutionary. In being asked to be a mirror of his time, he becomes the enemy of all those crippling institutions" (quoted in Lim, *Nationalism and Literature*, 13, 15).

26. "LOA Worldwide Program to Benefit Libraries in Iraq and Afghanistan," *News from the Library of America* (Fall 2004): 1. The summer 2006 newsletter revealed that the private foundation was the Horace W. Goldsmith Foundation.

27. Ibid., 7.

28. "LOA Sets Arrive in Iraq," *News from the Library of America* (Summer 2006): 1. Afghanistan number confirmed in e-mail correspondence with editors, October 7, 2008.

29. "U.S. Bringing Education Back to Iraq," presidential weekly radio address, October 18, 2003, White House transcript available at http://usgovinfo.about.com/b/a/36096.htm http://georgewbush-whitehouse.archives.gov/news/releases/2003/10/20031018.html.

30. Mary Zehr, "Iraq Gets Approval to Control Destiny of School System," *Education Week*, April 14, 2004.

31. Ibid.

32. Mary Zehr, "U.S. Withdraws from Education Reform in Iraq," *Education Week*, August 30, 2006.

33. Christine Asquith, "A New History of Iraq," *Guardian*, November 25, 2003.

34. "Another Vacuum Opens Up," *Economist*, November 6, 2003.

35. Bill Evers, U.S. Department of Defense, quoted in Asquith, "A New History of Iraq," November 25, 2003.

36. Asquith, "A New History of Iraq," November 25, 2003.

37. Ibid.

38. Christina Asquith, "U.S. Academic Brings Philosophy 101 to Iraqi Universities," EducationNews.org, March 1, 2004, www.ednews.org/articles/us-academic-brings-philosophy-101-to-iraqi-universities.html.

39. Christopher Hitchens, "Book Drive for Iraq: How You Can Do Your Bit to Build Democracy," *Slate.com*, June 30, 2008, www.slate.com/id/2194308/.

40. Quoted in Naomi Klein, "The Rise of Disaster Capitalism," *Nation*, May 2, 2005, 9.

41. San Juan Jr., *The Philippine Temptation*, 30.

Bibliography

ARCHIVAL SOURCES

David P. Barrows Papers. Bancroft Library, University of California, Berkeley.
Bureau of Insular Affairs. Record Group 350. National Archives and Record Administration, College Park, Maryland.
Jacob Gould Schurman Papers. Cornell University Library, Ithaca, New York.
William Holmes McGuffey Collection. King Library, Miami University, Oxford, Ohio.
William Howard Taft Papers. Library of Congress, Washington, D.C.
National Library of Education. Washington, D.C.

GOVERNMENT-PUBLISHED PRIMARY SOURCES

Adjutant General of the Army, *Correspondence Relating to the War with Spain.* Washington, D.C.: U. S. Government Printing Office, 1902.
Atkinson, Fred W. "Present Educational Movements in the Philippines." Undated manuscript, likely written 1902. In Scrapbook 5, Bernard Moses Papers.
Barrows, David P. *Annual Report of the General Superintendent of Education, September 1904.* Manila: Bureau of Public Printing, 1904.
[———]. *Course of Instruction for the Public Schools of the Philippine Islands.* Manila: Bureau of Public Printing, 1904.
———. "Education and Social Progress in the Philippines." *Annals of the American Academy of Political and Social Science* 30 (July 1907): 69–82.
———. "Review of the Year 1906." Carton 2, David Barrows Papers.
———. "Review of the Year 1908." Carton 3, David Barrows Papers.
Bureau of Education. *Approved Library Lists.* Manila: Bureau of Printing, 1928.
———. Libraries for Philippine Public Schools. Manila: Bureau of Printing, 1912.
———. *A Statement of Organization and Aims Published for General Information, December 1907.* Manila: Bureau of Printing, 1907.
———. *Suggested Course of Study.* Manila: Bureau of Printing, 1902.
Cook, Katherine. *Public Education in Hawaii, Bulletin, 1935, No. 10.* Washington, D.C.: U. S. Government Printing Office, 1935.
———. "Public Education in the Philippine Islands." In *U. S. Bureau of Education Bulletins, 1935.* Washington, D.C.: U. S. Government Printing Office, 1935.

Eaton, John. "Education in Puerto Rico" (1900). In *Annual Reports of the Department of the Interior for the Fiscal Year Ended June 30, 1900, Report of the Commissioner of Education*, 56th Cong, H. Doc. 5, 1:220–75. Washington, D.C.: U.S. Government Printing Office, 1901.

Hahn, Anna E. "A Plea for Filipino Girls." *Philippine Teacher* 2, no. 1 (June 1905): 16.

Jernegan, Prescott F. *Course of Study in Character Education and Citizenship*. Manila: Bureau of Printing, 1938.

———. *The Philippine Citizen: A Text-book of Civics, Describing the Nature of Government, the Philippine Government, and the Rights and Duties of Citizens of the Philippines*. Manila: Philippine Education Publishers, 1907.

Moses, Bernard. "American Control of the Philippines." Handwritten and printed manuscript, 1913. Carton 1, Bernard Moses Papers.

———. "The Education of the Stranger." *San Francisco Bulletin*, August 28, 1903. Carton 1, Bernard Moses Papers.

———. *First Annual Report of the Secretary of Public Instruction to the Philippine Commission, for the Year Ending October 15, 1902*. Manila: Bureau of Public Printing, 1902.

———. "In the Wilds of the Philippines." May 4, 1904. Carton 1, Bernard Moses Papers.

———. "The Philippine Assembly." Handwritten manuscript, n.d., pp. 2–3. Bernard Moses Papers.

———. "Use of the English Language in Schools." Handwritten manuscript, n.d. Carton 2, Bernard Moses Papers.

Prince, John T. "A Preliminary Report upon a Course of Studies for Elementary Schools." In *Sixtieth Annual Report: 1895–96*. Massachusetts Board of Education, 1896.

Reel, Estelle. *Course of Study for Indian Schools of the United States*. Washington, D.C.: U.S. Government Printing Office, 1901.

Report of the First Philippine Commission to the Secretary of War. Washington, D.C.: U.S. Government Printing Office, 1900.

Root, Elihu. *Education in the Philippines: Letter from the Secretary of War*. Washington, D.C.: U.S. Government Printing Office, 1901.

Selected Short Poems by Representative American Authors. Annotated by George W. St. Clair. Manila: Bureau of Printers, 1911.

Smith, General James F. "An Address Delivered at the Zorrilla Theatre, Manila, December 30, 1905." Printed in *Philippine Teacher: A Periodical for Philippine Progress* 2, no. 7 (December 1905): 4.

U.S. Adjutant General of the Army. *Correspondence Relating to the War with Spain*. 2 vols. Washington, D.C.: U.S. Government Printing Office, 1902.

U.S. Congress. House. *Papers Relating to the Foreign Relations of the United States with the Annual Message of the President*. 55th Cong., 2nd sess., 1898, H. Doc. I.

———. Senate. Committee on the Philippines. *Affairs in the Philippine Islands. Hearings before the Committee on the Philippines of the United States Senate*. 57th Cong., 1st sess., 1902. S. Doc. 331.

———. Senate. [Speech by Albert J. Beveridge.] 56th Cong., 1st sess., 1900, 704–11.

United States Insular Commission. *Report of the United States Insular Commission to the Secretary of War upon Investigations Made into the Civil Affairs of the Island of Porto Rico, with Recommendations.* United States War Department, Division of Customs and Insular Affairs, June 9, 1899. Washington, D.C.: U. S. Government Printing Office, 1899.

Worcester, Dean C. "The Native Peoples of the Philippines." *Report of the Philippine Commission.* Washington, D.C.: U.S. Government Printing Office, 1900.

Yule, Emma Sarepta. *An Introduction to the Study of Colonial History for Use in Secondary Schools.* Manila: Bureau of Printing, 1912.

OTHER PUBLISHED SOURCES

Alfonso, Oscar M., and Leslie E. Bauzon, eds. *The University of the Philippines: The First 75 Years.* Quezon City: University of the Philippines Press, 1985.

Alidio, Kimberly. "'When I Get Home I Want to Forget': Memory and Amnesia in the Occupied Philippines, 1901–1904." *Social Text* 59 (Summer 1999): 105–22.

Alquizola, Marilyn. "The Fictive Narrator of *America Is in the Heart*." In *Frontiers of Asian American Studies*, edited by Gail Nomura, Russell Endo, Stephen H. Sumida, and Russell C. Leong, 211–17. Pullman: Washington State University Press, 1989.

Althusser, Louis. "Ideology and Ideological State Apparatuses." In *Lenin and Philosophy and Other Essays*, 181–82. New York: Monthly Review Press, 1971.

Anderson, James D. *The Education of Blacks in the South, 1860–1935.* Chapel Hill: University of North Carolina Press, 1988.

Anderson, Warwick. *Colonial Pathologies: American Tropical Medicine, Race, and Hygiene in the Philippines.* Durham: Duke University Press, 2006.

Annual Report of the Commissioner of Indian Affairs to the Secretary of the Interior. Washington, D.C.: U.S. Government Printing Office, 1878.

"Another Vacuum Opens Up." *Economist,* November 6, 2003.

Applebee, Arthur N. *Tradition and Reform in the Teaching of English: A History.* Urbana, Ill.: National Council of Teachers of English, 1974.

Aquino, Belinda, ed. *The University Experience: Essays on the 82nd Anniversary of the University of the Philippines.* Quezon City: University of the Philippines Press, 1991.

Arnold, Matthew. *Culture and Anarchy: An Essay in Political and Social Criticism.* 1869. Reprint, Oxford: Oxford University Press, 2006.

Asquith, Christine. "A New History of Iraq." *Guardian,* November 25, 2003.

———. "U.S. Academic Brings Philosophy 101 to Iraqi Universities." EducationNews.org. March 1, 2004. www.ednews.org/articles/us-academic-brings-philosophy-101-to-iraqi-universities.html.

Auchincloss, Louis. "1908–1917: Idealism and Patriotism." In *A Century of Arts and Letters: The History of the National Institute of Arts & Letters,* edited by John Updike, 28–42. New York: Columbia University Press, 1998.

Baldwin, James. *School Reading by Grades*. New York: American Book Company, 1897.

Baron, Dennis. "Federal English," In *Language Loyalties: A Source Book on the Official English Controversy,* edited by James Crawford, 36–40. Chicago: University of Chicago Press, 1992.

Baym, Nina. "Early Histories of American Literature: A Chapter in the Institutionalization of New England." *American Literary History* 1 (1989): 459–88.

———. "Hawthorne's *Scarlet Letter*: Producing and Maintaining an American Literary Classic." *Journal of Aesthetic Education* 30, no. 2 (Summer 1996): 61–75.

Bederman, Gail. *Manliness and Civilization: A Cultural History of Gender and Race in the United States, 1880–1917.* Chicago: University of Chicago Press, 1996.

Bender, Thomas. "Introduction: Historians, the Nation and the Plentitude of Narratives," In *Rethinking American History in a Global Age.* Berkeley and Los Angeles: University of California Press, 2002.

Bennett, Bridget. "Spirited Away: The Death of Little Eva and the Farewell Performances of 'Katie King.'" *Journal of American Studies* 40, no. 1 (2006): 1–16.

Berlant, Lauren. "Uncle Sam Needs a Wife: Citizenship and Denegation." In *Materializing Democracy: Towards a Revitalized Cultural Politics,* edited by Russ Castronovo and Dana D. Nelson, 144–74. Durham: Duke University Press, 2002.

Berman, Carolyn Vellenga. "Creole Family Politics in *Uncle Tom's Cabin* and *Incidents in the Life of a Slave Girl.*" *NOVEL: A Forum on Fiction* 33, no. 3 (Summer 2000): 328–52.

Beveridge, Albert J. "The Development of a Colonial Policy for the United States." *Annals of the American Academy of Political and Social Science* 30, no. 1 (July 1907): 3–15.

———*The Meaning of the Times and Other Speeches*. Indianapolis: Bobbs-Merrill, 1908.

Blackburn, Robin. *The Overthrow of Colonial Slavery, 1776–1848*. New York: Verso, 1988.

Blanchard, William H. *Neocolonialism American Style, 1960–2000*. Westport, Conn.: Greenwood Press, 1996.

Blanco, John D. *Frontier Constitutions: Christianity and Colonial Empire in the Nineteenth-Century Philippines.* Berkeley and Los Angeles: University of California Press, 2009.

Blitz, Amy. *The Contested State: American Foreign Policy and Regime Change in the Philippines.* New York: Rowman and Littlefield, 2000.

Board of Educational Survey. *A Survey of the Educational System of the Philippine Islands.* Manila: Bureau of Printing, 1925.

Bourdieu, Pierre. *Outline of a Theory of Practice.* Cambridge: Cambridge University Press, 1977.

Brickhouse, Anna. *Transamerican Literary Relations and the Nineteenth-Century Public Sphere.* Cambridge: Cambridge University Press, 2004.

Briggs, Laura. *Reproducing Empire: Sex, Science, and U. S. Imperialism in Puerto Rico.* Berkeley and Los Angeles: University of California Press, 2002.

Brodhead, Richard. *Cultures of Letters: Scenes of Reading and Writing in Nineteenth-Century America.* Chicago: University of Chicago Press, 1993.

———. "Sparing the Rod: Discipline and Fiction in Antebellum America." *Representations* 21 (Winter 1988): 67–96.

Brown, Gillian. *Domestic Individualism: Imagining Self in Nineteenth-Century America.* Berkeley: University of California Press, 1990.

Bulosan, Carlos. *America Is in the Heart.* 1946. Reprint, Seattle: University of Washington, 1973).

Burnett, Christina Duffy, and Burke Marshall, eds. *Foreign in a Domestic Sense: Puerto Rico, American Expansion, and the Constitution.* Durham: Duke University Press, 2001.

Butts, R. Freeman, and Lawrence Cremin. *History of Education in American Culture.* New York: Holt, Rinehart and Winston, 1953.

Cameron, Kenneth Walter. *Longfellow among His Contemporaries.* Hartford: Transcendental Press, 1978.

Campomanes, Oscar V., and Todd S. Gernes. "Carlos Bulosan and the Act of Writing." *Philippine Studies* 40, no. 1 (1992): 68–82.

Carnegie, Andrew. "Distant Possessions—The Parting of the Ways." *North American Review* 167 (August 1898): 239–48.

Caronan, Faye. "Making History from U.S. Colonial Amnesia: Filipino American and U.S. Puerto Rican Poetic Genealogies." Ph.D. diss., University of California, San Diego, 2007.

Carpenter, George R., Franklin T. Baker, and Fred N. Scott, *The Teaching of English in the Elementary and the Secondary School.* New York: Longmans, Green, 1905.

Carroll, Henry K. *Report on the Island of Porto Rico; its Population, Civil Government, and Commerce, Industries, Productions, Roads, Tariff, and Currency, With Recommendations.* 1899. Reprint, New York: Arno Press, 1975.

Case, Henry L., and Robert A. Bunnell. *The University of the Philippines: External Assistance and Development.* East Lansing: Michigan State University, 1970.

Casper, Leonard. *New Writing from the Philippines: A Critique and Anthology.* Syracuse: Syracuse University Press, 1966.

Charvat, William. *The Profession of Authorship in America, 1800–1870.* Edited by Matthew J. Bruccoli. Columbus: Ohio State University Press, 1968.

Chauncey, George. *Gay New York: Gender, Urban Culture, and the Making of the Gay Male World, 1890–1940.* New York: Basic Books, 1994.

Cheyfitz, Eric. *The Poetics of Imperialism: Translation and Colonization from* The Tempest *to* Tarzan. New York: Oxford University Press, 1991.

Choy, Catherine Ceniza. *Empire of Care: Nursing and Migration in Filipino American History.* Durham: Duke University Press, 2003.

Chua, Jonathan. Introduction to *The Critical Villa: Essays in Literary Criticism.* Quezon City: Ateneo de Manila University Press, 2002.

Churchill, Ward. *Kill the Indian, Save the Man: The Genocidal Impact of American Indian Residential Schools.* San Francisco: City Lights Books, 2004.

Clark, Victor Selden. *Teachers' Manual for the Public Schools of Puerto Rico.* New York: Silver, Burdett 1900.

Cleveland, Charles D. *A Compendium of English Literature, Chronologically Arranged, from Sir John Mandeville to Wiliam Cowper.* 1849. Reprint, Philadelphia: E. C. and J. Biddle, 1851.

Conant, James Bryant. *Thomas Jefferson and American Public Education*. Berkeley and Los Angeles: University of California Press, 1962.

Constantino, Renato. *Insight and Foresight*. Quezon City: Foundation for Nationalist Studies, 1977.

———. *The Philippines: A Past Revisited*. Manila: Tala, 1975.

Crawford, James, ed. *Language Loyalties: A Source Book on the Official English Controversy*. Chicago: University of Chicago Press, 1992.

Cremin, Lawrence A. *American Education: The National Experience, 1783–1876*. New York: Harper and Row, 1980.

———. *Traditions of American Education*. New York: Basic Books, 1976.

———. *The Transformation of the School: Progressivism in American Education, 1876–1957*. New York: Knopf, 1961.

Csicsila, Joseph. *Canons by Consensus: Critical Trends and American Literature Anthologies*. Tuscaloosa: University of Alabama, 2004.

Dauncy, Campbell. *An Englishwoman in the Philippines*. New York: Dutton, 1906.

Delmendo, Sharon. *The Star-Entangled Banner: One Hundred Years of America in the Philippines*. New Brunswick, N.J.: Rutgers University Press, 2004.

Dennis, Michael. "Schooling along the Color Line: Progressives and the Education of Blacks in the New South." *Journal of Negro Education* 67, no. 2 (1998): 142–56.

Douglas, Ann. *The Feminization of American Culture*. New York: Knopf, 1977.

Douglass, Frederick. *Narrative of the Life of Frederick Douglass, an American Slave, Written by Himself.* 1845. Reprint, New York: Anchor Books, 1973.

Drinnon, Richard. *Facing West: The Metaphysics of Indian-Hating and Empire-Building*. Norman: University of Oklahoma Press, 1980.

Eley, George. "Nations, Publics, and Political Cultures: Placing Habermas in the Nineteenth Century." In *Habermas and the Public Sphere*, edited by Craig Calhoun, 289–339. Cambridge: MIT Press, 1992.

Elliott, Michael. *The Culture Concept: Writing and Difference in the Age of Realism*. Minneapolis: University of Minnesota Press, 2002.

Engs, Robert. *Freedom's First Generation: Black Hampton, Virginia, 1861–1890*. 1979. Reprint, New York: Fordham University Press, 2004.

Espiritu, Yen Le. *Filipino American Lives*. Philadelphia: Temple University Press, 1995.

———. *Home Bound: Filipino Lives across Cultures, Communities, and Countries*. Berkeley and Los Angeles: University of California Press, 2003.

Estioko, Leonardo. *History of Education: A Filipino Perspective*. Manila: Society of Divine Word, 1994.

Fear-Segal, Jacqueline. "Nineteenth-Century Indian Education: Universalism versus Evolutionism." *Journal of American Studies* 33, no. 2 (1999): 323–41.

Fee, Mary. *Constructive Lessons in English*. Manila: Bureau of Printing, 1910.

———. *The First Year Book*. New York and Manila: World Book Company, 1907.

———. "Learning English: A Plea for New Methods." *Teachers' Assembly Herald*, May 11, 1911, 113–15.

———. *A Woman's Impressions of the Philippines*. 1910. Reprint, Chicago: McClurg, 1912.

Fenton, Charles A. "The Founding of the National Institute of Arts and Letters in 1898." *New England Quarterly* 32, no. 4 (December 1959): 435–54.

Forbes, William Cameron. *The Philippine Islands.* Vol 1. Boston: Houghton Mifflin, 1928.

Ford, Paul Leicester. *The New England Primer.* New York: Teachers College, Columbia University, 1962.

Francia, Luis H. *Brown River, White Ocean: An Anthology of Twentieth-Century Philippine Literature in English.* New Brunswick, N.J.: Rutgers University Press, 1993.

Francia, Luis H., and Eric Gamalinda, eds. *Flippin': Filipinos on America.* New Brunswick, N.J.: Rutgers University Press, 1996.

Franciosi, Robert. *The Rise and Fall of American Public Schools: The Political Economy of Public Education in the Twentieth Century.* Westport, Conn.: Praeger, 2004.

Franklin, Benjamin. *Idea of the English School, sketch'd out for the consideration of the trustees of the Philadelphia Academy.* Philadelphia: Printed by B. Franklin, 1751.

Fraser, Nancy. "Rethinking the Public Sphere: A Contribution to the Critique of Actually Existing Democracy." In *Habermas and the Public Sphere,* edited by Craig Calhoun, 109–41. Cambridge: MIT Press, 1992.

Freer, William. *The Philippine Experiences of an American Teacher: A Narrative of Work and Travel in the Philippine Islands.* New York: Charles Scribner's Sons, 1906.

Gates, John Morgan. *Schoolbooks and Krags: The United States Army in the Philippines.* Westport, Conn.: Greenwood, 1973.

George, Rosemary Marangoly. *The Politics of Home: Postcolonial Relocations and Twentieth-Century Fiction.* Cambridge: Cambridge University Press, 1996.

Gibson, William M. "Mark Twain and Howells: Anti-Imperialists." *New England Quarterly* 20, no. 4 (December 1947): 435–70.

Gleason, Ronald P., ed. *The Log of the "Thomas," July 23 to August 21, 1901.* 1901.

Go, Julian, and Anne L. Foster, eds. *The American Colonial State in the Philippine: Global Perspectives.* Durham: Duke University Press, 2003.

Graff, Gerald. *Professing Literature: An Institutional History.* Chicago: University of Chicago Press, 1987.

Graff, Gerald, and Michael Warner, eds. *The Origins of Literary Studies in America: A Documentary Anthology.* New York: Routledge, 1989.

Gramsci, Antonio. *Selections from the Prison Notebooks.* Translated by Quintin Hoare and Geoffrey Nowell Smith. New York: International, 1971.

Gruesz, Kirsten Silva. "El Gran Poeta Longfellow and a Psalm of Exile." *American Literary History* 10, no. 3 (Autumn 1998): 395–427.

Guillory, John. *Cultural Capital: The Problem of Literary Canon-Formation.* Chicago: University of Chicago Press, 1993.

Habermas, Jürgen. "The Public Sphere: An Encyclopedia Article." *New German Critique* 3, no. 2 (Spring 1974): 49–55.

Harris, Wendell V. "Canonicity." *PMLA* 106, no. 1 (January 1991): 110–21.

Hartendorp, A. V. H. "The Importance of Philippine Literature in English." *Philippine Magazine* (January 1937): 18–19.

Hays, Edna. *College Entrance Requirements in English: Their Effects on the High Schools.* New York: Teachers College, Columbia University, 1936.

Hedrick, Joan D. *Harriet Beecher Stowe: A Life.* New York: Oxford University Press, 1994.

Hill, Patricia Ruth. *The World Their Household: The American Woman's Foreign Mission Movement and Cultural Transformation, 1870–1920.* Ann Arbor: University of Michigan Press, 1985.

Hitchens, Christopher. "Book Drive for Iraq: How You Can Do Your Bit to Build Democracy." *Slate.com,* June 30, 2008. www.slate.com/id/2194308/.

Historical Statistics of the United States. http://hsus.cambridge.org.

Hoganson, Kristin L. "'As Badly Off as the Filipinos': U. S. Women's Suffragists and the Imperial Issue at the Turn of the Twentieth Century." *Journal of Women's History* 13, no. 2 (Summer 2001): 9–33.

———. *Fighting for American Manhood: How Gender Politics Provoked the Spanish-American and Philippine-American Wars.* New Haven: Yale University Press, 1998.

———. "'Honor Comes First': The Imperatives of Manhood in the Congressional Debate over War." In *Whose America? The War of 1898 and the Battles to Define the Nation,* edited by Virginia M. Bouvier, 124–46. Westport, Conn.: Praeger, 2001.

Howells, William Dean. "Editor's Easy Chair." *Harper's Monthly Magazine* 102 (December 1900): 802–6.

"Industrial Work." *Philippine Teacher* 2, no. 2 (July 1905): 22.

———. "The New Historical Romances." *North American Review* 171, no. 6 (December 1900): 935–48.

———. "Opening Address of the President." *Proceedings of the American Academy of Arts and Letters and of the National Institute of Arts and Letters* 1, no. 1 (June 10, 1910): 5–8.

———. "The Philippine Problem: How to Secure the Peace." *New York Evening Post,* October 17, 1899.

Hoxie, Frederick E. *A Final Promise: The Campaign to Assimilate the Indians, 1880–1920.* 1984. Reprint, Lincoln: University of Nebraska, 1984.

Hunter, Jane. *The Gospel of Gentility: American Women Missionaries in Turn-of-the-Century China.* New Haven: Yale University Press, 1984.

Huntington, Ellsworth. *Civilization and Climate.* New Haven: Yale University Press, 1915.

Ignacio, Abe, Enrique de la Cruz, Jorge Emmanuel, and Helen Toribio. *The Forbidden Book: The Philippine-American War in Political Cartoons.* San Francisco: T'Boli, 2004.

Ileto, Reynaldo. "The Philippine Revolution of 1896 and U. S. Colonial Education." In *Knowing America's Colony: A Hundred Years from the Philippine War.* Manoa: University of Hawaii Press, 1999.

Jefferson, Thomas. *Notes on the State of Virginia.* Edited by Frank Shuffelton. New York: Penguin, 1999.

Jordan, David Starr. *The Question of the Philippines: An Address Delivered before the Graduate Club of Leland Stanford Junior University, February 14, 1899.* Palo Alto, Calif.: J. J. Valentine, 1899.

Joshi, Priya. *In Another Country: Colonialism, Culture, and the English Novel in India*. New York: Columbia University Press, 2002.

Jung, Moon-Ho. "Outlawing 'Coolies': Race, Nation, and Empire in the Age of Emancipation." *American Quarterly* (November 2005): 677–701.

Kalaw, Maximo M. *The Development of Philippine Politics, 1872–1920*. Manila: Oriental Book Company, 1926.

Kaplan, Amy. *The Anarchy of Empire in the Making of U.S. Culture*. Cambridge: Harvard University Press, 2002.

Kaplan, Amy, and Donald Pease. *Cultures of U.S. Imperialism*. Durham: Duke University Press, 1993.

Kim, Elaine. *Asian American Literature: An Introduction to the Writings and Their Social Context*. Philadelphia: Temple University Press, 1982.

Kirk, Donald. *Looted: The Philippines after the Bases*. New York: St. Martin's Press, 1998.

Kirstein, Lincoln, ed. *The Hampton Album*. New York: Museum of Modern Art, 1966.

Kitano, Harry, and Roger Daniels. *Asian Americans: Emerging Minorities*. Prentice Hall: New York, 1988.

Klein, Naomi. "The Rise of Disaster Capitalism," *Nation*, May 2, 2005.

Kramer, Paul, *The Blood of Government: Race, Empire, the United States, and the Philippines*. Chapel Hill: University of North Carolina Press, 2006.

———. "The Darkness That Enters the Home: The Politics of Prostitution during the Philippine American War." In *Haunted by Empire*, edited by Ann Laura Stoler, 366–404. Durham: Duke University Press, 2006.

Lachance, Paul F. "The Foreign French." In *Creole New Orleans: Race and Americanization*, edited by Arnold R. Hirsch and Joseph Logsdon, 101–30. Baton Rouge: Louisiana State University Press, 1992.

Lauter, Paul. *Canons and Contexts*. New York: Oxford University Press, 1991.

Lens, Sidney. *The Forging of the American Empire*. 1971. Reprint, Chicago: Haymarket Press, 2003.

Leonard, C. "Arnold in America: A Study of Matthew Arnold's Literary Relations with American and of His Visits to this Country in 1883 and 1886." PhD diss., Yale University, 1932.

Lewis, R. W. B. "1898–1907: The Founders' Story." In *A Century of Arts and Letters: The History of the National Institute of Arts & Letters*, edited by John Updike, 1–27. New York: Columbia University Press, 1998.

Lichauco, Alejandro. *Hunger, Corruption, and Betrayal: A Primer on U.S. Neocolonialism and the Philippines Crisis*. Manila: Citizens' Committee on the National Crisis, 2005.

Lim, Shirley Geok-Lin. *Nationalism and Literature: English-Language Writing from the Philippines and Singapore*. Quezon City: New Day, 1993.

Liu, John M., and Lucie Cheng, "Pacific Rim Development and the Duality of Post-1965 Immigration to the United States." In *The New Asian Immigration in Los Angeles and Global Restructuring*, edited by Paul Ong, Edna Bonacich, and Lucie Chang, 74–99. Philadelphia: Temple University Press, 1994.

"LOA Sets Arrive in Iraq." *News from the Library of America* (Summer 2006): 1.

"LOA Worldwide Program to Benefit Libraries in Iraq and Afghanistan." *News from the Library of America* (Fall 2004): 1.

Logan, Rayford W. *The Betrayal of the Negro: From Rutherford B. Hayes to Woodrow Wilson.* 1965. Reprint, New York: Da Capo Press, 1997.

Longfellow, Henry Wadsworth. *Evangeline.* Gretna: Pelican, 2003.

Lopez, Helen E. *At the Helm of the U.P.: Presidential Accents.* Quezon City: University of the Philippines Press, 1999.

Lowe, Lisa. *Immigrant Acts: On Asian American Cultural Politics.* Durham, N.C.: Duke University Press, 1996.

––––––. "The Intimacies of Four Continents." In *Haunted by Empire,* edited by Ann L. Stoler, 191–212. Durham: Duke University Press, 2006.

Macaulay, Thomas Babington. *Speeches by Lord Macaulay, with the Minute on Indian Education.* Edited by G. M. Young. London: Oxford University Press, 1935.

Luce, Henry. "The American Century." *Life* magazine, February 7, 1941. Reprinted in *The Ambiguous Legacy,* edited by Michael J Hogan. 11–29. Cambridge: Cambridge University Press, 1999.

Malmsheimer, Lonna M. "'Imitation White Man': Images of Transformation at the Carlisle Indian School." *Studies in Visual Communication* 2 (Fall 1985): 54–75.

Mann, Horace. *The Common School Controversy.* Boston: Dutton and Wentworth, 1844.

Manuud, Antonio G., ed. *Brown Heritage: Essays on Philippine Cultural Tradition and Literature.* Quezon City: Ateneo de Manila University Press, 1967.

Martin, Dalmacio. *A Century of Education in the Philippines: 1861–1961.* Manila: Philippine Historical Association, 1980.

Martin, Isabel Pefianco. "Longfellow's Legacy: Education and the Shaping of Philippine Writing." *World Englishes* 23, no. 1 (2004): 129–39.

May, Glenn. *Social Engineering in the Philippines: The Aims, Execution, and Impact of American Colonial Policy, 1900–1913.* Westport, Conn: Greenwood Press, 1980.

McHenry, Robert, ed. *Famous American Women: A Biographical Dictionary from the Colonial Times to the Present.* Boston: Dover, 1983.

McKinley, William. "Instructions to the Taft Commission, April 7, 1900." In Maximo M. Kalaw, *The Development of Philippine Politics, 1872–1920,* 452–59. Manila: Oriental Book Company, 1926.

––––––. "Remarks to Methodist Delegation." In *The Philippines Reader: A History of Colonialism, Neocolonialism, Dictatorship, and Resistance,* edited by Daniel B. Schirmer and Stephen Rosskamm Shalom, 22–23. Quezon City: KEN, 1987. Originally published in General James Rusling, "Interview with President William McKinley." *Christian Advocate,* January 22, 1903, 17.

McWilliams, Jim, and Cicero Bruce. "Matthew Arnold's Visit to St. Louis." *Nineteenth-Century Literature* 50, no. 2 (September 1995): 225–31.

Mersand, Joseph. "The Teaching of Literature in American High Schools, 1865–1900." In *Perspectives on English: Essays to Honor W. Wilbur Hatfield,* edited by Robert C. Pooley, 271–302. New York: Appleton-Century-Crofts, 1960.

Miller, Stuart Creighton. "Benevolent Assimilation": The American Conquest of the Philippines, 1899–1903. New Haven: Yale University Press, 1982.

Mohanty, Chandra Talpade. *Feminism without Borders: Decolonizing Theory, Practicing Solidarity.* Durham: Duke University Press, 2003.

Mojares, Resil B. *Panitikan: An Essay on the American Colonial and Contemporary Traditions in Philippine Literature.* Manila: Sentrong Pangkultura ng Pilipinas, 1994.

Moses, Edith. *Unofficial Letters of an Official's Wife.* New York: Appleton, 1908.

Mostern, Kenneth. "Why Is America in the Heart?" *Critical Mass: A Journal of Asian American Cultural Criticism* 2, no. 2 (1995): 35–65.

Nash, Frederick W. "Education in the Philippines." *Educational Review* 22, no. 3 (October 1901): 217–27.

Navarro, José-Manuel. *Creating Tropical Yankees: Social Science Textbooks and U.S. Ideological Control in Puerto Rico, 1898–1908.* New York: Routledge, 2002.

Negrón de Montilla, Aida. *Americanization in Puerto Rico and the Public School System, 1900–1930.* Río Piedras, Puerto Rico: Editorial Edil, 1971.

Newfield, Christopher. *Ivy and Industry: Business and the Making of the American University, 1880–1980.* Durham: Duke University Press, 2003.

Newman, Louise Michele. *White Woman's Rights: The Racial Origins of Feminism in the United States.* New York: Oxford University Press, 1999.

Newsom, Sidney C., and Levona Payne Newsom. *Primer.* Philippine English series. Boston: Ginn, 1904.

———. *Third Reader.* Philippine English series. Boston: Ginn, 1904.

Nieto, Sonia. "Puerto Rican Students in U.S. Schools: A Brief History." In *Puerto Rican Students in U.S. Schools,* edited by Sonia Nieto, 5–38. Mahwah, N.J.: Lawrence Erlbaum Associates, 2000.

Norton, Charles Eliot, ed. *Fairy Stories and Classic Tales of Adventure.* Third book of the Heart of Oak Books. Boston: D. C. Heath, 1901.

Novick, Peter. *That Noble Dream: The "Objectivity Question" and the American Historical Profession.* New York: Cambridge University Press, 1998.

Okihiro, Gary. *Margins and Mainstreams: Asians in American History and Culture.* Seattle: University of Washington Press, 1994.

———. *Pineapple Culture: A History of the Tropical and Temperate Zones.* Berkeley and Los Angeles: University of California Press, 2009.

Omi, Michael, and Howard Winant. *Racial Formation in the United States.* New York: Routledge, 1994.

Osuna, Juan José. *A History of Education in Puerto Rico.* New York: Arno Press, 1975

Parker, William Riley. "Where Do English Departments Come From?" *College English* 28, no. 5 (February 1967): 339–51.

Peabody, Francis Greenwood. *Education for Life: The Story of Hampton Institute.* New York: Doubleday, Page, 1918.

Pease, Donald, and Robyn Wiegman. *The Futures of American Studies.* Durham: Duke University Press, 2002.

Pecson, Geronima T., and Maria Racelis. *Tales of the American Teachers in the Philippines.* Manila: Carmelo and Bauermann, 1959.

"Philippine English." *Philippine Teacher* 2, no. 9 (February 1906): 1.

"The Philippine Report." *Harper's Weekly* 43, no. 2239 (1899): 1154.

Prucha, Francis Paul, ed. *Americanizing the American Indians.* Cambridge: Harvard University Press, 1973.

"Public Schools in Manila." *Washington Evening Star*, August 25, 1899.

Racelis, Mary, and Judy Celine Ick, eds. *Bearers of Benevolence: The Thomasites and Public Education in the Philippines.* Pasig City: Anvil Press, 2001.

Radway, Janice A. *A Feeling for Books: The Book-of-the-Month Club, Literary Taste, and Middle-Class Desire.* Chapel Hill: University of North Carolina Press, 1997.

Rafael, Vicente. "Translation, American English and the National Insecurities of Empire." *Social Text 101* 27, no. 4 (Winter 2009): 1–23.

———. *White Love and Other Events in Filipino History.* Durham: Duke University Press, 2000.

Reyhner, Jon Allan, and Jeanne Eder. *American Indian Education: A History.* Norman: University of Oklahoma Press, 2004.

Roces, Mina. "Filipino Identity in Fiction, 1945–1972." *Modern Asian Studies* 28, no. 2 (1994): 279–315.

Roe, Jae H. "Revisiting the Sign of 'America': The Postcolonial Humanism of *America Is in the Heart*." *English Language and Literature* 49, no. 9 (2003): 905–20.

Romero, Lora. *Home Fronts: Domesticity and Its Critics in the Antebellum United States.* Durham: Duke University Press, 1997.

Rosaldo, Renato. "Imperialist Nostalgia." *Representations* 26 (Spring 1989): 107–22.

Roseburg, Arturo G., ed. *Pathways to Philippine Literature in English: Anthology with Biographical and Critical Introduction.* Quezon City: Alemar-Phoenix, 1966.

Ross, Dorothy. *The Origins of American Social Science.* New York: Cambridge University Press, 1991.

Rowe, John Carlos. *Literary Culture and U. S. Imperialism: From the Revolution to World War II.* New York: Oxford University Press, 2000.

Saldívar, José David. *Border Matters: Remapping American Cultural Studies.* Berkeley and Los Angeles: University of California Press, 1997.

Salman, Michael. *The Embarrassment of Slavery: Controversies over Bondage and Nationalism in the American Colonial Philippines.* Berkeley and Los Angeles: University of California Press, 2001.

Samuels, Shirley, ed. *The Culture of Sentiment: Race, Gender, and Sentimentality in Nineteenth-Century America.* New York: Oxford University Press, 1992.

San Buenaventura, Steffi. "Filipino Immigration to the United States." *Asian American Encyclopedia*, 2: 439–53. New York: Marshall Cavendish, 1995.

Sandoval, Chela. *Methodology of the Oppressed.* Minneapolis: University of Minnesota Press, 2000.

Sangari, Kumkum, and Sudesh Vaid, eds. *Recasting Women: Essays in Indian Colonial History.* New Brunswick, N.J.: Rutgers University Press, 1990.

San Juan, E., Jr. *Carlos Bulosan and the Imagination of the Class Struggle.* Quezon City: University of the Philippines Press, 1972.

———. *The Philippine Temptation: Dialectics of Philippines–U. S. Literary Relations.* Philadelphia: Temple University Press, 1996.

———"Searching for the Heart of 'America.'" In *Teaching American Ethnic Literatures: Nineteen Essays,* edited by John Maitino and David R. Peck, 259–72. Albuquerque: University of New Mexico Press, 1996.

Sánchez-Eppler, Karen. *Dependent States: The Child's Part in Nineteenth-Century American Culture.* Chicago: University of Chicago Press, 2005.

Sand, George. "Review of *Uncle Tom's Cabin.*" In Harriet Beecher Stowe, *Uncle Tom's Cabin.* edited by Elizabeth Ammons. 459–63. New York: Norton, 1994. The review was originally published in *La Presse,* December 17, 1852.

Schirmer, Daniel B. "The Conception and Gestation of a Neocolony." In *The Philippines Reader: A History of Colonialism, Neocolonialism, Dictatorship, and Resistance,* edited by Daniel B. Schirmer and Stephen Rosskamm Shalom, 38–44. Quezon City: KEN, 1987. Originally published in *Journal of Contemporary Asia* 5, no. 1 (1975).

Schmidt, Peter. *Sitting in Darkness: New South Fiction, Education, and the Rise of Jim Crow Colonialism, 1865–1920.* Jackson: University of Mississippi Press, 2008.

Schott, Joseph L. *The Ordeal at Samar.* Indianapolis: Bobbs-Merrill, 1964.

Schurman, Jacob Gould. *Philippine Affairs: A Retrospect and Outlook.* New York: Charles Scribner's Sons, 1902.

Scudder, Horace E. "American Classics in School." In *Literature in School,* 44–60. Boston: Houghton Mifflin, 1888.

———"The Place of Literature in Common School Education." In *Literature in School,* 5–33. Boston: Houghton Mifflin, 1888.

Semple, Lewis B. Introduction to *Evangeline,* by Henry Wadsworth Longfellow, xiii–li. Gretna: Pelican, 2003.

Shell, Marc. "Babel in America; or, The Politics of Language Diversity in the United States." *Critical Inquiry* 20 (Autumn 1993): 103–27.

Shumway, David R. *Creating American Civilization: A Genealogy of American Literature as an Academic Discipline.* Minneapolis: University of Minnesota Press, 1994.

Shunk, Caroline S. *An Army Woman Writing in the Philippines.* Kansas City, Mo.: Franklin Hudson, 1914.

Sinha, Mrinalini. *Colonial Masculinity: The 'Manly Englishman' and the 'Effeminate Bengali' in the Late Nineteenth Century.* New York: Manchester University Press, 1995.

Slotkin, Richard. *Gunfighter Nation: The Myth of the Frontier in Twentieth-Century America.* New York: Macmillan, 1992.

———. *Regeneration through Violence: The Myth of the American Frontier.* Middletown, Conn.: Wesleyan University Press, 1973.

Smith, Neil. *American Empire: Roosevelt's Geographer and the Prelude to Globalization.* Berkeley and Los Angeles: University of California Press, 2003.

Sneider, Allison Lee. "Reconstruction, Expansion, and Empire: The U.S. Woman Suffrage Movement and the Re-Making of National Political Community, 1870–1900." Ph.D. diss., University of California, Los Angeles, 1999.

Snyder, Franklyn B., and Edward D. Snyder. "Henry Wadsworth Longfellow." In *A Book of American Literature.* New York: Macmillan, 1953.

Soldiers' Letters: Being Materials for the History of a War of Criminal Aggression. Boston: Anti-Imperialist League, 1899.

Soliongco, I. P. "Pan American Literature and Filipino Society." In *Rediscovery: Essays on Philippine Life and Culture,* edited by Cynthia Lumbera and Teresita Maceda, 209–18. Manila: National Bookstore, 1983.

Solís, José. *Public School Reform in Puerto Rico: Sustaining Colonial Models of Development.* Westport, Conn.: Greenwood Press, 1994.

Spillers, Hortense J. "Changing the Letter: The Yokes, the Jokes of Discourse, or, Mrs. Stowe, Mr. Reed." In *Slavery and the Literary Imagination,* edited by Deborah McDowell and Arnold Rampersad, 25–61. Baltimore: Johns Hopkins University Press, 1989.

Spivak, Gayatri Chakravorty. "Can the Subaltern Speak?" In *Marxism and the Interpretation of Culture,* edited Cary Nelson and Lawrence Grossberg, 271–316. Urbana: University of Illinois, 1988.

Starr, Mike. *Labor Looks at Education.* Cambridge: Harvard University Press, 1947.

Stoddard, Francis H. "Conference on Uniform Entrance Requirements in English." *Educational Review* (1905): 375–83.

Stoler, Ann Laura, *Carnal Knowledge and Imperial Power.* Berkeley and Los Angeles: University of California Press, 2002.

———. "Tense and Tender Ties: The Politics of Comparison in North American History and (Post) Colonial Studies." *Journal of American History* 88, no. 3 (December 2001): 829–65.

Storey, Moorfield, and Marcial P. Lichauco. *The Conquest of the Philippines by the United States, 1898–1925.* New York: G. P. Putnam's Sons, 1926.

Stout, John E. *The Development of High School Curricula in the North Central States from 1860–1918.* Chicago: University of Chicago Press, 1921.

Stowe, Harriet Beecher. *Palmetto Leaves.* 1873. Reprint, Gainesville: University of Florida Press, 1968.

———. *Uncle Tom's Cabin.* 1852. Edited by Elizabeth Ammons. New York: Norton, 1994.

Swinton, William. *A Condensed School History of the United States.* New York: Ivison, Blakeman and Taylor, 1875.

Taft, Helen Herron. *Recollections of Full Years.* New York: Dodd, Mead, 1914.

Taft, William Howard. "The Philippines." *National Geographic Magazine* 16, no. 8 (1905): 361–75.

Takaki, Ronald. *Iron Cages: Race and Culture in Nineteenth-Century America.* New York: Knopf, 1979.

———. *Strangers from a Different Shore: A History of Asian Americans.* New York: Penguin Books, 1989.

"The Teaching Process." *Philippine Teacher* 2, no. 2 (July 1905): 24.

Tinker, Hugh. *A New System of Slavery: The Export of Indian Labour Overseas, 1830–1920.* London: Oxford University Press, 1974.

Tompkins, Jane. *Sensational Designs: The Cultural Work of American Fiction, 1790–1860.* New York: Oxford University Press, 1985.

———. "Sentimental Power: *Uncle Tom's Cabin* and the Politics of Literary History." In *Uncle Tom's Cabin,* by Harriet Beecher Stowe. 1852. Edited by Elizabeth Ammons, 501–22. New York: Norton, 1994. Tompkins's article was originally published in *Glyph* 2 (1978).

Trask, Haunani-Kay. *From a Native Daughter: Colonialism and Sovereignty in Hawai'i.* Monroe, Me.: Common Courage Press, 1993.

Twain, Mark. "To the Person Sitting in Darkness." *North American Review* (February 1901): 161–76.

Tyrrell, Ian. "Making Nations/Making States: American Historians in the Context of Empire." *Journal of American History* 86 (1999): 1015–44.

Vanderbilt, Kermit. *American Literature and the Academy: The Roots, Growth, and Maturity of a Profession.* Philadelphia: University of Pennsylvania Press, 1986.

Veysey, Laurence. "The Plural Organized Worlds of the Humanities." In *The Organization of Knowledge in Modern America, 1860–1920,* edited by Alexandra Oleson and John Voss, 71. Baltimore: Johns Hopkins University Press, 1979.

Villa, J.G. "The Fence." In *The Best Short Stories of 1933,* edited by Edward J. O'Brien. Boston: Houghton Mifflin, 1933.

———. "Untitled Story." In *Best American Short Stories of 1932,* edited by Edward J. O'Brien. New York: Dodd, Mead, 1932.

Virtusio, Genario. "Vernacular Literature and Literary Quacks." *Philippines Herald,* August 7, 1935.

Viswanathan, Gauri. *Masks of Conquest: Literary Study and British Rule in India.* 1989. Reprint, New Delhi: Oxford University Press, 2003.

Visweswaran, Kamala. "'Wild West' Anthropology and the Disciplining of Gender." In *Gender and American Social Science: The Formative Years,* edited by Helene Silverberg, 87–123. Princeton, N.J.: Princeton University Press, 1998.

Volpp, Leti. "American Mestizo: Filipinos and Antimiscegenation Laws in California." *U.S. Davis Law Review* 33 (Summer 2000): 795–835.

Ware, Vron. *Beyond the Pale: White Women, Racism, and History.* London: Verso, 1992.

Warner, Michael. *The Letters of the Republic: Publication and the Public Sphere in Eighteenth-Century America.* Cambridge: Harvard University Press, 1990.

Webster, Noah. "Declaration of Linguistic Independence." In *Language Loyalties: A Source Book on the Official English Controversy,* edited by James Crawford, 33–36. Chicago: University of Chicago Press, 1992.

Wee, C. J. Wan-ling. *Culture, Empire, and the Question of Being Modern.* Lanham, Md.: Lexington Books, 2003.

Wexler, Laura. *Tender Violence: Domestic Visions in an Age of U.S. Imperialism.* Chapel Hill: University of North Carolina Press, 2000.

Williams, Raymond. *Culture and Society, 1780–1950.* 1958. Reprint, New York: Columbia University Press, 1983.

———. *Marxism and Literature.* New York: Oxford University Press, 1977.

Wilson, Woodrow. "Mere Literature." In *The Origins of Literary Studies in America: A Documentary Anthology,* edited by Gerald Graff and Michael Warner, 82–89. New York: Routledge, 1989. Originally published in *Atlantic Monthly* (1893).

Windhover, Ruth. "Literature in the Nineteenth Century." *English Journal: An Historical Primer on the Teaching of English* 68, no. 4 (April 1979): 28–33.

Wolff, Leon. *Little Brown Brother: How the United States Purchased and Pacified the Philippine Islands at the Century's Turn.* 1960. Reprint, New York: History Book Club, 2006.

Wong, Sau-Ling. *Reading Asian American Literature: From Necessity to Extravagance.* Princeton, N.J.: Princeton University Press, 1993.

Worcester, Dean C. "Knotty Problems of the Philippines." *Century Magazine* 56, no. 6 (October 1898): 873–80.

———. *The Philippines, Past and Present.* 2 vols. New York: Macmillan, 1914.

Zehr, Mary. "Iraq Gets Approval to Control Destiny of School System" *Education Week,* April 14, 2004.

———. "U. S. Withdraws from Education Reform in Iraq" *Education Week,* August 30, 2006.

Zwick, Jim. *Mark Twain's Weapons of Satire: Anti-Imperialist Writings on the Philippine-American War.* Syracuse: Syracuse University Press, 1992.

Index

Adams, Henry, 37

Afghanistan. *See* education: in Iraq and Afghanistan

African-Americans: comparison to Filipinos, 2, 11, 76–77, 84–86; domestication by sentimentality, 81–82; education, 3; and industrial education movement, 8, 18, 26–27, 84; as inferior in view of white Americans, 77–78; slavery and literacy, 22. *See also* Hampton Institute; slavery; Tuskegee Institute

Agresto, John, 173

Aguinaldo, Emilio, 39; as Topsy, 69–71, 76, 79–80

Alcott, Louisa May, 72

Althusser, Louis, 12–13

America is in the Heart, 33, 144; as collective autobiography, 145, 147, 205n16; critique of colonial education in, 153–55, 158; formal complexities in, 146–47, 206n17, 206n19, 207n26, 207nn28–29; knowledge production in, 149–51, 157; progress and teleology in, 159–62; uses of literature in, 145–47, 152, 156, 206n23, 206n25. *See also* Bulosan, Carlos

American Academy of Arts and Letters, 37–38

American Historical Association, 47

American Historical Review, 47

American Spelling Book (Webster), 43–44

Americanism: and education, 3, 15, 130; and the English language, 53, 58–59; and exceptionalism, 5, 8–10, 33, 47, 55, 64–65, 162; and literature, 6, 11, 20, 42, 88

Anderson, Warwick, 129, 204n70

Anglo-Saxon civilization: and American literature, 6, 8, 45, 63, 68; claims for superiority of, 2, 13, 35, 82, 112, 140; and the English language, 42, 56, 60, 166; and gender roles, 122, 128–29, 142

anthropology: comparison to study of English, 59; emergence as a field, 47, 190n86

anti-imperialist league, 3, 39, 105, 124, 164

antimiscegenation laws, 77

Applebee, Arthur, 8, 42, 185n24, 199n100

Armstrong, Samuel Chapman, 26, 81–82, 84–86, 196n48. *See also* Hampton Institute

Arnold, Matthew, 45, 87, 95, 198n87

Atkinson, Fred W., 189n58; and education in the Philippines, 36, 50–51, 53, 57, 61–62, 64, 91, 122; and industrial education movement, 18, 84–85

Baldwin Readers, 54, 64, 90–91

Barrows, David, 189n58; and education in the Philippines, 7, 19, 50–51, 54, 57, 61, 63–64, 93–94, 199n101; and emasculation in the Philippines, 129; and industrial education movement, 18

About the Author

Meg Wesling is Associate Professor of Literature at the University of California, San Diego.

CPSIA information can be obtained
at www.ICGtesting.com
Printed in the USA
BVOW01s1221081116
467223BV00005B/211/P